BEHIND ENEMY LINES

An In-Depth Insider's Guide To Spiritual Warfare

S. A. TOWER

Behind Enemy Lines

Copyright © 2025 by S. A. Tower

Published by Dwell Publishing LLC, dwellpublishing@gmail.com

Printed in the United States of America

All rights reserved. This book or parts thereof may not be reproduced in any form, stored in a retrieval system, or transmitted to any form by any means – electronic, mechanical, photocopy, recording, or otherwise – without prior written permission of the publisher, except as provided by United States of America copyright law.

ISBN: 978-0-9849523-7-3 (paperback)

Unless otherwise indicated Scripture is taken from the New King James Version of the Bible. Copyright © 1979, 1980, 1982 by Thomas Nelson, Inc. publishers.

Scripture quotations marked NIV are from the Holy Bible, New International Version®, NIV®. Copyright ©1973, 1978, 1984, 2011 by Biblica, Inc.™ Used by permission of Zondervan. All rights reserved worldwide. www.zondervan.com.

Scripture quotations marked ESV are from the ESV® Bible (The Holy Bible, English Standard Version®), copyright © 2001 by Crossway, a publishing ministry of Good News Publishers. Used by permission. All rights reserved. ESV Text Edition: 2025.

Scripture quotations marked MSG are from THE MESSAGE, copyright © 1993, 2002, 2018 by Eugene H. Peterson. Used by permission of NavPress. All rights reserved. Represented by Tyndale House Publishers, a Division of Tyndale House Ministries.

Scripture quotations marked CEV are from the Contemporary English Version Copyright © 1991, 1992, 1995 by American Bible Society, Used by Permission. Scripture quotations marked KJV are taken from the King James Version of the Bible. Public domain.

Scripture quotations marked NASB are from the (NASB®) New American Standard Bible®, Copyright © 1960, 1971, 1977, 1995, 2020 by The Lockman Foundation. Used by permission. All rights reserved. www.lockman.org.

To protect the privacy of some individuals referred to, names of persons, places, and some other details, have in some cases been changed.

Cover design by David Munoz Art – Additional art Adobe Stock licensed

Many say, and rightfully so,
"Deliverance is the children's bread,"
~ yet the crumbs fall to those with the
faith to receive them.
~ S.A. Tower
(see Matthew 15:26–27)

Contents

Foreword
Acknowledgments
Part I: A Clarion Call to Battle
   1   Awaken the Warrior Within 15
   2   The Mind Field 25
   3   The Earth Field 33
   4   The Spiritual Heavenlies 47
Part II: Kingdom of Darkness
   5   Uncloaking the Enemy 57
   6   Satan's Strategies 67
   7   The Strongman's Game 77
   8   Hooves of Satan 87
   9   Demon Hit List 97
Part III: Preparing for Battle
   10   Believer's Power and Authority 147
   11   Armor Up 155
   12   Weapons of Warfare 175
   13   Spiritual Discernment 189
Part IV: Set The Captive Free
   14   Healing the Brokenhearted 201
   15   Breaking Curses 215
   16   Deliver Us from Evil 227
   17   Walking Out Deliverance 243
Part V: Reclamation of Supernaturalism
   18   Waste Management 253
   19   Taking Back Ground 265
   20   Preparing for End Times Battles 275
   21   War of the Worlds 285
Appendix: Bondage Breaking Prayer
Also, by S. A. Tower

Foreword

When Ally asked me to write the foreword for her book, I told her integrity required me to read it, check all her scriptural references, and evaluate the theology she had written, and that she must be willing to discuss her viewpoints with me. She agreed. That began a dialogue that raised some questions for me. We were really examining reality—a reality that includes two dimensions, the natural and the supernatural.

To establish credibility or "street cred" for the reader, we should start with defining *reality*. I once heard it said that reality is really facts we can confirm with our five senses or our rational mind. Because I have known Ally since she was a beautiful young lady of eighteen who loved Jesus, and I have seen her living in both the natural and supernatural realities, I stand as a witness that Ally is the real deal. She is neither a wannabe or our media culture's typical influencer trolling for hits, nor an author just selling books. In this book, she presents life-saving information not commonly found elsewhere.

That leaves you to assess my history since in many ways, Ally has integrated some of my views into this book because I served as her pastor, counselor, and friend.

My history includes an athletic background, an MBA, and a senior executive position in research and development in New York City. At the age of thirty-two, I left business after literally hearing from God that I was to swap careers from business to ministry. My ministry experience included twenty-eight years of serving as a pastor, short-term missions in fourteen nations, presenting seminars in the USA and around the world on deliverance from demonic spiritual bondage, and praying for over three thousand people covering over nine thousand hours.

Ally became a household fixture in our home because my wife

took Ally under her wing, sensing Ally was gifted by the Lord in discernment (or identifying demons) and knew she loved Jesus. For several years, Ally attended our church and served where she could. After about four years in her marriage, we noticed a change in Ally and her husband. Our pastors joined me in six months of marriage counseling and prayer, but her husband's behavior deteriorated to the point that he lost a good job and left Ally to care for their three children with sparse support.

Our church sent food weekly and did some repairs on her rental home the landlord wouldn't provide, and one Christmas provided toys for her children.

But as you will read in this book, Ally grew despondent and gradually entered another part of the spiritual realm filled with Wicca, witchcraft, and experiences common only to leaders on the dark side.

What she presents to you is a unique perspective from someone who walked both sides of the spiritual world's sidewalks. She rose to be a candidate for a high priestess in Wicca, because they also recognized her gifting and wanted to use it for their own objectives. They groomed her with literature and occult knowledge.

For over ten years, I kept in contact with Ally while she was in the Craft, usually when she called with questions. My answers were often not to her liking while she was ensnared in the Wiccan world. Several calls stand out in my memory.

Ally had attended her first Halloween witches' ball, and to her surprise, a Philadelphia TV news station sent a crew to her coven's location to film an actual live ritual. While the camera rolled, Ally was filmed with two other witches while in the circle. The next morning, Ally called me in a panic. She had told no one in her family that she was a practicing witch, and she feared she would be outed on a major TV station. I said, "I can pray God will close the eyes of the people watching." I did pray, and Ally just sighed deeply, not entirely convinced prayer and God would be able to help. The program was scheduled to run that night on the ten o'clock news as a Halloween feature segment. Ally put the children to bed that night and sat nervously before her TV. The feature ran, and there were all her Wiccan friends dancing around in black robes, and then came the shot where she was standing in the circle with coven members. Ally couldn't believe her eyes! The other witches were there, but she wasn't!

She called back and told me what had happened, and I just said, "God is gracious and forgiving, Ally." And so, she had some hints that God was protecting her even while she was in the coven.

Ally went to one particular coven ritual in a barn where the windows were blackened out and total darkness hid everything. After they drew the circle, invited elemental spirits, and invoked a demon goddess to come, Ally told me she could feel things flying around her and they weren't birds or bats. She was falling deeper and deeper into the occult as we continued to pray for her.

Years later, Ally was awakened from a sound sleep to a voice asking her, "Who do you say I am?" The next day she called me and recounted the experience. Then she asked me, "Who was that voice?" I replied, "You know who it was, Ally. In the spiritual realm, I see you standing at the edge of a cliff, and the Lord is asking you, 'Who will you serve?' It is your last chance. Either you go over the cliff and into darkness and lose or you return to Jesus." Ally said, "I knew it!"

The last Halloween ritual she attended was the night before she accepted an invitation back to church. There were no camera lights for that one, and she almost didn't go, except that she thought it would prove that God couldn't touch her. God proved otherwise, and she gave her life back to Jesus. It took great courage, but she left the coven even though she knew the coven had taken revenge on those who left in the past.

After returning to the Lord, Ally was troubled by how she could have fallen away from the Lord. She did intensive repentance, prayer, and research. She also became active in helping other young girls come out of Wicca. Ally is a veteran of spiritual warfare and presents to you in these pages critically important knowledge for you and all other readers. Ally's ten-year passage through difficult times was redeemed by the Lord, who turned what the enemy meant for harm to our good.

Through our texts, I discovered things I did not know about the enemy's methods and attacks. Our focus was always on getting rid of demons, and we didn't really care about Wiccan practices. We knew they were blasphemous and prayed for people hurt by the enemy.

As Ally and I reviewed her work, I realized we had a different experience, history, and perspective on approaches. But I also realized we agreed on what I would call the "essentials," if not the process. Ally had success doing what she had learned, and so did we. My conclusion is that God will honor and bless those who will dedicate themselves to helping His bound and hurting children who came forth from Him.

May you be blessed, enlightened and prepared as you read *Behind Enemy Lines*.

Blessings,

Pastor Larry Arendas
Founder and Director,
Spirit and Truth Ministries International

Acknowledgments

How can I write acknowledgments without first acknowledging the Lord God Almighty, who saw me through the battle over my life before I knew it existed? He opened my spiritual eyes to reveal the battle that raged all around me. Even in my rebellion, when I made my bed in the depths of Sheol, He never left me; rather, He reached down with His mighty arm and rescued me from the dominion of darkness.

To each of my children and grandchildren, thank you for your forgiveness and willingness to love me despite my shortcomings and spiritual downfall; I pray they would serve as warning signs (of what to avoid) in your own lives. God has bestowed an amazing spiritual gift upon each of you, and I pray you grow into the fullness of those gifts and that you would discover all the goodness that He has for each of you. ~Love, Mom

I'd like to extend my sincere gratitude to Pastor Larry and the late Carole Arendas. Their leadership laid the foundation for spiritual warfare and deliverance in my life. Pastor Larry, words cannot express how much it means to me to have you write the foreword for this book. I am grateful for your vast knowledge of healing and deliverance, which our Lord has used to grace those hurting around the world, and I am especially thankful for having been a recipient of your ministry. Analyzing this book with you felt like a walk down memory lane, and I cherish the profound impact your teaching has made on my life. I will always remember Carole, although no longer with us, as one who touched the hearts of so many. A woman used by God to minister healing to the wounded and broken soul. In hindsight, having been a recipient of her occasional tough love, which was well deserved, has proven to be a true blessing and one that I hold dear to my heart.

To Robert from Dwell Publishing, the first thing that comes to mind is . . . at last. This "work" has been forthcoming for a long time. Thank you for your ongoing patience and encouragement through the hiccups and hurdles along the way and for helping me maintain accountability in fulfilling what the Lord placed on my heart. It's great to know you *will be* a continual part of future works.

I'm so grateful for my personal PC tech and would many times be at a standstill if it weren't for your ability to fix problems as they arise. Thank you for remaining on-call and keeping my computer protected and running smoothly. You're the best!

I want to acknowledge the following people, whose work was key in making this book what it is today. Thank you to my editor, Christy... for her insightful feedback and tireless effort in refining the manuscript. I also want to express my heartfelt gratitude to Pastor Larry for his editing assistance and for the biblical clarity he contributed to the book. Connie, thank you for your invaluable contributions to the layout, turning the content into a visually appealing and polished final product.

A shout out to David Munoz for another awesome cover design that stands out against the billions of others.

To all readers and my social media followers, thank you for your continual support. Watch and pray always.

PART I

A Clarion Call to Battle

CHAPTER 1

Awaken The Warrior Within

Years ago, a vision came to me one evening as I sat in my living room. I saw a dark, heinous creature burrowed deep underground. It ripped through the dirt, tossing it hastily aside as it raced toward the surface. The ground split open from the force of its hideous head, beneath the guise of night, and it crawled out of the ground. Once confined within the depths of the abyss, it now prowled down an isolated street in a sparsely populated area.

Shortly after its unleashing, this epitome of pure evil manifested. Its diabolical plan infiltrated our nation and beyond. Our world turned upside down, defining what is good as evil, and that which is evil as good. I don't know the name of this evil spirit, but I believe it ranked within the scope of a principality, yet its influence was widespread. It fed on spiritual disorder, and its target was on political corruption and pushing society toward chaos, darkness, and ultimately destruction.

We find a good example of what had become of our city streets in Isaiah 59:14: "Justice is turned back, and righteousness stands afar off; for truth is fallen in the street, and equity cannot enter." We watched lies and deception unfold as truth on the news and social media. I think what amazed me most was the number of people who fell in line behind the deception. Many minds appeared brainwashed and their eyes so blinded by the god of this world that they were clueless to the wickedness that had befallen them. Violence was unchecked, logic went out the window, and mindlessness became the new norm.

Demon's-Eye View

Sadly, at a time of increasing darkness—and when spiritual warfare is needed the most—it is not a popular pulpit topic. Believers need to be reawakened to the fact that not only do God, heaven, and angels exist, but the biblical enemy, known as Satan or the devil, and his demons are also as alive and real as humans are. The best analogy I've seen of this is from C. S. Lewis's *The Screwtape Letters*, which analyzes the theme of spiritual warfare from a demon's-eye view, with this illustrated in a ruling demon's training sessions with a lower-ranking demon.

Lewis begins with this observation: "There are two equal and opposite errors into which our race can fall about the devils. One is to disbelieve in their existence. The other is to believe and to feel an excessive and unhealthy interest in them. They themselves are equally pleased by both errors, and hail a materialist or magician with the same delight."[1]

Lewis provides excellent insight that exposes both the extreme of ignoring the existence of demonic influence and the unhealthy obsession with it. The enemy manipulates these thoughts to his advantage, keeping us ineffective on the battlefield; our belief, unbelief, or indifference pleases him. I know, because I've been on both sides of the spiritual fence and witnessed the daily spiritual victories and casualties of this unseen war.

Spiritually Fatigued

Early in my Christian walk, I attended a church focused on healing and deliverance, and was therefore trained in spiritual

---

[1] *The Screwtape Letters* by C. S. Lewis © copyright 1942 CS Lewis Pte Ltd. Extract used with permission.

warfare. Despite my spiritual preparedness, my prayers failed to help my marriage. In fact, over time, I grew spiritually fatigued from fighting an uphill battle for many years and ultimately falling into the allure of the enemy's deception. How could this have happened? Perhaps more important was the question Carole, my pastor's wife hurled at me: How could someone with the spiritual discernment that I had, become involved in of all things... witchcraft? My fall from grace landed me right in the enemy's camp, where I spent over a decade as a practicing witch (as foretold in my memoir, *A Witch's Encounter With God*[2]).

In that season of my life, the enemy was having a field day. Coming out of the deception I had bought into was no simple task, and certainly not without battle scars. But praise Jesus, He delivered and restored me back into a relationship with God Almighty. Amid the struggle, the Holy Spirit led me to a song that resonated in my spirit, based on Isaiah 61:1. This song, "The Spirit of the Sovereign Lord,"[3] became my battle anthem, proclaiming my deliverance from the occult and the darkness that once held me. This Scripture instilled in me God's divine purpose for my life: sharing the good news to those in spiritual darkness, praying for healing of the brokenhearted, proclaiming freedom to the captives, and opening the eyes of those blinded by the darkness of the god of this age.

Much later, after my deliverance and return to church, I consulted with Pastor Lyndon, one of my church's pastors, about participating in a spiritual warfare class at my favorite Christian coffee shop. He responded, "Ally, why go to the class when you could teach it?" He suggested I focus on another theological topic that I wasn't as familiar with, such as eschatology. At the time, I wasn't exactly feeling like a spiritual warrior, but in hindsight I see how God used for good what the enemy had intended for evil. Now I share how crucial it is for Christians to stay armored and anointed to avoid the enemy's trenches.

---

[2] S.A. Tower, *A Witch's Encounter With God: Taken From the Night* (Dwell Publishing LLC, 2017).
[3] Andy Park, "Spirit of the Sovereign Lord" on *Sampler* (Vineyard Music, 1994), CD.

In this book, I share what I learned from my original training in spiritual warfare, along with additional insights I've gained. Even more importantly, I share from my personal experience on both sides of the battlefield. My goal is to expose my vulnerability, share the strategic intelligence I gained, and show how to overcome enemy advances.

Opposing Armies

Our current age has blurred the lines between religions. This is by no mistake, but rather is a calculated plan by Satan, the enemy of our souls. One of the common themes that must be exposed is how the devil uses just enough of God's Word to make his translation sound good and godly, but then distorts it to fit his agenda. Our belief alone won't deter him, and just like he uses our belief or unbelief in demons to his advantage, he uses the same strategy with religion. He knows that every human soul has a void that only God can satisfy, so he tries to distort our view of who God is and offers a religious system that appeals to each individual. He will do anything to keep us from worshipping the one true God. He knows that any philosophy, other than God, that we buy into will eventually direct us right into his grasp.

I rejected God's truth and became entangled in Satan's lies. God rescued me from the depths of darkness, and I responded to His all-consuming love. But my mind still needed to be renewed. One Sunday while in church, to my surprise, God opened my spiritual eyes and revealed the army of God, comprised of thousands of angels and people who were wearing bright white robes. The radiance of Jesus, who sat upon a white horse leading the way, enthralled me. I then saw another army, a multitude of pagans donning many-colored robes and their leader carrying the scepter of the goddess. I finally realized, after so long, that their paths were heading in opposite directions; there was more than discord between them. I knew in my spirit that they opposed one another. This was war, and the battle for each had a different ending.

A deceived mind lacks logical reasoning. My obstructed

spiritual vision prevented me from understanding spiritual truth without divine intervention. I, like so many others, believed the illusion that the path I followed was enlightening. Many have believed the pagan mindset that every path eventually leads to the same place (i.e., heaven). However, we as Christians know that is a lie. Jesus makes that clear in Matthew 7:13–14: "Enter by the narrow gate; for wide is the gate and broad is the way that leads to destruction, and there are many who go in by it. Because narrow is the gate and difficult is the way which leads to life, and there are few who find it." There are not many ways to God. The truth is there is only one way to God, and that is through His Son, Jesus Christ (see John 14:6).

This Present Darkness

The vision I shared at the beginning of this chapter, I believe, was a precursor to the increasing spiritual darkness that now overshadows our world. We've been slowly descending into this depraved darkness since pure evil reared its ugly head, but now it is more apparent than ever before, though many people remain ignorant. We've watched with apprehension as our culture stumbled further into chaos and confusion. And as a nation, we have turned from God and fallen under the influence of the heinous creature described above. The previous administration was the catalyst to spoil the goods of our nation, and they quickly went to work. Rather than God-fearing politicians who wrote law into legislation that upheld godly principles, those who openly mocked God replaced them, creating laws that opposed the Word of God. The repercussions of this led to the drastic downfall of a nation that was once considered number one economically and militarily. We had fallen into a state of moral relativism and spiritual illiteracy. Violence, greed, corruption, and immorality soon plagued our world. Our one nation under God was close to becoming a secular humanist society—being destroyed from right within our very walls.

To make matters worse, many churches compromised their faith in order to assimilate into society, rather than provide the spiritual and moral compass for mankind to embrace. Because of our nation's nefarious climate, the political, economic, cultural, and social state of society suppressed our freedoms. We can't ignore the decline in church attendance or the profane comments on social media that show a progressive falling away from the traditional basic tenets of the gospel. This sudden darkness didn't come from out of nowhere; the ruler of darkness is an opportunist and seizes ground whenever and wherever possible.

Enduring Till the End

Considering the current state of the world, many Christians believe we are near the end times. While light has pierced through the spiritual darkness that befell upon our land, and the Lord has graciously lifted the oppression we were recently under for a time, we may have had a glimpse of what it would feel like to lose our freedoms and live under a demonic dictatorship. We've also seen an increase in wars and rumors of them, as well as other natural disasters. Yet, this is nothing compared to what the end times will be. If indeed the latter days are upon us, it might explain the apostasy growing at an alarming rate within the church; it is no longer limited to traditional church denominations but has spread throughout Christendom. Even so, we haven't reached a comparison to the "days of Noah." Not yet.

Still, regardless whether the coming of the Lord is nigh, the question is the same: What shall we do? Some may become discouraged and feel there is no time left to get right with God and/or share the gospel with a hostile and rebellious world. Others have become fearful and paralyzed as the impending day of doom closes in, while others joyfully cry out, "Come quickly, Lord Jesus!" and consider their labor complete.

Should we wave the timbrels and resolve that the day is done while waiting to see Him coming in the clouds? Is there no one left to bring the gospel to? Are there none remaining who are bound in chains in need of deliverance? Do we refrain from taking back the ground that the enemy has stolen? Is there anything left for us to do?

Woe to us if we just sit idle, waiting for the day of the Lord.

While the Lord tarries, we should continue to run the race (see 1 Corinthians 15:58), taking the gospel to the ends of the earth (see Mark 16:15) and setting the captives free (see Luke 4:18–21). We are to continue on course. It's business as usual. Matthew 24:36 tells us, "But of that day and hour no one knows, not even the angels of heaven, but My Father only." We may discern the times and realize that day is nearing, but a day in the Lord's timing we do not know. Therefore, let us press onward and do as Matthew 24:13–14 says: "But he who endures to the end shall be saved. And this gospel of the kingdom will be preached in all the world as a witness to all the nations, and then the end will come."

As Christian warriors, we cannot become complacent, silently picking and choosing the skirmishes close to home. Before long, we'll find the thorns and thistles in our own backyard if we don't conquer the evil that is spreading across the land. We need to look beyond and be ready to accept the marching orders that take us out of our comfort zone and into unknown territory. The war is raging, and we each have a position in the army of God. It's time we arise, armor up, and face the Goliath of our day. We are Jesus' hands and feet on this earth. It is not by might, nor by power, but by my Spirit, says the Lord (see Zechariah 4:6).

Our God Is Greater

If gearing up to take on giants in our flesh seems intimidating, that is not without reason; our enemy is a powerful unseen foe. Yet, we also need to remember that he is a defeated one. Colossians 2:15 says, "And having disarmed the powers and authorities, he made a public spectacle of them, triumphing over them by the cross." We stand at the foot of the cross, the place where Jesus defeated Satan and where we now have the power and authority to win the battle the devil wages against us.

As we engage in spiritual warfare, we must always remember how great our God is. Psalm 89:7 tells us He is "above all gods." The first thing we must grasp is that Satan and his demonic foes are nothing in comparison to our God. Psalm 113:5 asks who can compare with our God, and emphasizes His supremacy over anyone and anything. We cannot fall into the trap of fear, for the battle is not ours but the Lord's (see 2 Chronicles 20:15). No matter how daunting the situation we face, remember the Lord is the one who fights our battles. He is our Commander-in-Chief and we, His warrior soldiers, are under His command.

Enlisted in God's Army

As warriors for Christ, we are called to the front lines. As soon as our feet hit the ground, we boldly profess the gospel despite any opposition we face. That doesn't mean we aren't sweating in our boots the first few times we step on the battlefield, but in due time we learn what boldness really means. It's not a complete absence of fear by any means, but there is total reliance on the strength that comes from the Holy Spirit. In fact, by facing our fears and boldly advancing forward, we engage in warfare that enables us to overcome any obstacles that stand in the way. By applying intelligence from behind enemy lines, we can prayerfully adjust our strategies to avoid pitfalls and successfully carry out our mission.

Whether you're a recruit, a re-enlistee, or an active soldier in the army of God, you'll discover new intelligence and strategies on the pages that follow. As soldiers for our Savior, we are called to war. As His boots on the ground, we rely on the direction of the Holy Spirit—marching in confidence on the promises of God. To prepare for this spiritual battle, we must bunker down with God's Word, as it serves as both a defensive and offensive weapon in spiritual warfare.

We have the assurance that the Lord God will never abandon us in the midst of the battlefield. He will always have our backs. Deuteronomy 31:6 says, "Be strong and of good courage, do not fear nor be afraid of them; for the Lord your God, He is One who goes with you. He will not leave you nor forsake you." Our preparation is to develop the kind of faith that moves mountains by learning to trust the Lord with our whole being.

We must not rely on our own strength, which is limited by biological, neurological, and spiritual constraints. Remember,

"I can do all things through Christ who strengthens me" (Philippians 4:13). To overcome these barriers, we must rely on God, whose power is incomparably great and surpasses any measure of strength that we can possibly muster up.

We must know our identity in Christ and His weapons against the enemy. First John 5:4 tells us, "Everyone who has been born of God overcomes the world. And this is the victory that has overcome the world—our faith." One of the first things that the enemy will attack is our identity in order to weaken our faith and separate us from God. We're not a threat on the battlefield if we're isolated in self-pity. When we put our faith in Jesus, we gain a new identity in Him. We are no longer defined by our past, but by who God says we are, which is a child of God and co-heir with Christ.

Before we step out onto the battlefield, we need to know and resist our enemy, the devil, and not fall for his schemes. James 4:7 tells us, "Submit yourselves to God, resist the devil and he will flee from you." Engaging in battle against an unseen enemy is challenging. In order to find out who we're up against, we must study the Scriptures to learn who our adversary is, and in order to resist him, we must learn what it means to stand firm in our faith and rely on God's power instead of our own strength.

As Christians, we live out our calling and anointing as ambassadors of God's kingdom, actively taking part in the fight against evil. First John 4:4 says, "You are from God, little children, and have overcome them: because greater is He in you than he who is in the world." By default, we are called into spiritual warfare in the army of God at our salvation. In order to fulfill that calling, we receive God's anointing, which empowers us to engage the weapons of our warfare against the enemy.

Now that I've shared with you the vision, my warfare history, and our current nefarious spiritual climate, it's time we prepare for battle. In the next chapter, we'll evaluate the first of three spiritual battlefields, the mind.

Behind Enemy Lines

CHAPTER 2

The Mind Field

The most talked-about field of warfare is the battlefield of the mind, and while the mind is certainly the most direct attack we face, it is by far not the only battlefield. There are three battlegrounds where good and evil engage in warfare: the mind field, earth field, and the heavenlies. As Christians, our warfare is fought in both the mind field and the earth field, which leaves the heavenlies to the angelic and demonic host. While we refrain from waging war in heavenly places, it is important to have a basic understanding of the spiritual battles that take place there simultaneously, as they have a significant impact here on earth. Let's begin with the battlefield closest to home, the mind field. But before we step foot on the mind field, we need to make sure our minds are battle ready.

The Battle of the Mind

God created man "in the image of God" (see Genesis 1:26–27) and gave him a fascinating mind that empowers godlike abilities. Unlike any other of God's creations, the human mind mirrors divine qualities, such as moral thought, creativity, and spiritual insight. We often associate the brain with the mind, but actually the mind is to the brain what the spirit is to the body. We read in Job 32:8, "But there is a spirit in man, and the breath of the Almighty gives him understanding"; therefore, the spirit in man given to us by God is what provides our mind's intelligence. The mind is also where thought and comprehension take place and decisions to choose good or evil are formed. No wonder our mind is a primary target of attack.

One of the things the human mind is capable of is carving a neurological pathway within the brain in which our thoughts travel, and in turn our brain constructs its own expressway, thus providing a bustling of thoughts to traverse on a day-to-day basis. To change our behavior after constructing this pathway, we must deconstruct the expressway and begin again to reprogram our behavior. The Bible tells us in Romans 12:2, "And do not be conformed to this world, but be transformed by the renewing of your mind that you may prove what is good and acceptable and the perfect will of God." As believers, we must commit to renewing our minds daily through the power of God's Word, and in time, God will create a new righteous road map.

The enemy knows how God created the human mind and how it works. The last thing he wants is for the Spirit of God to impart spiritual knowledge to the human mind, gradually shaping and molding us into the likeness of God. Here again, Satan takes the Word of God and distorts it for his purpose. The enemy's tactic follows God's design except that rather than impart wisdom, it strips the mind of all godly thoughts, knowledge, and nature. That's exactly what he did with mine. After convincing me to doubt God, Satan went on the attack. Not surprisingly, a magazine ad put me in direct communication with a high priest shortly after I discovered Wicca. I must say, the devil's strategy was clever. I began my studies by stripping my mind of all godly beliefs, which others had supposedly implanted, and believe it or not, the Bible was the resource used to do it. The high priest assigned me selected Scriptures to dissect—verses that seemed to contradict one another and ultimately were used to discredit the Bible as truth.

Once my mind had been stripped of everything I once

believed, the high priest's next step was to rebuild. He emphasized the need to research and form my own conclusions, thus creating my own truth, rather than rely on information imposed by others, such as the Christian church. A clever method indeed, for it makes us feel as though no one is forcing their beliefs on us. Next, they led me into self-discovery. Considering man's fallen nature, this proves disastrous in itself, but the deception goes much farther. This opened my mind to demons who went right to work providing me with ungodly books, magazines, internet sites, and people. It was like selecting my favorite ice-cream flavor; I could choose from an unbeknownst list of demonic doctrines. Brick by brick, the fortress in my mind rose until the stronghold was fortified. I was tricked into believing I was in control; the truth is, demons had hijacked my mind. That's how cunning Satan is. Here I thought I was in control when actually he was.

The Devil's Mind Games

In order to defeat the devil on the mind field, we must first crucify our thoughts at the foot of the cross. We must "put off our old self, which belongs to our former manner of life and is corrupt through deceitful desires, and to be renewed in the spirit of our minds, and to put on the new self, created after the likeness of God in true righteousness and holiness" (Ephesians 4:22–24). It is not enough to know the Scriptures intellectually; we must believe, declare, and meditate on them so the Holy Spirit can bring revelation to our minds.

If we have not brought our every thought into captivity to the obedience of Christ (see 2 Corinthians 10:5), we have an unguarded mind, which is an easy target. All the enemy and demons have to do is drop a thought bomb, then sit back and watch as our own humanness sets a domino effect into action and takes over our way of thinking. It only takes one little lie whispered in our ear to separate spouses, split families, or divide an entire church.

The subtle maneuver of a few demonic forces easily succeeds

in implanting "thought seeds" into their human targets, our minds. Seemingly out of nowhere, a thought pops into our heads, and we have but a few seconds to take it captive or entertain it (see 2 Corinthians 10:5). These are the devil's mind games, and it's a game we must refuse to play. Instead, we should fill our mind with "whatever is true, whatever is honorable, whatever is just, whatever is pure, whatever is lovely, whatever is commendable, if there is any excellence, if there is anything worthy of praise, think about these things" (Philippians 4:28).

Another game the enemy likes to play is creating a landmine in our subconscious mind. Satan does not fight fair, and he will use anything within his power to manipulate and control our thoughts. The attack can come when we're distracted, not feeling well, and especially when we're asleep. The thought is silently and precisely hidden away in our subconscious mind, undetected in its vast reservoir, while it weaves a web of destructive thoughts that will play a big role in our interactions with ourselves and others. It's so hidden that it can take months or even years before it's exposed, and by then it's already repatterned our habits and rewired our thinking. These thoughts can be game changers and will require us to not only dissect the lies that are at the heart of these intrusive thoughts but to also fill our mind with the truth of the gospel in order to restructure our thinking patterns that have been spiritually crippled.

Not all evil thoughts come from the enemy or his demons. Sometimes they come from our own sinfulness and the enemy simply provides the justification our mind uses to engage in it. A good example of this is Judas Iscariot at the Last Supper. Judas wasn't exactly a disciple after God's own heart. He had already yielded to his sinful nature by stealing from the disciple's money bag (see John 12:6). Then Satan used Judas's greed and love of money to betray Jesus for a bag of silver. It's not always Satan's seeds that have been sown into our mind that led us down the path of destruction; sometimes it's our own fleshly lust, and Satan simply provides the opportunity.

Satan's Search Engine

Many times, the devil uses what I call "Satan's Search Engine" to tempt our sinful nature and provide the opportunity for us to fall. It's yet another mind game and works in much the same way as the internet. Have you ever noticed when you search for, say, a car on your search engine, every social media platform that you visit suddenly displays the car that you're looking for? In fact, you can't navigate or web surf anywhere without seeing that car, in all different colors and loaded with luxurious features, flash before your eyes. And they tend to have some pretty good price tags too.

Satan's Search Engine works in the same way. The devil or his demons know what you searched for. They've watched the movie you turned on last night that showed a man's lust for another man's wife. Or that music video that invoked demons in a ritualistic performance. What was it that you searched for on Satan's Search Engine? You may think it was innocent enough, that you only looked and didn't actually commit the sin, and that, really, compared to what's in the world nowadays, it was quite mild. Yet now it seems the word is out and the entire world marketing system is suggesting every lustful movie, demonic video, or occult book—all kinds of dark entertainment. Those hidden sins haven't stayed in Vegas. No, every possible temptation catered specifically for you is flashing before your mind night and day.

That's Satan, and that's how his search engine works. Before we know it, our subtle interest becomes a compulsive addiction.

Subtle Attacks

Sometimes the battle begins in the heavenlies, before being passed down to earth demons who harass us before attacking our mind. Here is an example from my life.

Soon after I began writing my memoir, the subtle attacks began. I'd finish writing an entire section only to have my computer crash and lose hours of saved data. It was decision time—I would either choose to give in to a spirit of fear or stand firm. I chose to stand firm, following Psalm 27:1: "The Lord is my light and my salvation whom shall, I fear? The Lord is the stronghold of my life, of whom shall I be afraid?" I began rewriting entire chapters, and this time backing them up. The computer crashes soon became only temporary nuisances, and God provided me with personal computer techs for quick computer repairs and retrieval of lost data.

The attack then moved on to the battlefield of my mind. Reminders of my past and guilt flooded my thoughts. Although I had forgiven myself, I struggled to accept the grace given to me. Pastor Lyndon urged me to persevere, reminding me of the actual date I'd given my life back to the Lord, and would reinforce my identity as a child of God.

To silence these thoughts, the Bible instructs us to "demolish arguments and every pretension that sets itself up against the knowledge of God, and we take captive every thought to make it obedient to Christ" (2 Corinthians 10:5 NIV). And that's exactly what I did. I rejected any guilt-ridden thoughts and filled my mind with Scripture and psalms.

Even today, the enemy tries to use the same old tactics with me. I've come to expect demonic interference whenever writing; it's no longer a surprise attack. The challenges include random computer problems, attempted hacks, missing texts, constant phone interruptions, and social media attacks, among other things. Obviously, the issue isn't the writing itself, but rather its subject matter. It's really become more of a nuisance than anything else, and one that requires my preparation, prayer, and perseverance.

Forty Years in Bewilderment

In Numbers 13, we find Moses sending twelve spies to scope out the Promised Land. Ten of them brought back a negative report. They returned fearful, saying they were like grasshoppers compared next to the Anak giants who occupied the land. Only two, Joshua and Caleb, weren't afraid and encouraged the Israelites to trust God and subdue the land. The Israelites discouraged by reports of giants, hesitated to claim the Promised

Land. They would spend another forty years wandering in the wilderness when the land that flowed with milk and honey was theirs for the taking.

In this story, we see what happens when we allow the enemy to plant doubt and fear in our mind. Despite the promise of God, they believed the lie and continued to wander in the desert. How many times have we done the same? We know God has given us His blessings, but the enemy whispers in our ear, and rather than tear down the doubt and unbelief, we listen to the lies and miss out on God's promised blessing. Interestingly, after forty long years, the Israelites finally went in to possess the land. And once there, they found the Canaanites were fearful of them because they feared their God. Forty years they lived a lie and missed out on the blessings of God.

Let their mistake be a lesson to us. The battle that rages in the mind is a struggle where a worldly mind falls for the devil's lies instead of being Christ-centered. We must commit to aligning our thoughts with the Word of God and rejecting anything contrary. We don't want to miss out on God's blessings.

Now let's look at the earth field.

Behind Enemy Lines

CHAPTER 3

The Earth Field

While spiritual warfare is a means of equipping ourselves to ward off a direct attack on our mind, our warfare goes beyond self-preservation. Many times, the battle begins in the mind field, but warfare does not confine itself to the mind and extends beyond it. This next field is the earthly battlefield. The earth is more than a dwelling place for us to live; it's also the place God uses for our spiritual growth and preparation for our eternal dwelling place.

It only takes one quick glance around the world today to see the brunt of spiritual darkness that has befallen us. Certainly, Satan and his angels established this present darkness when they fell to earth thousands of years ago. But if our eyes are open, we see the blatant evil running rampant in our world today. The enemy no longer even attempts to hide; he operates in plain sight. We need to set our sights beyond ourselves and be ready to embark outside our comfort zone and onto the front lines of this battlefield.

It is helpful to understand that we're not lone soldiers left to conquer an enemy whose sole purpose is our personal defeat. We're gearing up for the battles we face today, and preparing for the greatest battle of all time, and the enemy knows it. He may be already working to advance his army, but remember that our God is greater. First Peter 5:9 instructs us to resist him and stand firm in the faith because our brothers and sisters around the world are enduring the same suffering. We're not in this alone. We have other soldiers in this war alongside us, both human and angelic.

Remember, our God is omnipresent (see Proverbs 15:3; Jeremiah 23:24; Job 28:24; Romans 1:20), and we therefore have the assurance that He is always with us. Satan is not omnipresent. Job 1:7 confirms this: "And the Lord said to Satan, 'From where do you come?' So, Satan answered the Lord and said, 'From going to and fro on the earth, and from walking back and forth on it.'" We are not always his primary target. His range of attack spreads far and wide, but he cannot be in our camp all the time. He comes and attempts to cause havoc before going off to another place, instead sending demons in his place to do his bidding.

The Seven Key Earthly Battlefields

The world continues to evolve. However, certain things remain unchanged, such as the battlefields where we engage in spiritual warfare. In 1975, Loren Cunningham (Youth With A Mission) and Bill Bright (Campus Crusade) identified seven key cultural areas needing leadership for societal change: the home; the church; schools; government and politics; the media; arts, entertainment and sports; and commerce, science, and technology. According to Jeff Fountain, a YWAM member for over forty years who was present when Loren Cunningham revealed the Seven Mountains of Influence revelation, "In my understanding, Loren (who passed away October 6, 2023) was not encouraging others to 'storm these mountains' or take them by force. Rather, he was urging faithful engagement in the various spheres of life, as salt and light, as yeast, as planted mustard seeds."[4] Over the years, Cunningham's original teaching was hijacked by those encouraging Christian dominionism, adding mandate to its title.

If we look closer, we find that these aren't just areas of

---

4   Jeff Fountain, "The distortion of inspiration that led to toxic Christian nationalism," *Christianity Today*, November 26, 2024, https://www.christiandaily.com/news/distortion-of-inspiration-leading-to-toxic-christian-nationlism.

influence, but the earthly battlegrounds where the bulk of our warfare occurs. Bill Bright of Campus Crusade had a similar epiphany around the same time as Cunningham. Bright penned "Kingdoms at War," which dealt with exploring how biblical influences were being eroded from the foundational structures of society. Both Cunningham's and Bright's revelations together became known as The Seven Spheres.[5] In retrospect, their revelation might have been a warning about Christians ignoring societal influence while living in but not of the world. The church's long disengagement from worldly matters left a void readily filled by the enemy. Principalities now control a majority of the seven spheres, wielding considerable societal influence. We have lost a seat at the table because of our absence. The battle to regain our place is the spiritual warfare we now face. As Fountain says, it's a "bottom-up approach," one that we fight on our knees. These are the key battlefronts of our earthly warfare.

The Attack on the Home

God planned for His kingdom on earth to be established through Adam's lineage (Genesis 1). As part of His grand design, He assigned Adam and Eve the critical role of caring for the earth. He established the traditional family unit—a man, a woman, and their children—on a God-sanctioned lifelong commitment of holy matrimony. The family, as God intended, forms the base of His earthly kingdom, reflecting the bond between Christ and the church.

Knowing this, we see that Satan wasted no time in his attack on God's plan. His vilest attack is the depravity of the holy union by same-sex marriage. This deception tries to justify itself by claiming not to discriminate against the love two people have for one another outside of the traditional mold. Satan, however, will exploit our compassion, to fulfill his global agenda. Many churches have compromised their values due to societal pressure, adding insult to injury. We find major denominations failing to protect the sanctity of marriage between one man and one woman. Yet, it is possible to love all people while remaining

---

[5] "Seven Spiritual Battlefields," Spirit & Truth, June 17, 2019, https://spiritandtruthonline.org/seven-spiritual-battlefields/.

unwavering in our commitment to God's will. Our focus shouldn't be on numbers in our pews, but on the number of names written in the book of life.

Satan doesn't care whether a couple lives together before marriage, divorces, or engages in a same-sex union. All of these destroy a God-ordained marriage designed within a family unit, which is the backbone of our society. Broken marriages impact the children and disrupt the stability of the family unit. Same-sex unions and living-together arrangements are not God-ordained replacements for holy matrimony. This battlefront is multi-layered, and it is targeted for the destruction of the holy union of man and woman. Make no mistake, this attack goes deeper than marriage itself. It also aims at the representation of marriage, which is the relationship between Christ and His church.

The Attack on the Church

One of the most prevalent battlefronts is on the front line of the church. As Christians, we know there is only one true God, and that the only way to reach Him is through Jesus. However, as we look around our world, we find many religions with many gods and many paths to follow. As of 2024, Christianity is the world's largest religion, with 2.6 percent of the global population identifying as Christian; however, Islam's 1.9 percent population is the fastest growing.[6] This shows that demonic obstacles have hindered the spread of the good news through evangelism.

Within mankind is an internal desire to seek God, but he often rebels, finding a faux replacement for God instead. By doing so, he violates God's first commandment: to worship the one true God. In God's place, man worships various foreign gods and engages in forms of worship that are forbidden in Scripture. Behind this demonic activity is the enemy's calculated plan to occupy this nation, and the world at large, before Christ's return. If we're to reclaim territory, we need to stand our ground and withstand the enemy's advances.

---

6 "Religious People by Country 2025," World Population Review, accessed June 19, 2025, https://worldpopulationreview.com/country-rankings/religion-by-country.

The Attack on Schools

How many hours in a day would you have your child sit at the feet of demons who indoctrinate them with immorality? Of course, the answer would be a flat-out zero, yet we send our children into public schools taken over by an anti-Christian worldview. Most children begin school as early as four or five years old (pre-K4 and kindergarten) and continue until graduation (twelfth grade), an average of 14,040 hours. That's 14,040 hours spent in a classroom setting with an educator who likely does not share the same moral conviction or values as Christian parents.

As well, the curriculum used by most public schools now includes white privilege (racism), equity (unfairness), lack of parental rights (parent's voice silenced), and the existence of widespread systemic racism, which pollutes the minds of our most vulnerable.

History is being rewritten to exclude the foundations of our country. Children are being told that our society's history was evil, resulting in the removal of statues, books, and anything that could spark discussion about our historical past. The system prevents teachers from teaching certain topics and discourages student patriotism.

During the COVID-19 pandemic, many parents, for the first time, got an actual glimpse of what their children are being taught. There was a time when teachers and parents worked together to help the child achieve their highest potential, but unbeknownst to a lot of parents, that agenda changed. There is now an underlying agenda that teaches the child to conform and believe whatever is taught, rather than use critical thinking skills and conclude on their own.

Even worse, the child's very own godly identity is under attack, and it has Satan written all over it. Children are taught that they can change their God-given body into the opposite gender. The movement for transgender equality has become a trend that mutilates our youths' bodies, thus preventing them from living a normal life. While children cannot take Tylenol at school without parental approval, schools provide them access to gender blockers—and often, authorities charge parents with child endangerment for attempting to refuse this access.

The battlefront in schools and education is treacherous. All opposing parties know the significance of the prize that awaits them—our children. As noted in Parent Power, an online resource for protecting children, Adolf Hitler boldly stated, "He alone who owns the youth, gains the future," showing not just the importance of early education, but providing an object lesson in the attempts to manipulate and impose control through it.[7] In the United States, the states recently resumed control of the education system, a move many people welcome. Those in democratic states who currently oppose these harmful ideologies in schools are the exception. For these families, the lack of governmental oversight will do nothing to deter using this strategy to control the minds of the next generation and convert their thinking to a godless, socialist worldview.

The Attack on Government and Politics

Government is a God-ordained institution that enacts justice, punishes evil, and protects the people. Government that governs by God's design benefits its people and establishes a system that enables all men to be treated fairly. As long as the governing authority remains within this framework, the society prospers, but when the government becomes corrupt and self-serving, it quickly becomes a suppressed society within the scope of a political hierarchy. This type of government has set a time clock for its future collapse.

Our government has its share of political corruption, namely those who support their own (many times bought) agendas rather than the people they vowed to serve. In the past, we have witnessed money laundering, as well as the exchange of money with foreign governments that could jeopardize the sovereignty of our nation. This corruption has affected each citizen, and forged a

---

[7] "Give Me a Child Till He's 7, and I Will Show You the Man – The Next Step," Parent Power, January 18, 2021, https://parentpower.family/give-me-a-child-till-hes-7-and-i-will-show-you-the-man/.

moral and ethical divide between party lines. It's illogical reasoning that we would find those hard-bent on supporting social unrest, lawlessness, and criminal activity that contribute to both a moral and economic decline. But *illogical* is the key, as this disordered behavior is often the result of demonic influences.

Satan's battle plan exceeds far beyond our nation to a globalist agenda. Many have claimed a "New World Order" has existed for years, but people have dismissed it as a conspiracy. This is not the case any longer, for the elite and powerful now openly admit to their desire to establish a one-world government. Satan's agenda is no longer done in complete secrecy. Nor is it hidden just within the walls of Freemasonry or the Bohemian Grove. Revelation 13 and 17 tell of a global world system that the beast will introduce to prepare for the last war between good and evil. Until then, we must fall to our knees before God, repent of our nation's sins, and pray that God removes wicked political parties from power and that He raises up those who spearhead righteousness to govern. Then, with much prayer and intercession, we must execute our liberty at the voting polls.

The Attack on Media

Media communication includes all forms of print and digital media, comprising visual and audio communication with the ability to reach target audiences. In today's technological world, we can communicate globally. Not only do we have the means to reach the world, but computers can translate the language used into the native tongue of the receiver. This field of communication is wide open.

While media communication enables many good things, such as access for people everywhere to buy books, read websites, and use social media to spread the gospel globally, it also serves as an ungodly source to spread evil on the same scale. One conflict we face is with the social media companies who have influence on political or other religious views. They use algorithms to filter, rank, and select content for users. By doing so, they control who sees what is communicated on social media and many times can limit the audience of those they oppose. In addition, hidden on the dark web are all kinds of dark, illegal, dangerous, and diabolical forms of telecommunication, unbeknownst to most except those who lurk there. This limitless form of illicit activities available to people provides the opportunity for a global-scale evil agenda.

In the Bible, the story of the Tower of Babel foretells of a similar situation. Satan used mankind's singular language to unite man in his evil plan of rebellion against God (see Genesis 11). The people who God had set up to be divided into tribes instead converged into one land and contrived to build a city and a tower to reach the heavens. *Matthew Henry's Commentary* on Genesis 11 explains, "They would be like the Most High, or would come as near him as they could, not in holiness but in height. They forgot their place, and scorning to creep on the earth, resolved to climb to heaven, not by the door or ladder, but some other way."[8] Satan also desired to ascend above the clouds and to be like God (see Isaiah 14:14).

With the language barrier broken by internet language translation, the enemy can gather those whose minds he has blinded to many evil practices. The internet has become

- a tool for terrorist groups to recruit, and to plan and set attacks in motion;
- a source for child sex traffickers to move and sell children, both within and beyond our country's borders; and
- a place to communicate for drug smugglers to carry out distribution of drugs both within and from one country to another.

We know that with the Tower of Babel, God stepped in and the tower fell. God scattered the people abroad and confused their languages. I believe that through this example from Scripture, God revealed our combat prayer strategy which is twofold:

1. When entering this battle zone, we can pray for language

---

8 "Genesis 11:1–4," *Matthew Henry's Commentary* on Bible Gateway, accessed June 19, 2025, https://www.biblegateway.com/resources/matthew-henry/Gen.11.1-Gen.11.4.

barriers between evildoers that would confuse their plans and cause them to fall through. Here is an example of this prayer strategy: After coming out of witchcraft, I struggled with temptation and, on one such occasion, I failed to resist and ended up going to a ritual. Pastor Lyndon told me later that, knowing this, he had prayed for confusion in our midst. I can confirm that there was chaos within the coven and no successful magick done that night.

2. When we pray, we can use our prayer language, which is a Spirit-led form of communication that exceeds human and even demonic understanding, thus preventing interference.

The Attack on Arts and Entertainment

Visual and performing arts, television, movies, books, and music are only some of the creative expressions included in the arts and entertainment industry's diverse tapestry. Through the internet, people can access all art forms within the comfort of their own home. The explicit content that is entering our homes is alarming. Many movies, music videos, and television shows portray unwholesome methods of dealing with life issues. They instill fear and violence and promote lies to their audience. Even more alarming, they encourage sexuality and occult practices, especially focused on our youth, desensitizing and creating a vacuum of demonic activity to be absorbed in their minds and spirits.

Social media is not the only limit of arts and entertainment, as the silver screen and music concerts also follow suit. Although people spend less time at these venues of entertainment, they can be more influential. Movies create a live effect with their 3D screen and surround sound, and it's almost like the viewer is part of the motion picture itself. Concerts are even more extreme, with concert goers interactively taking part in the event. Added high-tech special effects illuminate the event to an even greater degree.

The stars themselves will have God to contend with for their actions as they engage in ritualistic performances, incorporating occult symbolism and singing lyrics with subliminal messages.

They evoke mystical imagery regardless whether the performer endorses occultism or not. By incorporating these types of practices, they are evoking demons while subjecting themselves, as well as their fans, to demonic influences. The examples below provide a glimpse of the arts and entertainment battlefront.

As reported by a major magazine, fans who attended a pop star's concert reported bizarre experiences following the event. Many later took to social media platforms like Reddit to describe their inability to recall details or even large parts of the performance. One Philadelphia fan stated, "Looking back, it feels like an out-of-body experience, as though it didn't really happen to me."[9] Psychiatrists attempt to explain the phenomenon away as overstimulation and sensory overload, but people have been going to concerts for many years without expressing "post-concert amnesia," let alone out-of-body experiences (unless perhaps drug induced). This pop-star icon, who many young teens and tweens look up to, incorporates occult imagery and rituals into her performances, which may invoke demons and manifest a trancelike state.

Another example is that of a young eccentric woman slithering on stage. During the concert, the camera captured her experiencing kundalini activation, bending her body completely backward and exhibiting strange facial contortions. One of her songs tells of a fallen angel landing on earth, although she claims she is not a Satanist and her song is about climate change. Despite what she says, the evidence is in the poisonous fruit being served up to her unsuspecting audience.[10]

The sports arena attack has had a major impact on the youth, many of whom idolize star players who are not always the best role models. But the most grievous attack is on women's sports, where biological males identifying as females insist on competing with biological females. They even want to share locker

---

9   Angela Haupt, "Why You Can't Remember That Taylor Swift Concert All Too Well," TIME, May 26, 2023, https://time.com/6282468/taylor-swift-concert-memory/.
10 Claudia Willen, "Billie Eilish says that she was 'super religious' as a kid even though her family wasn't: That went on for years," Business Insider, July 21, 2020, https://www.businessinsider.com/billie-eilish-super-religious-as-a-kid-2020-7.

rooms with their teammates, attempting to create the illusion that there is no biological difference between the two. Of course, a male player's biological makeup is physically dominant in comparison to that of a female, making for unfair competition.

The Attack on Commerce, Science, and Technology

Here I want to look at the battleground of commerce, or business and the economy. This is a large playing field promoting good or evil. It funds all other battlefronts, thus determining their success or failure. Money is powerful and buys influence, thus making the love of money the root of all evil (see 1 Timothy 6:10). Business can be a blood-thirsty battle of greed where one will sell their soul to reach the top. Along the way, the enemy has planted many snares that cause many to lose sight of ethically achieving their goal. Reaching the top of the ladder while stepping on others along the way, and pushing others off the corporate ladder while making a few shady deals, may make a person wealthy on earth, but remember, our goal is to run the race of heaven, where the treasures of earth can't go.

As it stands, there are many legal ways to conduct business unethically, enabling fraud that goes undetected and circumventing our government tax dollars to unelected bureaucrats. The last place we'd like to find flawed business practices is within the church, but if we're not covering our finances with prayer, we're leaving our safe deposit box wide open.

I'd like to share a story of the Lord's protection of me. It happened at a large church that started an LLC as a side business to raise funds for their school. The LLC purchased liens of homes where owners had fallen behind paying utility bills and held them for an allotted two-year period, then forced homeowners struggling to put food on their table to pay the unpaid lien, including 18 percent interest and an additional penalty, or have their home foreclosed on. That allowed the business to gain thousands of dollars from homeowners unable to come up with the money, and to enrich itself by reselling the homes of those who were less fortunate and unable to pay. These homes became the cash cow for the shell corporation tied to the church. One woman was told to pay $57,000 to avoid foreclosure. The LLC took her home, leaving her homeless. Church officials scolded another woman for her tax delinquency and then, in front of the media, gave her a bag of groceries as a token of goodwill.

A similar scenario could have happened to me. After my marital separation, an enormous amount of debt, including unpaid utilities, fell on me. At first, although I had found full-time work, I was struggling just to meet current bills, let alone those overdue. But praise God, when the foreclosure notice came, I had just received a sizable income tax return and unexpected unclaimed funds that enabled me to pay off the debt. Years later, I received an additional financial blessing: Apparently, the church had pleaded guilty to the criminal charge of "conspiring to eliminate the competitive nature of public bids," which started a public lawsuit action, and I received a check for overpayment fees and additional interest that I had paid to keep my home out of foreclosure. It took time, but justice was served.

Signs of demonic influence are all over this. To begin with, the enemy oppresses the poor—the down-and-out individuals who suffer circumstances that cause financial crises resulting in the inability to pay their taxes and utilities. Next, Satan weasels his way into the government and influences it to ignore its godly purpose of protecting its people and their property (see Romans 13:1). In this case, the government created an environment of taking advantage of the needy and those living below the poverty line, while the devil cunningly used, of all things, his adversary the church to deliver the final blow. It only takes a little greed. After all, the church claimed it was for expanding the ministry. Astronomical fees left the disheartened homeless. To further the insult to injury, the enemy, by manipulating the church's arm, set a negative precedent to the community that this is how Jesus cares for the poor. This real-life example exposed the level of evil this church leadership was totally content with, and issues a warning to us all against financial compromise.

Now that you have a better understanding of how the enemy

attacks the seven key areas, we're going to look at the warfare that occurs in the heavenlies.

Behind Enemy Lines

CHAPTER 4

The Spiritual Heavenlies

Warfare in the heavenlies is often downplayed as an "out of sight, out of mind" scenario, or it's viewed as the end times battle as described in Revelation 12. But a continuous warfare in the heavenlies began when Lucifer, the devil, rebelled against God and God then cast him and his angels out. This confrontation was a pivotal moment that set the stage for the ongoing conflict that continues to this day. It's not expected to end until the last war, when one word spoken by Jesus will destroy all the armies that have gathered against Him. That's pretty impressive, but think about what power the sword of the Spirit (the Bible) holds. Even more amazing is what it gives to us to ward off the enemy.

We may put off thinking about the heavenly battles since they can seem so far away and out of touch with our reality. Yet, what we may not understand is that there is a very real spiritual reality in heaven that parallels the events on earth. We experience the fallout of heavenly warfare more often than most people realize. Part of our problem is that we place our focus on the physical and material levels, neglecting our spiritual self for a materialistic worldview. Think of it this way: Standing on the East Coast shore, we cannot witness an amphibious landing and assault on a West Coast beach, but we will still experience the effects of it, thousands of miles away.

Evidence of the Heavenlies

It's difficult to comprehend an existing battlefield without knowing its location, so let's answer this question: Where exactly are "the heavenlies"? In our physical state of mind, we think of the heavenlies as the sky since it's visible to the naked eye; or the celestial plane that encompasses the sun, moon, and stars; or perhaps beyond that to outer space. However, our world is not simply one-dimensional. The Bible references the heavenlies as a spiritual realm that coexists alongside our physical world (see Ephesians 6:12 NIV).

While unseen, the spiritual realm is just as real as the air we breathe and is subject to interaction with our natural world. The spiritual heavenlies, also known as simply the heavenlies, are within the stellar heaven, though it's not limited to a set place high above our earthly atmosphere. It is rather a spiritual realm, with boundaries running between earth and the third heaven, which is where God's glory resides. Spiritual beings of both good (the angels of God) and evil (the enemy's demons) occupy this ethereal location. Therefore, since both angelic and demonic activity operate in this realm, angels and demons both can move and operate between the spiritual and physical dimensions. Angels pass through this area to deliver messages and minister to God's people. They're also sent to come against the powers of darkness when demons attempt to thwart the purposes of God. However, the devil also uses this place as a base to exert his power over wicked spiritual forces in the heavens, and execute his attack on the church. You may find it strange that God would allow demonic activity in the heavenlies to war against humanity, but it is part of His sovereign plan in allowing free will, testing our faith, and demonstrating His power and authority.

This is the area where conflicts arise and angelic warfare between the kingdom of darkness and the kingdom of God is engaged. The outcome of this ongoing warfare affects individual people on earth as well as real-world events. The best place to form our understanding of this spiritual reality is Scripture. In the beginning, the Spirit of God hovered over the waters that surrounded the earth (Genesis 1:2). This placed God not in some distant dimension, but near and interactive in our earthly dwelling place. The problem has come because, over time, man has grown ignorant of the spiritual dimension, not trusting God and even His existence, and choosing to rely on his own human inventions or scientific methods.

One example of this is air. Although unseen to our physical eyes, the evidence of its existence is everywhere around us. What man discovered only three hundred years ago as scientific evidence, God revealed by establishing the weight for the wind in Job 28:25. Through this example, we can understand the existence of things beyond what science can physically prove, at least for the time being. While we cannot see the spiritual dimension with our physical eyes, it parallels our physical existence and shapes our earthly reality. We also can affect the spiritual realm depending on our own prayerful engagement or lack thereof.

Biblical Encounters of the Heavenlies

A search of the Scriptures reveals many encounters with, or glimpses into, the heavenlies that have been granted to man. Jacob received a glimpse into the heavenlies through a dream of a staircase resting on the earth and extending into heaven where God was (Genesis 23:12). Angels were ascending and descending on the stairway between the physical and spiritual realms, giving Jacob a view of the angelic interaction between heaven and earth. Many times, what happens in the heavenlies is executed here on earth. Through this example in Scripture, we gain an understanding of how the spiritual realm operates in continuity with our physical world.

We find another example in the burning bush (Exodus 3:2–4). The angel of the Lord appeared to Moses from within flames that miraculously did not consume the bush. Once the angel stepped aside, God spoke to Moses, which was the starting point of Moses's ability to hear God's voice. Further on, God traveled in a cloud by day and fire by night, leading Moses and His people out of Egypt (Exodus 40:36). Instructed by God, Moses built the tabernacle, which became God's dwelling place, thus revealing heaven here on earth.

Ezekiel's vision of moving wheels showed that prophets could see into the heavenlies. This vision symbolized God's omnipresence and omniscience, thus showing that His presence exists both in heaven and on earth, eternally. The description positions the wheels on the earth, but their height connects them to God's Spirit, highlighting the link between heaven and earth (see Ezekiel 1). In addition, Isaiah saw the Lord, high and exalted, seated on a throne; his train filled the temple and above him were angels (Isaiah 6:1). The temple envisioned is the house of the Lord, of which the temple on earth is its shadow—two spiritual realms running parallel to one another that assisted Isaiah in his ministry.

In 2 Kings 6, we find Elisha's servant awakening to find the city surrounded by an army of horses and chariots. In order to relieve his servant's fear, Elisha opened the man's spiritual eyes so that he could see what was happening in the spiritual realm. The servant saw the mountain was full of horses and chariots of fire all around Elisha. When looking through only physical eyes, we are many times unaware of what is occurring in the heavenlies.

Testimonial Evidence of the Heavenlies

The Bible recounts many people's spiritual encounters, providing the best testimonial evidence of the spiritual realm. These encounters extend beyond the Old and New Testaments. Today, by utilizing our gift of discernment, we still can see glimpses into the heavenlies. During the time I was being lured into the occult, I witnessed the battle over my soul and watched the struggle between angels and demons in the heavenlies on numerous occasions. Then I lived out the results here on earth. The situation presented a strange dichotomy: my gift of discernment persisted through my occult involvement, though significantly hampered. Here is one of those occasions.

I was at home talking on the phone with Pastor Larry and his wife, Carole, who were like spiritual parents to me. Suddenly, it was as though I was looking down into their kitchen and witnessing both sides of our conversation. Pastor Larry was sharing the Word of the Lord with me, but then Carole interrupted, offering her own opinion. It then appeared as though a veil lifted, and I saw into the spiritual realm.

I saw God's angels grasping at my pastor's words, which slipped past me, while attempting to stop the words being hurled at me. The angels took the words and ascended upward toward heaven, while others descended, bringing unfamiliar words back down. They were carrying these words back and forth. Simultaneously, I saw beings the color of smoky quartz, who held thought-forms, tauntingly projecting them like arrows at both their heads. The beings then watched their tempers flare as words spewed back and forth between them.

In an instant, the angels were gone, and I was back in my kitchen. Through the phone I heard Carole make an ultimate declaration, which was that I was a waste of his time and didn't want the truth. I could sense the frustration in Pastor Larry's voice as he promised to keep me in prayer before hanging up. At the sound of the dial tone coming from my phone, I was speechless.

Interpreting this event revealed that the angels of God were intervening in the conversation by removing the word assaults that were being hurled at me and taking them up to God. The words the angels brought down were words of encouragement meant to be spoken to me. The demons were the darkened beings who provoked anger, projected harmful thoughts, and provoked the explosive exchange that ended the conversation. It seemed their sheer delight was to witness the frustration and chaos that had escalated. God's angels had withdrawn from this skirmish. Despite my spiritual state, it was disappointing, as I silently hoped good would have won over evil.

This experience shows not only a glimpse into the heavenly/spiritual realm, but the battles that are a normal daily occurrence.

Pastor Larry used to always say, "There is no such thing as coincidence," which is a truth revealed here. The warfare that occurred had a far greater purpose than simply changing the direction of a conversation. It would be one of many greater battles fought over many years with the purpose of changing the direction of my soul. This kind of warfare is happening all around us all the time, but we're mostly unaware.

While we believe the angelic realm ultimately triumphs, temporary setbacks can make it seem otherwise. But God will use even these defeats for His greater purpose and glory. Trust Him.

Heavenly Messenger

The book of Daniel describes the interaction in the heavenlies between God's angel, whom God had sent with a message to Daniel, and the prince of Persia. The prince here is the fallen angel who was in charge of the territory of the Persian Empire. He was the ruling power over this region that opposed God's plan, and worked to take as many with him as he could. The angel told Daniel that he would have responded sooner, but the prince of Persia withstood him for twenty-one days until Michael, the archangel, came to his aid. Both archangels and principalities belong to the same high-ranking order of angels; however, archangels serve God, whereas principalities serve Satan while ruling over nations and the powers within them. These classes comprise mighty warrior angels—two-thirds holy angels and one-third fallen angels. So it comes as no surprise that this messenger angel would need a high-ranking angel to resist the prince of Persia.

The next time it appears heaven is as brass and the answer you seek is long in coming, remember there may be obstacles in the way of you receiving God's response. God's angels are maneuvering through hostile territory and interacting with enemy fire in order to thwart Satan's attack on God's plan on earth. Be patient and continue to pray, because ultimately there will be a breakthrough. Now that we've learned to recognize the enemy through his many attributes, we move on to examining the strategies he uses to execute his diabolical plan.

Human Interaction in the Heavenlies

"Witchcraft in the heavenlies" refers to the spiritual battle against evil powers that operate in the spiritual realm. Witchcraft is a demonic power working in the heavenlies, usually connected to evil entities that aim to manipulate, intimidate, and control. Its influence is not limited to this realm and affects human actions and events through demonic means. Occasionally, ruling demons operating in this realm, leave their abode and carry out earthly assignments. However, the unseen realm's spiritual activity is far more complex and profound than that of demons interacting on earth. Some occult practitioners also engage in astral projection within the spiritual realm. Serious occultists are aware of the danger that lurks there but engage anyway. Principalities war not only against angels, but also in opposition with one another. No wonder angels often have to fight their way through cosmic chaos to complete their mission.

Heavenly Perspective

In today's society, man's own technology has become his god. We've so consumed our lives with technical devices that we've lost sight of acknowledging the supernatural events that occur in the world. We're no longer heavenly minded. While the ancient church interpreted "in the heavenlies" as the spiritual realm of angels, demons, and spiritual conflict (Ephesians 6:12), many contemporary believers have adopted a more restricted physical perspective. Understanding the multidimensional realm alongside our physical reality is vital to prevent our ignorance from empowering Satan against the church. If we ignore the spiritual dimension where battles often begin before manifesting physically, and leave our spiritual defenses unused, how can we hope to win in spiritual warfare against the fiery darts thrown our way?

In the next chapter, the first in Part II: The Kingdom of Darkness, we're going to uncloak the enemy and reveal his true colors.

Behind Enemy Lines

PART II

Kingdom of Darkness

Behind Enemy Lines

CHAPTER 5

Uncloaking The Enemy

Humanity's downfall began with the devil's seduction in the garden of Eden. Satan is just as busy today and plans to achieve two goals: to usurp God's glory unto himself and to separate mankind from God's eternal purpose. People frequently find it hard to take Satan seriously, often picturing him as a small red devil on their shoulder, wielding a pitchfork and with a pointed tail, whispering temptations in our ear. His modern depiction is a muscular, monstrous figure with red skin, horns, pointed ears, and glowing eyes, embodying the darker aspects of man. But everything aside, would you recognize him if you met him face-to-face?

We read in Ezekiel 28:13 that God adorned Satan with precious stones, timbrels, and prepared pipes for him. Ezekiel 28:12 describes him as "full of wisdom, perfect in beauty." He had the privilege of covering the glory of God's throne with worship until the iniquity of pride was found within him. It is sometimes unclear whether the Ezekiel 28 passage refers to the king of Tyre or the devil, as it seems to address both, but most Bible scholars consider it a dual prophecy, as it compares the pride of both. I interpret it as addressing the king of Tyre, who is under the devil's influence or possession, thus addressing Satan through his dominion. We find a similar situation in Matthew 16:23, where

Jesus rebuked Peter, saying, "Get behind me, Satan! You are an offense to Me, for you are not mindful of the things of God, but the things of men." Again, Peter is not being addressed as Satan; rather, Satan is being rebuked for having influenced Peter.

Satan was once a cherub (see Ezekiel 28:14). Since he's a spirit, we can't see him without God opening our spiritual eyes. We ought to be able to discern him and other demonic beings, and observe supernatural activity around us. However, we mustn't assume his invisibility means he's nonexistent or imprisoned, for, as we'll learn, he's very active on earth today.

Satan's ambition to be "like the Most High," as described in Isaiah 14:13-15, led to his downfall. He desired more than the position of the highest cherubim closest to God's throne. Pride filled his heart, and he coveted God's throne and rebelled against Him. Because of this, he was cast out of heaven, along with a third of the angels, who sided with him in his rebellion. In Luke 10:18, Jesus describes his descent: "I saw Satan fall from heaven like lightning."

The devil, having been cast down to earth, isn't sitting idle. He roams back and forth across the land (see 1 Peter 5:8). Like a wild animal, he is on the prowl, and if we're not careful, his search won't be in vain. He may play the part of a jokester or trickster, but he plans to consume us entirely and spit out the pieces into the fiery pit that awaits him and those who fall for his deception. God's enemy is our enemy, and while we need to be on guard, we also need to remember that "He who is in [us] is greater than he who is in the world" (1 John 4:4).

Not only did God create Satan beautiful, but he also made him "full of wisdom"; therefore, he is a highly intelligent being. The fall of humankind (Genesis 3) demonstrates his understanding of Scripture. He was also well aware of the prophecy of the Messiah's birth, though he didn't know the day, the time, or the manner in which God would bring forth the birth of our Savior (see Isaiah 7:14). But just as the wise men knew to watch the stars, Satan knew enough to be on the lookout for the Savior's birth.

Satan still watches today. He is aware of the book of Revelation's contents and knows of his impending doom coming at the end of the age. How do we know this? Because Satan is the god of this world, and even this world is aware of Christ's eventual return, regardless of whether or not they believe it. Satan, in his arrogance, may consider himself powerful enough to change the end times results, but he is not. He is well aware of the Bible prophecy, and he is busy preparing for the global worldwide war. His demons have assignments: some lead people astray, others ushered in the antichrist and prepare unrestrainedly, and still others gear up for the end times war.

Satan the Serpent

The portrayal of the devil as a serpent is based on Genesis 3:1-7. Here, the devil is a talking serpent who convinces Eve to take a bite of the forbidden fruit. But let's stop for a moment and talk about this snake. This obviously wasn't an ordinary serpent. As we know, snakes don't talk, they hiss. They also don't have the intelligence to convey this crafty conversation to tempt Eve into rebellion. So, what makes this serpent different?

Revelation 12:1-17 and 20:2 describe Satan, identified as the serpent or devil, being cast down to earth and attempting to devour the Christ child. Clearly, the serpent in the garden wasn't an ordinary snake; some claim it was a literal snake that could talk, others view it as a metaphor, and still others believe it was a snake that was used by the devil as a vessel in deceiving Eve. I believe the latter—a genuine snake, operating as Satan's mouthpiece, controlled through demonic influence. The Hebrew word *Nachash*, used in this Scripture, has three meanings for us to draw from: it means a snake or serpent, the one who shines, and a deceiver or diviner. Consequently, the serpent, mirroring Satan's traits, craftily tempted Eve through its deceptive charm and cunning language.

No wonder it caught her attention and she gave in to its temptation.

Angel of Light

Satan, as an angel, reflected the light of God, which magnified his brilliance. His name, Lucifer, means "shining one."[11] But it wasn't enough for him to bear the light of God; he wanted to become the light. His poisoned ambition led to his demise and landed him on earth. After his fall, Satan no longer shone with the brilliance of God's glory. The fall caused the once-brilliant cherub to lose his heavenly position and the light of God that shone through him.

Yet, as a master counterfeiter, he knows how to mimic the appearance of light. To deceive people, he cloaks himself with light and presents himself as righteous. He is anything but. The cloak he wraps himself in covers his true identity, which is an angel void of light. We must not be fooled by his disguise. He'll come to us as everything we've ever dreamed of. His words will sound convincing, and he'll entice with empty promises. Nothing good can come out of him, for he is the embodiment of evil.

Prince of the Air

Ephesians 2:2 calls Satan "the prince of the power of the air, the spirit who now works in the sons of disobedience." But what exactly does this mean? Let's break it down.

The Greek word Paul uses for a prince is *archon*, which means ruler or the leader.[12] Therefore, Satan leads the powers of the air. The power referenced is a singular superhuman power within the air, or the invisible realm above the earth and below the heavenly throne of God. According to Ephesians 6:12, Satan, the ruler of the air, handles all demonic spirits and wicked entities that are known to be active in the heavenly realms.

Satan's influence, according to Ephesians 2:2, encompasses both demons and those who disobey God. In verse 3, we find a

---

[11] "Genesis 3:1 – 'Serpent' or 'Shining One'?" Biblical Hermeneutics Stack Exchange, accessed June 19, 2025, https://hermeneutics.stackexchange.com/questions/47317/genesis-31-serpent-or-shining-one.

[12] "758. Archon," *Strong's Exhaustive Concordance: Greek* on Bible Hub, accessed July 16, 2025, https://biblehub.com/greek/758.htm.

self-reflective passage: "We all once lived in the passions of our flesh, carrying out the desires of the body and the mind, and were by nature children of wrath, like the rest of mankind." We remember that we, as sons of disobedience, were once Satan's instruments. It's a humbling experience to admit that we once lived according to the flesh, just as the unbelievers who the enemy works through today do. That humility turns to joy when we recall Christ's liberation from the enemy, and see unbelievers converted.

The god of This World

Satan is called the god of this world, with "this world" defined as the earthly realm. He holds ultimate power over demons and dark forces and uses them to manipulate humanity. Second Corinthians 4:4 speaks of those "whose minds the god of this age has blinded, who do not believe, lest the light of the gospel of the glory of Christ, who is the image of God, should shine upon them." Satan covers man's eyes with a veil of deception that prevents him from seeing the truth and deceives him into believing his lies, which are interwoven into the false philosophies of the world. As this world's god, Satan establishes mankind's worldview, causing their blind following to lead them to their destruction. No wonder Scripture also calls Satan the father of lies.

Father of Lies

In John 8:44, Jesus, in a confrontation with the Pharisees, tells them, "You are of your father the devil, and the desires of your father you want to do." Here, he recognizes their murderous hearts and satanic influence, and redirects their accusations found in John 8:39, where they claimed that Abraham, and therefore God, was their father, yet they failed by their own ignorance to acknowledge that the Father sent Jesus.

Satan has been a liar from the beginning, and he's still a liar today. If we go back to the garden of Eden (Genesis 3), we find his first lie to mankind, which was that Eve assuredly wouldn't die if she ate the forbidden fruit. Rather, she would receive immortality and godlike status, he said. In this act, he introduced death and sin into the world, committing humanity's first murder. He continues to recycle the same lies, and sadly I too fell victim to them. The same deceptive tactic was the source of my fall. Like Eve, I fell for the enemy's lie and doubted God's Word as truth. Satan offered me the forbidden fruit of occult knowledge, and I took it and ate, resulting in my fall from grace.

When Satan lies, he speaks from his own resources, for he is a liar and the father of lies. He disperses lies throughout the entire world system, which is another of his strategies to destroy God's plan for mankind. He has even convinced some people that he is God's rightful heir, saying God usurped the throne from him. *Satan* means "adversary," as he is the enemy of God and the origin of evil. He will stop at nothing in his attempt to lure humanity away from God and prevent us from receiving the salvation God has provided for us. In John 8:44, Jesus confirms that Satan was a murderer from the beginning and does not stand in the truth because he does not have truth within him.

The Great Dragon

In Revelation 12:4, we read, "Its tail swept one-third of the heavenly stars to Earth. And the dragon stood before the woman who was ready to give birth, to devour her Child as soon as it was born." This verse reveals the spiritual assault against Israel and believers in Christ. The fiery dragon is Satan, the stars cast down are the fallen angels, and the child the dragon tries to eat is Jesus. This symbolizes Satan's attack on Christ.

After the fall of mankind, God told Satan, "And I will put enmity between you and the woman, and between your offspring and hers; he will crush your head, and you will strike his heel" (Genesis 3:15). Satan knew from that point that his time was limited and that God had a plan for man's salvation. Thus began his quest to defile the bloodline of David and prevent the Savior's birth. When he failed at preventing the Christ child from being born, he influenced King Herod to murder all the male babies under the age of two. God, however, ensured the Christ child's safe escape. The dragon finally believed he had killed Jesus Christ, the Son of God, on the cross, but what he didn't realize was that Jesus' death was part of God's plan for redemption. Nor had he counted on Jesus being resurrected, defeating death.

The Bible uses the dragon as a symbol of rebellion, evil, chaos, and destruction; these are already present but will worsen with Satan's unrestricted reign during the tribulation. Ultimately, the "great, fiery red dragon" (Revelation 12:3) will face his ultimate demise. Revelation 20:10 tells us that he will meet his end in the lake of fire along with the beast and prophet, to be tormented day and night.

The Kingdom of Darkness

As a primary counterfeiter, Satan mimics the things of God in a perverted evil fashion. He has even replicated God's kingdom in building his own as a hierarchical organizational structure. God's kingdom will reign eternally, while Satan's kingdom has limits and will ultimately fail. Still, his legion is an organized unit with orders of rank and file, and we are all his targets. Remember, as Christians we have something Satan and his forces lack: eternal life and a connection with God. The devil tempts men to replace their worship of God with worship of him. As Ephesians 6:12 explains, the battle is not physical but spiritual—against wicked forces in the heavens.

Principalities

Paul refers to the first rank of Satan's kingdom as "principalities." Translators derive the word *principalities* from the word *arché*, which, according to *Strong's Exhaustive Concordance: Greek,* means "what comes first and therefore is chief (foremost)."[13] Principalities rule over continents or territories and assign lesser demons and dark powers with evil tasks in order to accomplish Satan's plans in a specific area.

God has chained some from this rank, and they await judgment for crossing His boundaries and rebelling against Him (see Jude 1:6). It is likely that the result described in Genesis 6:1–22 is what

---

13   "746. ἀρχή (arché)," *Strong's Exhaustive Concordance: Greek* on Bible Hub, accessed June 19, 2025, https://biblehub.com/greek/746.htm.

contributed to their fate, as they took wives from the daughters of men (female humans) and bore children with them against God's plan. Their release to join with the rest of their warrior rank for an appointed time will not occur until the tribulation (see Jude 6).

Dark Powers

The "powers" are ranked second. These demonic powers, which are spirit beings without bodies, strive for world control and are often mentioned in association with principalities. They exert the authority of the higher-ranking principalities by carrying out evil operations and exhorting the power of sin in the world. As hands-on manipulators, they're sent to lead mankind away from God, and teach them according to their expertise, at Satan's command.

Rulers of Darkness

The "rulers of darkness of this world" is the name given to those ranked third. The term *the ruler of this world* translates to *kosmokratór* in Greek.[14] The word *kosmos* means "an arrangement, order, government," and *kratos* means a work of power. The two words combined, *kosmokrator*, mean to seize or take hold of for the purpose of evil.

The rulers of darkness are high-ranking demonic spirits who influence the lives of worldly people in various forms of witchcraft, occultism, and false religions. Many whom these spirits have deceived believe they are in control, when in actuality the evil spirits have control over them. This rank, therefore, encompasses not just demonic forces opposing God but also humans practicing sorcery and following demonic doctrine.

Spiritual Wickedness

Paul's fourth rank is what he calls "spiritual wickedness in high places." The word *wickedness* comes from the Greek word *kakos*, signifying evil, malice, trouble, and wickedness. The

---

[14] "2888. κοσμοκράτωρ (kosmokratór)," *Strong's Exhaustive Concordance: Greek* on Bible Hub, accessed June 19, 2025, https://biblehub.com/strongs/greek/2888.htm.

phrase refers to "Satan's demonic horde," including all who inhabit the "high places," the rulers of principalities and the rulers of darkness among them.[15]

High places were natural hills or artificially made elevations that were set up with altars and sacred objects for worshipping false gods. Many times, they were found in groves of trees or among standing stones. People held festivals and performed abominations there, including divinations, cult prostitution, burnt offerings, and sacrifices. These types of festivals still happen today. Demonic forces, in control of the area, unleash all manner of wickedness.

Demonic Spirits

A demon is a disembodied spiritual entity. In the Gospels, they are often called unclean spirits, evil spirits, or devils. The term *unclean* means defiled, which is morally or spiritually impure. These spirits, or demons, oppose God and commit immoral and rebellious acts against Him. Their names reflect their characteristics, which also determine their methods of attack. Their purpose is threefold: 1) to harass, torture, and harm; 2) to prevent a person from coming to a saving knowledge of Jesus; and 3) to keep an individual from fulfilling their God-given purpose in life.

Demons are earth-bound spirits that attempt to harm and deceive humanity. These are the spirits that we contend with in spiritual warfare. If permitted, they will demonize, or take control of a person, where they can do the most harm; this is their preference. However, if unable to gain access, they will cling to the outside of a person, oppressing them with their torment. This form of harassment causes physical and/or emotional distress. Because they are social entities, they frequently inhabit their host in groups, and occasionally, legions. They work together under the direction of a ruling demon, as part of the dominion of darkness ruled by Satan. They are enemies of God and mankind.

---

15 "2556. κακός (kakos)," *Strong's Exhaustive Concordance: Greek* on Bible Hub, accessed June 19, 2025, https://biblehub.com/greek/2556.htm.

Manifestation Turned Deadly

A highly publicized incident points to a deadly demonic manifestation. A woman contacted the sheriff about a noise next to her residence, prompting an investigation. Upon arrival, two officers checked out the property and informed the resident that no one was there. They were wrapping up the call when the officer saw boiling water on the stove and instructed her to tend to it. Things went terribly south from there.

The woman moved the pot from the stove to the sink's edge. A quick exchange about the water provoked a strange remark from the sheriff, insinuating she might throw it at him. The woman paused, then said, "I rebuke you in Jesus' name" and with that, the scene turned deadly. The deputy sheriff's entire demeanor changed from caring and kind to confrontational and aggressive. He told her she had better not (rebuke him in the name of Jesus) or he swore to God that he'd shoot her in the face.

She didn't have a chance. He immediately drew his weapon, and as she raised her hands, pleading and ducking for cover, he shot her in the face. The demonic manifestation showed in his personality change, anger, and aggression. The violent, unmerciful act exposed it. As she lay on the floor in a pool of blood, the deputy had no remorse; rather, he told his assistant officer a medical kit was pointless. Moments later, he told dispatch she was still breathing. He displayed other evidence of demonic manifestation through his disdain of the Lord's Holy name, his bizarre laugh while relaying the woman's death, and his coughs at the crime scene.[16]

Now, don't get me wrong, I fully support law enforcement and consider this a rare occurrence. Authorities arrested the deputy sheriff for murder, and he is currently in jail awaiting trial. Of course, he is innocent until proven guilty, but it goes to show that no one is exempt from demons. Now that we've exposed the devil and all his evil empire, we move on to learning what his tactics and strategies are.

---

16 Abby Trivett, "Isaiah Saldivar Breaks Down the Demonic Manifestation of a Police Officer," Charisma News, July 21, 2024, https://charismanews.com/culture/isaiah-saldivar-breaks-down-the-demonic-manifestation-of-a-police-officer/.

CHAPTER 6

Satan's Strategies

Satan will do anything within his power to stop the salvation of mankind, and to turn man's worship to himself. He doesn't care how these come about, just so long as he accomplishes his goal. While we don't know the tactic used to convince one-third of the angels to align with him, I surmise it was similar to the tactic he uses with believers today. He's been using the same strategies to come against God's people since the garden; the people and places change, but his schemes remain the same. It's important that we recognize these strategies so we can avoid being taken advantage of.

Satan will use whatever influence best deceives the unbeliever as well, be it a false religion or a twisting of Scripture. One example would be convincing the unbeliever that works earns salvation. He personalizes the tactic to each person; whichever will keep the individual believing they are not good enough, or are too far gone, to attain God's love and redemption, is utilized.

Twisting God's Word

In Genesis 3:1–6, we see that Satan is well-versed in the Bible. He loves to turn the Word of God (our sword) against us. Yes, he fights dirty and does not play by the rules of engagement, instead manipulating our own weapon, twisting its intended use and counterstriking us.

Remember the play on words he used when tempting Eve in the garden? He distorted God's own words, asking, "Did God really say you must not eat from any tree in the garden?" Notice how he twisted them ever so slightly to instill doubt in Eve's mind. What God said was that they could eat from any tree *except* for one. Next, he persuaded her into rebellion by telling her she would not actually die but would become "like God" if she ate the fruit. That was his hook, and when she bought into it as truth, he went in for the sinker by rushing Eve from thought to action. She took the apple and tasted its goodness. Sin always tastes sweet, but while some sins look good on the outside, they're always bad on the inside.

Satan cunningly uses the same strategy today. He takes the very Word of God and distorts it so that if we're not careful, we'll fall into a similar trap. Then, he'll attempt to turn our sword (the Word) against us.

Temptation

Temptation is the enticement to sin. There are many temptations known to man, such as gambling, drug and alcohol abuse, boasting, pornography, nicotine, overeating, gossip, and the list goes on. As "the tempter," Satan strategically uses temptation to lure humans into sinful behavior, establishing a foothold and planting seeds of sin to increase his influence.

In Luke 22:3-6, Satan tempted Judas Iscariot, one of the Twelve, to betray Jesus. Satan entered Judas, and after conferring with the chief priests on how he might betray Jesus to them, they agreed to give him money for leading them to Jesus. When Judas realized the consequences of his actions, he had remorse, but that didn't stop the demonic influence that led to his violent death (see Acts 1:18).

Temptation does not always stem from Satan. It can also result from sin, such as the lust of the flesh, the lust of the eyes, and the pride of life. It's not the temptation itself that is a sin, but succumbing to the temptation. Satan uses our ungodly desires as a strategy to tempt us to sin and turn away from God. Once he has his grip on us, our decisions are not ours alone and can lead us to fall away from God's grace without repentance.

Lies and Deception

Satan is the father of lies. While lying is making a false statement, deception is more sinister because its intent is to cause harm. Satan's deception isn't just to make us believe his lies, but to cause us great harm and, ultimately, spiritual death.

Nehemiah 6 recounts how the Lord moved Nehemiah to return to Jerusalem, inspiring the remnant to rebuild the city wall and restore worship. Using one hand to build and the other to hold a weapon, they worked against opposition until the wall was complete, except for the gates. Nehemiah then received word from his enemies: "Come, let us meet together in one of the villages on the plain of Ono" (v. 2). A meeting on neutral ground to promote peace would seem beneficial—except that Nehemiah discerned it was a plan to harm him. Nehemiah responded that he could not go down to meet them because he was working on a significant project.[17]

Spiritual warfare is not always when we're down on our knees in our prayer closet. The enemy's attack comes when we least expect it. Satan's goal is to harm us and prevent us from walking in God's calling in our lives. Here's how he did this in my life.

One of my virtues has always been compassion. It's not a bad thing. In fact, as Christians, we are called to have compassion. But the very things that enable us to do the work God has called us to do are also the enemy's targets. After I had been out of witchcraft for many years, I received a call out of the blue from the high priestess requesting me to go with her to the home of a craft elder who was in failing health and needed assistance, as if I were the only one who could help. Being a compassionate person, it was only natural for me to want to help. However,

---

17   "7. Recognizing the Tactics of the Enemy," Bible.Org, accessed June 12, 2025, https://bible.org/seriespage/7-recognizing-tactics-enemy.

upon discerning the situation, I knew it was a ploy to get me to meet with them, and I'm sure the intent wasn't to celebrate my conversion to Christianity. Much to her surprise, I declined the invitation—and later learned the elder had been in fine health.

Many times, the enemy will attempt to lure us away from God's protection to a neutral ground for something that looks good. He will target part of our Christlike character to lure us in. It's deception, and the enemy is persistent. Like Nehemiah, we must learn to identify and discern the devil in situations and respond accordingly.

Masquerading as Light

Another of Satan's tactics is masking himself as an angel of light (see 2 Corinthians 11:14-15). He appears to us as righteous and good, but he's the originator behind a false prophet masquerading as a true one, thus spreading deceit and diverting many from God. He fools many by using those who identify as "Christian" but work as psychics or mediums. Regardless of what these people may tell you, the information they provide is not coming from heaven, but from the realm occupied by demons. They are, like their master, imitators of light and righteousness, and some are even unknowingly sent to trick and deceive people into thinking they are doing them a service.

Satan's deceptive appearance can make some see him as being on God's side and promoting righteousness, when he actually opposes God and is unrighteous in all his ways. In some cases, he actually makes angelic visitations and introduces false religious beliefs that will lead many astray. We find him appearing as an angel of light when we research false religions such as Jehovah's Witness, Mormonism, Islam, and New Age. Each of these believe an angel appeared to an individual and gave them a divine revelation from which to base their beliefs. Sometimes Satan even takes on the persona of a biblical angel, but we can tell by the message that it contradicts the Word of God. Not surprisingly, these great revelations, which have captured the hearts and minds of billions, deny the deity of Jesus Christ as well as His death and resurrection for our sins. Beneath this cloak of light and enlightenment, he is an angel of darkness and deception who plans to take many with him into the lake of fire.

Affliction and Oppression

Affliction and oppression are physical or mental suffering over a long period. The enemy will use both to put us in a holding pattern and prevent us from fulfilling our God-given purpose. Affliction can manifest itself as physical conditions such as epilepsy, deafness, blindness, or oppression (e.g., depression, anxiety, irrational fear, chronic pain, or insomnia). A telltale sign of demonic influence is behavioral or mental extremism, such as extreme isolation, irrational fear, intense anxiety, persistent hopelessness, a sudden shift in personality, increased aggression, or undefined diagnoses.

We can learn from the biblical example of Saul, who struggled with a tormenting spirit. Deeply troubled and terrified, Saul experienced fretfulness and melancholy, and he occasionally acted as a madman. Saul would call upon David to come play his harp, and when the troubling spirit left Saul, he was revitalized and restored to health (1 Samuel 16:23). David surely was a gifted musician, but his playing did more than calm Saul's weary soul.

Satan afflicts people with demons that cause distress, which results in people becoming withdrawn and isolated. The nagging pain and sorrow stir up anger, and in their bitterness, people blame God. When this happens, Satan has succeeded in his mission. But like in the time of Saul and David, scripturally based worship music is a powerful weapon of spiritual warfare today. God dwells in the praises of His people, which dispel demons and release the ministry of angels.

Stealing, Killing, and Destroying

Another strategy of Satan is to "steal, and to kill, and to destroy" (John 10:10). As the god of this world, the devil attempts to distract us into believing our happiness is based on worldly ideals and accomplishments. However, the world offers us only emptiness, thus discouraging us and causing us to lose our joy, which only Jesus can fulfill (see John 15:11).

Satan attempts to steal the life right out of us by causing us to feel hopeless and defeated in all areas of life. He persistently pounds away at our faith, our emotions, and our identity until he weakens us to the point of surrendering to his lies. Satan is jealous of God, and jealous of us because of God's promises to us in His Word. He will make every attempt to choke the Word of God out of us in order to keep us from walking in faith (see 1 Thessalonians 3:5). While these tactics will kill a person's will to pursue their godly purpose in life, the enemy inflicts rage and violence, enticing the demon-influenced to commit murder or suicide.

Satan's plan is to destroy the plan God has for each of us and the world. The devil opposes anything that benefits God's children and the earth, striving to destroy relationships, homes, and marriages. It is important that we don't grow weary and give up, allowing Satan control over our life. Instead, we must stand strong, remembering that our God is for us and He will "cause our enemies to be defeated" (Deuteronomy 28:7).

Accusing the Brethren

This strategy of the enemy is right in his name, as Satan means the accuser. As if it's not bad enough that the enemy attacks to get us to fall, when we do, he is quick to head to the throne room to accuse us before God. Zechariah 3:1–10 shows Satan standing before God, accusing Joshua, a priest of God, after the angel of the Lord brought him there, attempting to secure his condemnation. But Christ, the advocate for His people, rebuked Satan.

In Zechariah 3:4, God told his priest, "Your iniquity is removed, and I will clothe you with splendid garments."

Satan, the accuser of the brethren, does the same by bringing charges against us before God's throne. He's like the snitch who keeps track of everything we do wrong and can't wait to run and squeal on us. It gives him great joy to stand before God and tell Him of our failings. And before he does, he will remind us of the wrong we've done and condemn us. It's another of his strategies because if he can convince us to wallow in guilt, he's left us incapacitated. However, in the throne room, Christ our mediator will remind him of His blood washing us and of our being clothed in His garments of righteousness. To avoid giving the enemy a leg to stand on, we must repent of any sin in our life and ask Jesus to cleanse us from unrighteousness. The enemy loves to bring unrepentance before God's throne.

Sowing Discord

Another common strategy Satan uses is sowing discord by pitting believer against believer. In Proverbs 6:16-19, the Lord lists the things He hates the most, one of which is sowing discord among brethren. Someone who sows discord gossips, lies, makes unfounded accusations, gives negative criticism, or engages in backbiting. This divides friendships, and sometimes entire churches. It unravels the unity of believers, which makes them much easier targets. Ecclesiastes 4:12 tells us, "A single person may be overcome, but two can withstand him. And a threefold cord is not quickly broken." The third cord in the threefold cord is Jesus, who joins Himself in the covenant of believers, strengthening the love and fellowship between them. Believers unified with Christ and one another are better able to withstand the attacks of the enemy. Those who reside in love, reside in God, and He in them. No wonder Satan attempts to tear them apart.

In Galatians 1, Paul asserts his authority by addressing the Galatians who were attacking his credentials. False teachers were accusing him of being an apostle of men, and that the church of Antioch had made him an apostle. These accusations challenged Paul's authority; after all, "the gospel which he preached was not *after man; he neither received it of man, nor was he taught it by man,* but by immediate inspiration, or revelation from Christ himself."[18] The importance of Paul's authority stemmed from his refutation of the false teachings on circumcision that had misled the Galatians.

---

18 "Verses 10-24," Matthew Henry's Commentary on Bible Gateway, accessed August 6, 2025, https://www.biblegateway.com/resources/matthew-henry/Gal.1.10-Gal.1.24.

When Satan attacks our relationship or ministry, we can bet he's put his claws into our weakest link. We must take authority over the accusation and attempt to reconcile with the person doing the accusing, backbiting, or slander. Regardless of their ability or lack thereof to seek forgiveness or reconciliation, we must forgive them (see Matthew 6:14–15). Forgiving them strengthens and enables us to stand firm against any ongoing attacks.

Discouragement

Perhaps one of the enemy's most obvious strategies is discouragement. He'll discourage us through various circumstances or obstacles that he sets before us. It doesn't matter the type of disheartenment he uses, it's sure to be whatever will hit us the hardest. And sometimes he'll use a bombardment of multiple sources of despair. His goal is to cause us such great dispiritedness that we will forget the promises of God. Or we will become so focused on the sorrows of our circumstances that we lose all hope and faith.

The story of Job shows how Satan gained permission from God to attack Job, a blameless and upright man in practically every area of his life. Job lost his sheep, his servants, and even his ten children because of intruders or natural disasters. He responded by ripping his clothes, shaving his head, and praising God. Satan then afflicted him with skin sores over his entire body in hope that Job would curse God. Job's wife eventually urged him to denounce God, but Job's response was, "Though He slay me, I will hope in Him" (Job 13:15). The suffering became so great that Job turned bitter and anxious, and his friends came to sit with him for comfort for seven days. When Job could endure no more, God came to Him and restored his health, property, and children. Throughout it all, Job never lost hope or faith.

It's hard to grasp why God would allow Job such suffering at the hands of the enemy, and to come to terms with the fact that God may allow him access to believers' lives. We see that, though limited, Satan was permitted to use natural disasters, as well as health, financial, and relationship problems. These trials tested Job's faith, and the same is true for us. When the enemy bombards us with an array of discouraging circumstances, we can remember Job and trust that God has limits on what Satan can and cannot do.

Spiritual Blindness

Satan attempts to keep the entire world in darkness, but he cannot keep the light of the gospel out of this world, so his next strategy is to keep men from the gospel. To accomplish this, he "blinded the minds of unbelievers, hindering them from seeing the gospel's light, which reveals Christ's glory and the message of salvation" (2 Corinthians 4:4). He does the same today. Even a tiny speck of dust can blur our vision. Once a person is in darkness, Satan turns them against the light of the gospel message, and the rejection of the gospel becomes willful blindness that veils the wickedness of the heart.

Satan sometimes changes this strategy to use it against believers who don't fall for his first tactic of unbelief. To accomplish this, he uses doubt. This snare strategy is exactly how he trapped me. It came when I had grown weary and had a few maladjustments in my armor. The temptation was occult books and a thirst for knowledge. The lie went like this: "You aren't receiving any blessings from God, so do you really think any curse will come upon you?" It wasn't that God had never blessed me, for certainly He had, but I wasn't feeling blessed. In fact, I was in a state of desperation and had believed another lie—that God had abandoned me. Satan gave me a counterfeit for my thirst for God. He gave me a thirst that was never quenched but became increasingly obsessive, leaving me thirsting for more. It was like an addiction, always wanting more and never having enough.

The strategy the enemy used on me began with doubt in God's Word, which caused my unbelief. He then proceeded as though I was an unbeliever, because at that point I had become one. From there, the enemy implemented the strategy to blind me to the gospel's light—my lifeline—and darkness closed in. We must guard our vision and be sure to rebuke any obstacle the enemy places within our sight so that deception does not blind us.

Our Response

These are some of the strategies that the enemy uses to entrap us and render us helpless. It's important that we recognize his impending attack, as the best time to rebuke it is before he strikes. When we are attacked, we must resist and stand firm against his schemes. Often, the enemy will use a multi-strategy approach, combining several strategies into one attack. This increases his chance of succeeding because we tend to focus on only one area and he strikes from another angle. By understanding his methods of attack, we can ward off any advances before his strikes cripple us.

With a solid understanding of Satan's strategies, we now will examine the strongman and his method of footholds.

CHAPTER 7

The Strongman's Game

The enemy is an opportunist and cunningly looks for a way to get into your house and influence your life. Think of a thief who stalks your home—watching your comings and goings, waiting for the day you forget to lock the door or leave a window ajar. He seizes the moment and gains access to your home, and now that he's gained entry, he'll ransack your house, eventually establishing a stronghold along with a revolving door for other unclean spirits to operate.

Footholds

Spiritually thinking, when we put our guard down, we give Satan or his demons open access to our lives. We allow a spiritual foothold to be gained by him. This could result from our ignorance or laziness and not be an intentional act on our part, but in that moment, he took advantage of us. Or it could come from undiagnosed or unrepented sin, which has propped open the door and provided an entryway for demonic invasion. Ephesians 4:26-27 says, "'Be angry, and do not sin': do not let the sun go down on your wrath, nor give place to the devil." Either way, the opportunity presented itself and the enemy took full advantage of it.

Open doors can also come through family lineage. We may be unaware that our ancestors left more than their heritage behind, and that a hidden access point even exists (see Exodus 20:5). The access comes as a surprise when we discover that something evil is lurking like a skeleton in our closet. When we discover it, we need to be diligent and shut the door and perhaps install a Ring cam (aka the Holy Spirit) to warn us (aka discernment) of an impending intruder.

Footholds are not demons, but are works of our flesh that, if not dealt with, will progress to strongholds. It's best we slam the door on them immediately, for they serve as access points that, if left open, will become the gateway of our fleshly entertainment. Romans 13:12–14 says, "Therefore let us cast off the works of darkness, and let us put on the armor of light. Let us walk properly, as in the day, not in revelry and drunkenness, not in lewdness and lust, not in strife and envy. But put on the Lord Jesus Christ, and make no provision for the flesh, to fulfill its lusts."

Works of the Flesh

The Bible provides a list of the works of the flesh in Galatians 5:16–24, Colossians 3:5–8, Mark 7:21–23, Romans 1:28–32, Ephesians 5:3–6, 1 Corinthians 6:9, and 2 Timothy 3:2–5. These transgressions serve as access points for the enemy to plant inroads into our lives. You see, the devil and his demons are not our only enemies. Our flesh wars against our spirit in sinful behaviors. Romans 8:13 says, "For if you live according to the flesh, you will die; but if by the Spirit you put to death the deeds of the body, you will live." Our flesh holds the door open for the next in line, which are demons associated with our sin of choice. It's spiritual suicide to continue to satisfy our fleshly desires. According to Galatians 5:24, we are to crucify the flesh with its passions and desires. That is the best way to prevent demonic footholds from gaining ground.

Works of the Flesh List

Adultery	Drunkenness	Envy	Covetousness	Filthiness
Fornication	Foolish talking	Strife	Boastfulness	Theft
Lying	Anger	Idolatry	Lewdness	Revelries
Slander	Dissentions	Hatred	Sorcery	Being unloving
Pride	Murder	Blaspheming	Being unforgiving	Disobedience
Contentions	Deceit	Uncleanness	Brutality	Jealousies
Wrath	Lasciviousness	Heresies	Homosexuality	Divisiveness
Malice	Backbiting	Gossip	Obscenities	Selfish ambitions
Sensuality	Evil desires	Sexual immorality	Witchcraft	Greed

Enjoying God's Blessings in the Flesh Without Sinning

The works of the flesh shouldn't make us doubt our salvation or lead to invasive thought patterns. Instead, it can liberate by informing us how to avoid demonic influence. Proverbs 23:21-23 highlights three important steps: a warning against overindulgence, the importance of seeking guidance from parents and spiritually mature individuals, and the need to value truth, wisdom, and understanding through God's Word. The Bible, being the ultimate source of truth, identifies Jesus as "the Way, the Truth, and the Life" (John 14:6). Biblical teachings should guide our life choices to find true satisfaction and joy. The text illustrates how past sins can distort our identity, leading to guilt and despair, but God offers mercy for those who confess and forsake their sins. Proverbs 28:13 and Micah 7:19 remind us of the importance of acknowledging and moving beyond our past wrongs. Ultimately, we have the choice to follow God's way, which leads to life, or our own path, which can lead to destruction. Choose life!

Access Granted

Here is one way the devil can gain a foothold in our life. In this case, it begins with an offense. It doesn't matter whether it was a deliberate offense against us; it could just as likely be, and many times is, a reaction to a hidden insecurity of our own that has nothing to do with the person we feel offended by.

This is what happened to me on social media. I believe this insecurity resulted from an online Christian friend's self-esteem triggering an unexpected retaliatory strike. Just before the "assault," this person had uploaded a new profile picture on social media using an app that enhances the user's appearance. About the same time, another friend of mine posted a funny meme aimed at profile pictures with idealized images that look nothing like the real person, and I clicked "like" on the post, not putting much thought into it. A few days later, I posted a meme on my page about how we as believers should not focus so much on being attractive on the outside, but on our heart and soul. Within a New York minute, the friend with the new profile picture retaliated. A burst of anger must have welled up inside, for the response was in fury. After hammering out a few warfare Scriptures aimed at me, this person posted a comment that "I shouldn't have gone public with this." I was unfriended, blocked, and banned. Surprised, I wondered what had happened, especially since the Scripture verses didn't apply to the random meme I posted.

That is how the enemy can use our insecurity as bait, and if we don't nip it in the bud, it will arouse us to anger and incite an emotional reaction. At that moment, the devil seizes the opportunity and slips his foot in the door. He has gained a foothold. This one sly maneuver, if not brought under submission to Christ's instruction of forgiveness, will gain ground for further advances into his target's actions, which escalate into outlandish accusations and sow discord between believers, which is his ultimate plan. The spirit of offense has now entered the home.

It's also possible that a spirit of offense has already occupied the residence, and now uses this opportunity to wreak havoc.

If we lack humility, hold on to unforgiveness, and cannot love as Jesus commands, there's a good chance we have an unwanted house guest to expel. The body of Christ is stronger when in unity, and the enemy always attempts to put a wedge between us. We need to guard our hearts against the wiles of the devil, and that means guarding our access points. Spiritual protection from offense is found in Scriptures such as 1 Corinthians 10:32 ("Give no offense"), Matthew 18:7 ("Woe to the world because of offenses"), and Luke 17:3-4 ("Forgive those who repent, even repeatedly"). This points to bringing grace to every offense. Conclusion: Believers should mature into people who cannot be easily offended.

Strongholds

A stronghold is a spiritual force or compulsive sin in our lives that needs to be overcome. If not pulled down, and we continue in habitual sin, we create a fortified wall or a "safe place" to conceal and harbor it. This becomes a vicious cycle of entertaining sin and justifying our indulgence in it, to the point that it occupies a good portion of our thoughts and creates patterns in our way of thinking that further embeds it into our mind. We no longer control it; it controls us.

Second Corinthians 10:4-5 tells us, "For the weapons of our warfare are not carnal but mighty in God for pulling down strongholds, casting down arguments and every high thing that exalts itself against the knowledge of God, bringing every thought into captivity to the obedience of Christ." In this Scripture, Paul's analogy of a fortress describes the fortified wall we build in our mind; it harbors worldly philosophies and Satan's lies so that he can exalt himself against the knowledge and plans of God. At first, we may be ignorant of how we are believing the lies of the enemy. He cunningly convinces us that all is well, and that we are acting in our own moral principles. But the devil operates under the cloak of invisibility, and his lies slowly become ingrained traits that, if we don't tear them down, will grow into twisted roots firmly planted in our mind. By this point, it takes more effort to discard our "trunk in the attic" and pull the traits down on our own. That means it's time to call on the fervent prayers of others to help yank them down.

Access Secured

As an example of how a stronghold develops and how intense it can become, consider the story of a friend of a friend from our local Christian coffee shop. Shortly after I came full circle out of the occult, she called me regarding her mother (we'll call her Anita). In her youth, Anita had experimented with a Ouija board, experiencing success not only in receiving answers to her questions but also in making future predictions—until she encountered something so frightening that she couldn't speak about it.

She immediately threw the board away, but bad things continued to happen, which she concluded were repercussions for discarding it. With great trepidation, at a garage sale she purchased a used replica of the board she got rid of. She kept it in a cabinet in the living room, and said that despite her husband closing the cabinet door multiple times, the door kept opening and she would hear faint screaming coming from within. Sometimes in the middle of the night, she would awaken and go downstairs to peer into the living room—although she dared not enter—to find the cabinet door wide open.

The enemy gained a foothold through her sin of engaging in occult activity, which the Bible strictly prohibits (see Leviticus 19:31). At first, Anita received answers, which kept her coming back for more. Often, demons will provide answers, even correct ones, to lure us into believing in the power we've accessed. It's meant to draw us away from God and replace prayer with demonic devices as our go-to source. Through her repeatedly returning to the Ouija board, the enemy could establish a stronghold in her mind, and that eventually gave access to the strongman.

The traumatic experience then exposed the demonic dark side of the Ouija board, causing Anita to throw it away. But even though the board was gone, she still had a fortified wall within her mind that allowed the strongman to continually access her thoughts, and his demons were free to manipulate the board in her home. So strong was this hold that both she and her husband were captive to fear in their own home.

My friend Bo and I spent the most part of an afternoon praying and sharing Scripture with Anita until she had to leave for work. We then asked if she was ready to get rid of the board once and for all, and she acknowledged that she wanted nothing more to do with it but was too fearful to remove it from the cabinet herself. We walked into the living room, Bo grabbed it from the shelf in the cabinet, and we all left together, her to work and us to take the board to its ultimate destruction. As far as we know, there has not been any other paranormal activity since.

We have two offensive weapons that can take down these strongholds: the sword of the Spirit (God's Word) and prayer (see 2 Corinthians 10:4–5). Allowing a stronghold to remain and gain strength opens the door for a strongman to enter.

Strongman (Ruling Demonic Spirit)

If we haven't resisted, rejected, and pulled down the strongholds of sin, and have instead allowed the flesh to operate in our life, we're sitting on a time bomb. That revolving door, enabling sinful behavior and demonic influences, also allows a strongman, or ruling demon, to become firmly established. The strongman is a powerful demonic spirit that rules over the stronghold and other demons. As Satan's delegated authority, he is the mastermind carrying out Satan's mandate (see John 10:10), and he doesn't want to be held responsible for failing to achieve that goal. Once the strongman takes root, we experience demonic oppression, and a spirit influences our behavior and enslaves us. Nonbelievers can become demonized, or demon-controlled.

Like a squatter who illegally occupies another's house, the strongman is an intruder. The squatter doesn't take over the entire house immediately. With the owner absent, the squatter gradually takes one room at a time. The true owner has lost authority to kick him out, and will have to go before a judge and prove ownership in order to have the squatter evicted. Similarly, we must show our ownership through God, for Jesus Christ's blood purchased us. We first must reject the enemy's claim of ownership and reaffirm our faith in Jesus, and then we can cast him and his unclean spirits out of our home and the squatter has to flee.

Simon the Sorcerer

Acts 8:9–24 provides an example of a strongman in the Bible. Simon Magus amazed the people of Samaria "for a long time with his sorcery" (Acts 8:11). Possibly, the devil sent him soon after Jesus had visited several years earlier, to counteract Jesus' work. Satan's plan is always to rob the seeds planted to prevent them from spiritually maturing (see Luke 8:11–12). Many Samaritans declared Simon "the great power of God," mistaking that which was done by the power of Satan and attributing it to the power of God. Either Simon had bewitched the people of Samaria by his magic arts (performing signs and wonders that basically mimicked miracles equivalent to those the Egyptian magicians did) or Satan himself had filled their hearts with deceit to follow Simon.

The Holy Spirit sent Philip to the Samaritans to preach Christ to them. When he reached them, he shared the gospel of Jesus and performed miracles. Acts 8:7 tells us, "For unclean spirits, crying with a loud voice, came out of many who were possessed; and many who were paralyzed and lame were healed." The people of Samaria believed and received baptism "and there was great joy in that city" (Acts 8:8). How mighty is the power of our God, who brought those held captive by Satan to obedience to Christ (see 2 Corinthians 10:5).

The strongman over Simon and the city of Samaria is an example of a principality. Simon held his possessions (Samaritans) concealed in the fortified palace built within his mind, and had considered his goods safe, until Christ, who was stronger than he, was called upon by Philip to dispossess him and divide the spoil. This released those who had been prisoners of the kingdom of darkness, and who the devil had once triumphed over.

Philip's announcement of the kingdom of God and Jesus led

to Simon's belief and subsequent baptism. He continued to follow Philip, amazed at the signs and miracles Philip performed. When the news from Samaria reached Jerusalem, the apostles sent Peter and John, who laid hands on the new believers to receive the Holy Spirit. When Simon saw this, he offered money for the power so that he, too, could lay hands on others to receive the Holy Spirit. Peter reprimanded him, telling him that the gifts of God cannot be bought. He advised Simon that his heart wasn't right and that he needed to repent of his wickedness and pray for God's forgiveness. Simon, fearful of what he was told, asked Peter to pray to the Lord on his behalf.

Our Response

The difference between footholds and strongholds is subtle but significant. A foothold is the work of the flesh, or unrepentant sin. By entertaining that sin, we enable a stronghold to be built within the confines of our mind. Failure to pull down the stronghold over time adds strength and fortification to its walls and makes way for a strongman (a demonic spirit) to enter and hold us in bondage. Our thinking becomes clouded, our eyes are blinded, and Satan has secured his right to operate in our lives. Initially, he remains undetected until he gains a firm grip, and then more demons join him. We can identify the demons associated with the strongman by their roots, which stem from the works of the flesh, and their fruits that make them recognizable. But our identification cannot stop there, for as we'll learn in the next chapter, the devil also uses many people to accomplish his works of darkness through the power source of witchcraft.

Behind Enemy Lines

CHAPTER 8

Hooves Of Satan

I cannot write a spiritual warfare book without touching on witchcraft and the occult. Witchcraft is a major playing field that the enemy uses to advance upon the people of God and manipulate his plan into action. As we saw in the three battlefield chapters, we know that the heavenlies is where the rebellious angels (the host of wickedness) operate, and the earth is the natural world in which we live. Witchcraft traverses both realms. It is best described as having a dual nature, combining both physical and spiritual practices. For now, we're going to focus on its earthly operations.

The Devil's Playground

Satan's plan is to influence humankind to interact with demons rather than God. He does this by slowly taking people from the straight and narrow path and leading them into his kingdom. Witchcraft is one of his strategies for accomplishing this, as it uses spiritual power to manipulate change in people, nature, and the spirit world for ungodly purposes.

The field of witchcraft has a wide range of shiny trinkets, magical energies, and mystical powers to entice. For the average person, the allurement seems like innocent fun. It includes zodiac signs that tell us about our personality traits and daily horoscopes that predict our day, as well as tarot cards, shiny pendulums, crystal balls, and many other prediction devices to answer all of life's questions. Typically, people don't take them seriously—until they find that some of the predictions actually came true. Then they realize there must be something more to it. So, they make them part of their routine, especially when they have something important coming up in their life. Then a loved one passes unexpectedly, and they're off to the friendly neighborhood medium to attempt contact with their lost loved one to find out what happened. Each of these leave a foothold open for demons to come and play in the person's life.

The ruler of the field is Satan, and the shiny trinkets are just some of his devices. The answers come from demons, and the human conduit (a witch, medium, psychic, or fortuneteller) belongs to the kingdom of darkness. Despite what these conduits may say, there are only two power sources: God and Satan. God forbids the practice of witchcraft (see Deuteronomy 18:10–12), so their source is always demonic. If people don't slam that door, they'll soon be lighting candles for money, taking a bath in rose petals to draw love, burning sage to chase away negativity, etc. The demons have set up shop. We can't play on the devil's playground without paying the price.

Hooves of Satan

First Samuel 15:22–23 tells us, "Rebellion is as the sin of witchcraft, and stubbornness is as iniquity and idolatry." So, anyone who practices witchcraft rebels against God, including the fallen angels, demons, and fallen humanity. They are, knowingly or unknowingly, all part of Satan's kingdom and are his hooves here on the ground. The countless ceremonies, rituals, and spells sent forth invoke demons and work toward Satan's agenda. People may believe its self-will and self-intent, but Satan empowers them and he uses them to implement his will.

During my involvement in the craft, I observed many outcasts and fringe groups drawn to the occult. They were looking for empowerment to change their circumstances, or a place to find acceptance in practicing spirituality. Interesting to note, though, is that the craft elders always looked for the "attractive witch" to be the face of witchcraft. They sought a pretty, sensual, or, at the least, good-looking witch in alluring garb, considering her to be the perfect platform to market the dance with the devil. It's Satan's disguise, as replicated throughout his kingdom—alluring, beautiful, and charming on the outside. But Proverbs 31:30 says, "Charm is deceitful and beauty is passing, but a woman who fears the Lord, she shall be praised."

Carnal Man

The works of the flesh are man's carnal, fallen nature being manifested on the earth (see Galatians 5:19). These fleshly works appear in sin, one of which is witchcraft. Derek Prince explained, "Witchcraft is primarily a work of the flesh, as it reflects the carnal nature of man, which seeks to control and manipulate others."[19] While the flesh may be its root, it invokes spiritual entities into its practice, attempting to exert its will over God's.

Some witches perform skyclad (naked) rituals to raise energy and increase power, a practice Scripture warns against as "uncovering the nakedness of another" (see Habakkuk 2:15; Job 31:1; Leviticus 18:18; Ezekiel 23:10). Witchcraft rituals include, sorcery, spells, and divination, all of which are considered an abomination to the Lord (see Deuteronomy 18:10–12). Many ceremonies and rituals also venerate or call upon pagan gods and goddesses, which are fallen angels in disguise. In Exodus 20:3–5, God says, "You shall have no other gods before me," so invoking a god or goddess is the same as spirit demonization (from the Greek word *daimonizomai* meaning "under the influence of demons"), which we are to cast out, and not invite in.[20]

---

[19] "The Nature of Witchcraft (Part 2): The Enemies We Face | Part 7 of 20" Derek Prince Ministries, accessed August 6, 2025, https://www.derekprince.com/radio/102.
[20] "Demonized," *Topical Bible* on Bible Hub, accessed August 6, 2025, https://biblehub.com/topical/d/demonized.htm#:~:text=Definition%20and%20Terminology:,2.

Witchcraft as Rebellion

Rebellion and witchcraft are frequently linked together, as both stem from disobedience and defy divine authority. In the Bible, disobedience often signifies a rejection of God's authority. Witchcraft rejects God's authority and engages in disobedience through idolatry and other occult practices, thus closely linking with rebellion. The Bible clearly warns against seeking guidance from mediums, familiar spirits, and those who practice witchcraft (see Leviticus 19:31). Satan's prideful heart initiated his rebellion against God, and this became the origin of all rebellion. Consequently, rebellion mirrors Satan's actions, aligning it with witchcraft and his influence. Rebellion and witchcraft are alike in their opposition to God's power and government, and God commands us to avoid rebellion and submit to His will (see Isaiah 1:19–20).

If we don't submit to God's authority, we will, by nature, end up replacing it with an illegitimate authority. Witchcraft will become this illegitimate authority.

Exodus 7:8–13 describes God's authority over Egypt's false gods, with Moses and Aaron standing before Pharaoh to demand the Israelites' release; thus, the showdown began. Aaron threw down his rod, which transformed into a snake. Summoned by Pharaoh, the wise men and sorcerers cast their enchantments to mimic Aaron, only to have Aaron's serpent devour theirs. This demonstration distinguished the genuine divine authority of Moses and Aaron, from the illegitimate power asserted by Pharaoh and his magicians. Subsequently, a clash of miraculous feats unfolded, with the sorcerers replicating some of Aaron's miracles. However, in the end, their defeat humiliated them, and the Israelites went free.

The powers of darkness, not God, enabled the Egyptian sorcerers to perform their miracles. However, as shown, these powers are inferior to God's power. While intelligent, the Egyptian sorcerers lacked divine wisdom only obtainable from God. This example reveals the demonic power they showed was from Satan, whose power and authority are limited, but it reveals something more: Wherever we find rebellion against God's authority, we will discover witchcraft as its power source.

Religions Engaging in Witchcraft

Wicca, New Age, Druidry, Kabbalah, Luciferianism, and Theistic Satanism are a few examples of belief systems that incorporate witchcraft into their practice. These vary widely in their actual beliefs and in their chosen deities, but they have two major things in common: they deny the sovereign deity of God Almighty of the Bible, and they adhere to doctrines of demons. Now, depending on the belief system, some believe that their magick is from a neutral source, while others will acknowledge that their source is Lucifer (aka Satan) or malevolent demons. Regardless, Satan or his fallen angels influence their beliefs, which are grounded in false doctrines that contradict the God of the Bible.

Some go as far as claiming to be Christian witches, but while the practice of witchcraft adheres to any belief system, the Bible is strictly against it. Make no mistake, those who practice witchcraft, regardless of what religion they claim, are taking part in the works of the devil.

Witchcraft as a Spiritual Power

Witchcraft is not limited to works of the flesh. Its power is not from human ability; rather it comes from an evil source. As we know, if the power is not from God, it comes from Satan. Satan wields his power over the earth to its fullest extent. He may tempt us in our flesh and appeal to our fleshly desires, but the power behind that is anything but flesh. Since Satan and his kingdom are spiritual entities, resisting him requires not just physically rejecting temptation but also spiritually opposing the manipulative spirits he uses in an attempt to control us.

There are three major spiritual access points that operate under the kingdom of darkness:

1. Witchcraft is a spiritual influence that draws on demonic powers to move and manipulate people or situations by exerting

one's will through the use of spells or curses. Curses and spells are powerful instruments used intentionally to block God's will for a person. A spell can be as simple as a prayer, or can incorporate candles, herbs, oils, incense, crystals and magickal words.

2. Divination is revelation from demons associated with witchcraft. This demonic entity taps into hidden knowledge, power, and the supernatural. Spirits communicate through people like witches, mediums, and fortunetellers. Tarot, oracle cards, runes, pendulums, and crystal balls are among the various tools used to access forbidden knowledge. Gaining knowledge isn't inherently evil. Its source—divine or demonic—is what decides whether we ought to desire it.

3. Sorcery, which is a demonic spirit associated with the spirit of witchcraft, is an abomination to the Lord, and those who practice it are an abomination to Him. Both practices use spells, divination, consulting mediums, and communicating with spirits to bypass God's authority and seek power and knowledge from demonic and false powers. The Greek word used in the New Testament for sorcery is *pharmakeia*, which refers to the use of drugs, potions, or poisons for both medicinal and other purposes, including abortion (*pharmakeia* refers to occult use, not including conventional medicine).

Rachel and the Mandrakes

Genesis 30:14-24 tells the story of Rachel, whom Jacob desired as his wife. Her father, Laban, tricked Jacob; after he worked for seven years to marry Rachel, Laban gave him her sister Leah instead. Jacob worked seven more years to take Rachel as his second wife. Leah gave Jacob children, which was her only source of his affection, because he favored Rachel. Not surprisingly, there was competition and jealousy between the sister wives. Rachel was barren and desperately wanted a child, and one day, a son of Leah's came home with a mandrake that he had found in the field. In ancient times, mandrakes were believed to have aphrodisiac and fertility-enhancing properties, which is reflected in their biblical mentions. The root's human-like shape contributed to various pagan superstitions and appeared in many potent ingredients list not only in biblical times but also in many pagan practices today.

Rachel was aware of the mandrake's reputed fertility magick—a God-forbidden practice and a remnant of pagan customs that still plagued the Israelites—and bartered a night with her husband to Leah in exchange for the mandrakes. Despite the warnings against it, many fall for the allure of witchcraft in their desperation. Rachel was no different. Having grown up in a household that acknowledged God but continued in pagan practices, when the opportunity presented itself, she seized the pagan solution instead of trusting God. Rachel's use of the mandrake failed, and Leah conceived instead. Much later, it was God, and not some potent charm, that opened Rachel's womb, enabling her to conceive a son.

Rachel's story offers some valuable insights. First, it warns of the dangers of being misled by the wrong spirits and falling into the trap of witchcraft. Second, it warns that some dangerously straddle the spiritual fence. But as the Bible says, we cannot serve two masters (Matthew 6:24). Third, it reveals that despite the power behind witchcraft, God has the ultimate power and can use our mistakes for something good.

Witchcraft in the Church

One example I can share is that of a couple and a young girl who were attending the same church I had just returned to. They appeared to be knowledgeable in God's Word and in deliverance, which made them fit well in this body of believers. Yet, within my spirit, I sensed red flags everywhere. Despite their claims, I recognized a familiar spirit. At first, to me, it seemed no one had picked up on it, and I thought I was just overreacting because my occult involvement was still fresh. But I avoided receiving prayer from them. When they prayed, I sensed a subtle twisting of God's Word. Then one evening, I received encouragement to receive prayer from the man I assumed was her husband. This time, as he prayed, I literally heard him asking for Satan to keep hold of me. I rejected his prayers and walked away, confused. Praise God, others discerned it too. They soon discovered that the couple had been making rounds through different churches on the East Coast, feeding off the hospitality of believers who offered their homes, money, and transportation.

I later learned the details from my pastor. Apparently, the family appeared in church when holy laughter was spreading throughout many charismatic congregations. They needed a place to stay, so someone at the church housed them. The woman, who identified herself as a prophetess, described how she felt drawn to and purchased a lovely vase from a craft store, claiming that God had told her the vapor inside would give holy laughter to any mouth she poured it into. After one Sunday service, the woman began pouring the vapor into the mouths of those wanting to receive it. She said the reason some didn't get holy laughter was because they were harboring bitterness. By then, several people had discerned that something was off. My pastor intervened, and after he made several calls to verify their background and found several deceptions, he asked the family to leave.

This is an example of Satan's manipulation of believers right in a house of God. As Christians, we are sometimes vulnerable to falling prey to someone taking advantage of our kindness. We need to remember to balance our compassion with wisdom and, in all things, use discernment in every situation. Just because someone looks and acts spiritual doesn't mean it's the Holy Spirit guiding them. Remember, the devil is an expert counterfeiter, as are his followers, mimicking the things of God. This is one of his favorite tactics to use on God's children because it's the least likely they will pick up on and pray against.

The Serpent in the Pew

The enemy is subtle, and he lures us with things that look good or even seem godly. He masks deceiving practices, which we attribute to a move of God, but in reality, the allure comes from witchcraft. Now I'm not condemning the entire prophetic signs and wonders movement. I believe God still speaks through prophets today and exhibits signs and wonders. However, we cannot deny that a counterfeit spirituality lurks in the shadows. Therefore, it is crucial that we hold all things, including our practices, in the light of Scripture. That means we compare the practice or manifestation to ensure it fits with what the Bible says, and not the other way around. The enemy would have us twist Scripture to justify a non-biblical act.

On one occasion, I visited a church where a well-known woman of God gave a prophetic word, all while shaking her head so vigorously that it could have ended with a concussion. Examining Scripture, we don't find any examples of prophets shaking their heads while prophesying. We do, though, find an example of a demon thrashing and gnashing the teeth of a young boy (see Mark 9:20). I resisted intervening and laying hands on her to cast out the demonic spirit, but instead prayed silently. However, the next time I found myself in a similar situation, it was a prayer meeting where I was one of its leaders. I followed the lead of the Holy Spirit and verbally told the spirit to flee in Jesus' name. We must be careful and test all spirits to make sure they align with God's Word. If they do not, we know that the manifestation is from the spirit of the antichrist.

Our Response

We are seeing more churches compromise with society and engage in evil practices that are not of God. They do so while claiming to be Christian churches and are quick to call people a Pharisee if they uphold biblical principles. First Timothy 4:1 tells us, "Now the Spirit expressly says that in latter times some will depart from the faith, giving heed to deceiving spirits and doctrines of demons." We are seeing evidence of this at an alarming rate; therefore, we must stand firm in the faith and resist the wiles of the devil (see Ephesians 6:11).

If we are to discern the true prophet from the false, the work of the Holy Spirit from other spirits, and the signs and wonders from God as opposed to manifestations of evil, we need to immerse ourselves in the Word and sit at the feet of Jesus. Witchcraft is the most deceptive practice that Satan uses against us. While it encompasses most of his schemes, the power of God within us surpasses his worldly demons (see 1 John 4:4). To God be all the glory.

In the next chapter, we'll learn to identify demons and their manifestations.

CHAPTER 9

Demon Hit List

In the spiritual realm, the hosts of wickedness understand the authority inherent in rank. Therefore, the lesser spirits that are under ruling spirits are subject to their leadership. Casting out a strongman or ruling spirit makes all lesser demons flee, and we easily uproot any remaining.

When casting out demons, we learn from Jesus' example and use discernment to identify the strongman that is attacking the person. By starting at the top of rank, we eliminate the exhaustive list of lesser demons that may have taken up residence along with the strongman. We also want to maintain a spiritually healthy balance here. If we're to cast out demons, we need to have some knowledge about them. On the other hand, we don't want to delve too deep into the study of them, but at the very least, we can identify them as unclean, impure, or evil spirits, so gaining further insight is helpful.

Since our ability to identify demons is a key point in deliverance, understanding which demonic influence is affecting the person we're praying for is essential and works hand in hand with our gift of discernment. In 1994, Robeson and Robeson initially created a list of strongmen[21] that I have used as a source for the following list of strongmen or ruling spirits, along with additional insight from my own personal experience. I've included some biblical and personal examples of demons at work in people's lives so you can not only learn about them but also see them in action.

Demonic spirits manifest in many ways, as shown in the manifestations listed at the end of each section. Their root stems from the works of the flesh, and their fruit makes them identifiable. Each demon, regardless of its rank, is clever, cunning, and deceptive; therefore, we should use discernment to identify the demons that are present, and should the Holy Spirit bring to light one of the lesser spirits, we should heed what the Spirit of God says and cast out the exposed demon by name. We'll want to use this list as a guide in chapter sixteen, but for now let's familiarize ourselves so we can identify them and their manifestations.

Strongman: Spirit of Fear

Spirit of Fear, Torment, Nightmares, Fear of Death

Cast out: Spirit of fear (and any lesser demons discerned)

Pray for: Power, love, and a sound mind (see 2 Timothy 1:7)

The spirit of fear paralyzes, torments, and locks us in bondage. God has not given us a spirit of fear (see 2 Timothy 1:7); we give the spirit of fear access when we don't view things through God's Word. As human beings, we have three natural reactions to danger: fight, flight, or freeze. When faced with fear, we should first discern and identify what specific fears we are facing, and then bind and cast them out. It is important to differentiate between standing firm in faith, guided by the Holy Spirit, and "freezing," which can be perilous. This concept is illustrated in 1 Peter 5:8, warning to be vigilant against the devil, likened to a roaring lion seeking prey. Understanding lions is crucial;

---

21   Robeson and Robeson, Strongman's His Name . . . What's His Game?: An Authoritative Biblical Approach to Spiritual Warfare (Whitaker House, 1984).

lionesses do the hunting, but once a lion grows old, they abandon him, causing him to go hungry. Thus, their roar becomes its tactic to scare smaller animals into a state of paralysis, making them easy targets for the older lions to consume. Don't become easy prey; bind and cast out demons of fear!

During my teen years, my English teacher witnessed to me after she read a drug-related poem I'd written in class. I insisted that since God made pot (cannabis), it must be okay. Her advice to me was to pray and ask God about that, but only if I really wanted to know. Months passed, and I forgot all about it. Then one evening, I was smoking with a few friends in a nearby schoolyard when I had what can only be described as an out-of-body experience. I remember walking past a lit-up cross that said "Jesus Saves, Jesus Heals."

Before long, I felt like I couldn't keep up with my friends or my body. An auburn ambiance covered the area, and buildings were but shadows. I then felt as though I was being drawn into some type of magnetic opening. I attempted to resist, wanting out of the dark, reddened abyss. When it was about to devour me, I screamed. My friends tried to calm me down, but it wasn't until my best friend, knowing of my teachers' witness to me, began calling on God. That's when it stopped.

The experience traumatized and confused me. Things like that didn't happen with pot, at least not back then. But the thought that God had actually answered my prayer meant He could actually interact with me on earth. You'd think I would've run to Him, but I didn't. I ran from Him, attempting to find another explanation, and when I couldn't, I hid from everything and everybody. I took flight to a whole new level. You can read the full story on my website in my free download "My Life Before the Encounter."

I wasn't a born-again believer at the time and had no spiritual knowledge, so Satan took full advantage of my ignorance and used the fear of God against me. It kept me bound in fear and hiding from God for years.

Demons Under the Spirit of Fear

Spirit of Anxiety: The Greek word for anxiety is *merimnao*, which means to divide or separate. We can describe it as a person torn in two different directions, or between God's will and way and their own. The spirit of anxiety inflicts extreme worry, terror, phobias, and feelings of impending doom. Cardiophobia, or the irrational fear of having a heart attack, and can mimic symptoms of a heart attack. Philippians 4:6 "Be anxious for nothing, but in everything by prayer and supplication, with thanksgiving, let your requests be made known to God."

Tormenting Spirit: A tormenting spirit hounds, harasses, and pressures an individual, thus preventing the person from experiencing peace. In Samuel 16:14, we see that the Lord left Saul and a tormenting spirit filled him with depression and fear.

Nightmare Spirit: Such as the incubus, which is a spirit of perversion that attacks women. This tormenting spirit disturbs one's sleep, causing terrifying hallucinations. The victim often sees and feels a faceless presence on her chest, causing a feeling of suffocation. A temporary paralysis induced by the spirit prevents the individual from moving or screaming. A succubus, associated with Lilith, is a spirit of perversion similar to an incubus, only it attacks men. Both incubus and succubus involve unnatural relations. Psalm 91:5-6: "You shall not be afraid of the terror by night, nor of the arrow that flies by day, nor of the pestilence that walks in darkness, nor of the destruction that lays waste at noonday."

Fear of Death Spirit: The fear of death spirit manifests as a foreboding sense of death looming over a person. It can also cause an irrational fear of dying, intrusive thoughts, or a fascination with death. The spirit torments the mind and can cause physical symptoms such as panic attacks, dizziness or lightheadedness, sweating, and irregular heart rate. Psalm 55:4: "My heart is severely pained within me, and the terrors of death have fallen upon me."

Manifestations: Phobias, the foreboding sense of death, fear of man, heart attacks, horror, inferiority, inadequacy, timidity, stress, torment, worry, panic attacks, irregular heart rate, heart palpitations, chest pain, shortness of breath, insomnia, fear of impending death.

Strongman: Spirit of Heaviness

Spirit of Rejection, Spirit of Despair, Spirit of Insomnia, Spirit of Depression

Cast out: Spirit of heaviness (and any lesser demons discerned)

Pray for: Garment of praise, oil of joy, and the Holy Spirit

Feelings of despondency, or being weighed down, burdened, or brokenhearted, and the feeling that a dark cloud is constantly hanging overhead characterize the spirit of heaviness. All of these are symptoms of demonic oppression. This spirit gains access during natural times of grief, mourning, or despair, and causes us to focus on our feelings of inadequacy and self-pity. It's the enemy's attempt to steal our joy and keep us bound in an endless cycle of spiritual oppression.

Whenever we're in a place of despair, and as difficult as it may seem at first, if we lift our voices in praise to the Lord, the Lord will free our spirit from our burdens and joy will well up within our soul. Psalm 22:3 says that God inhabits the praises of His people, so when we praise, He is in our midst. All else falls away in the shadow of the Lord God Almighty. And where God is, the enemy flees.

Demons Under the Spirit of Heaviness

Spirit of Rejection: The spirit of rejection attaches itself to our God-given need to be loved, and distorts our view, turning incidences in our lives into feelings of rejection. The emotional pain of rejection can be debilitating; it's one of the leading causes of depression and anxiety. 1 Samuel 8:7: "And the Lord said to Samuel, 'Heed the voice of the people in all that they say to you; for they have not rejected you, but they have rejected Me, that I should not reign over them.'"

Spirit of Insomnia: The spirit of insomnia attacks our sleep and either denies us the ability to fall asleep or interrupts our sleep during the night. The victim lies there for hours, unable to calm the thoughts racing through their mind, even awakening throughout the night for no apparent reason. Ecclesiastes 2:22–23: "For what has man for all his labor, and for the striving of his heart with which he has toiled under the sun? For all his days *are* sorrowful, and his work burdensome; even in the night his heart takes no rest."

Spirit of Despair: The spirit of despair instills a state of despair within a person's mind. It uses every negative situation possible to make it appear that there's no use in expecting anything good out of life. 2 Corinthians 1:8–9: "For we do not want you to be ignorant, brethren, of our trouble which came to us in Asia: that we were burdened beyond measure, above strength, so that we despaired even of life."

Spirit of Depression: The spirit of depression is like a heavy vacuum sucking the life right out of a person. This malevolent spirit dumps an overwhelming amount of grief, brokenness, and despair on our shoulders. Isaiah 61:3: "To console those who mourn in Zion, to give them beauty for ashes, the oil of joy for mourning, the garment of praise for the spirit of heaviness; that they may be called trees of righteousness, the planting of the Lord, that He may be glorified."

Manifestations: Broken heart, depression, despair, discouragement, excessive mourning, heaviness, hopelessness, inner hurts, insomnia, loneliness, rejection, self-pity, sorrow, grief, sadness, suicidal thoughts (suicidal thoughts should be taken seriously).

Strongman: Spirit of Jealousy

Spirit of Envy, Spirit of Offense, Murder Spirit, Spirit of Revenge, Spirit of Anger, Spirit of Hatred

Cast out: Spirit of Jealousy

Pray for: Love of God

The spirit of jealousy provokes us to covet that which is not rightfully ours. It works with pride so that we believe we are the deserving one—and no one else had best take it away. A jealous spirit can cause a person to lust after someone other than their spouse, or can cause a spouse to suspect an unfounded affair. It splits friendships when one feels the other has undeserving favor that they themselves deserve. Furthermore, it breeds unnecessary competition and division among churches. It is a dangerous spirit that the devil uses to convince us we should feel threatened by someone else's success.

In Genesis 37, we find an exceptional example of jealousy. Jacob loved his son Joseph more than his brothers. Jacob gave his favorite son a coat of many colors, which caused his brothers to resent and hate him. So great was their hatred that they ended up selling him to the Ishmaelites, even lying to their father, saying he was dead. In the end, their hatred and revenge cost the brothers more than they could have ever dreamed because the Ishmaelites took Joseph to Egypt as a slave, yet he remained faithful to God. Through God's divine plan, Joseph rose to become the second most powerful man in Egypt. When famine struck, Joseph's brothers traveled there to buy grain and ran into their discarded brother, which forced them to admit their actions as they stood before him. Joseph, though brokenhearted by what they had done, did not harbor resentment or hatred. God used him to teach his brothers a valuable lesson. It's best if we recognize we are not to avenge, but to put all things into God's hands and trust He will take care of it (see Romans 12:19–21).

Demons Under the Spirit of Jealousy

Spirit of Envy: The spirit of envy doesn't want anyone else to have what it lacks. It causes resentment, anger, and bitterness toward someone who has a quality or possession that a person desires. The spirit of envy creates anger when someone else has reached a higher achievement. If left to its devices, it can provoke murderous thoughts and even murderous actions. Matthew 27:18: "For he knew they had handed [Jesus] over because of envy."

Spirit of Offense: The spirit of offense often uses a person's insecurity as its entrance point. Often, the person's self-esteem hinges on receiving validation and respect from others. This insecurity leads to hypersensitivity, causing them to interpret even harmless comments negatively. The spirit of offense's primary target is to cause division either in relationships, families, or within the church. It frequently accompanies pride, which legitimizes its existence and strengthens its grip. This is one of Satan's most effective tools for breaking the unity of believers (see Proverbs 18:19).

Spirit of Murder: The spirit of murder enters through the heart of a person who has housed the spirits of anger and envy for some time. Upon reaching a boiling point, the well-thought-out act snuffs out another person's life. Words, too, can express the spirit of murder; while not killing the body, they destroy another person's spirit (self-esteem, hopes). The tongue can be a ruthless weapon that a murderous spirit will use. Matthew 5:21: "You have heard that it was said to those of old, 'You shall not murder, and whoever murders will be in danger of the judgment.'"

Spirit of Revenge: The spirit of revenge seeks to injure in retaliation for a wrong suffered. The spirit preys on our natural inclination as humans to seek revenge against injustice. It strives to keep its victims bound in a maelstrom of vengeance and hate. Romans 12:19–21: "Never take your own revenge, beloved, but leave room for the wrath *of God*, for it is written: "Vengeance is Mine, I will repay," says the Lord" (NASB).

Spirit of Anger: The spirit of anger works to discredit your identity as a believer. It pushes its victims to lose their temper and react according to the flesh to discredit their witness and rob their peace. This spirit causes one to harbor grudges that become more and more destructive. Deep-rooted anger may go back several generations within a family. Ephesians 4:26 states, "Be ye angry, and sin not." Note: Not all anger is forbidden. We should be angry at the things that anger God, but avoid sin by not acting in unsanctified areas of one's flesh.

Spirit of Hate: The spirit of hate has its roots in the beginning of time when Satan, out of jealousy and envy, held perpetual hatred toward God and His creation because he fell short of and wasn't equal to God. This destructive spirit fosters animosity and vindictiveness and entices mankind to harbor hatred in their hearts against one another and God. 1 John 3:15: "Whoever hates his brother is a murderer, and you know that no murderer has eternal life abiding in him."

Manifestations: Anger, competition, cruelty, envy, hatred, murder, rage, revenge, selfishness, spite, suspicion, strife, covertness, contention, quarreling, division, adultery, resentment, bitterness.

Strongman: Spirit of Infirmity

Spirit of Oppression, Crippling or Disabling Spirit, Any Type of Disease

Cast out: Spirit of infirmity (and any lesser demons discerned)

Pray for: Spirit of life (John 6:63)

The spirit of infirmity is spiritual oppression that affects the whole body and can cause a variety of ailments, such as physical illness or injury, mental anguish, and emotional distress. *The Encyclopedia of the Bible* defines a disease as "a definite entity of sickness affecting part or all of the body."[22] We find, upon examining Jesus' and his disciples' healings, that some illnesses were attributed to demonic spirits, while others were documented as healings that do not mention demons.

Even mild illnesses, like the common cold, temporarily weaken our body, but we are more concerned about serious illnesses, from which recovery is rare. Some of these illnesses are hereditary, passing through generations; however, we don't have to accept them like family heirlooms. Rather, we can resist and reject them in the name of Jesus and stop their progression

---

[22] "Diseases of the Bible" in Encyclopedia of the Bible on Bible Gateway, accessed July 16, 2025,. https://www.biblegateway.com/resources/encyclopedia-of-the-bible/Diseases-Bible.

through our family line. Many times, the spirit of infirmity gains entry through unconfessed sin. It also will take hold after an assault by other demons, such as the spirit of fear manifested as a fear of illness or death. A weakened immune system abused by lack of rest and proper nutrition can also be the culprit. Regardless of how it enters, this spirit slowly sucks the life force out of its host and renders them ineffective.

While Satan uses spiritual oppression to keep mankind bound and inoperable, God anointed Jesus with the power to heal all who were oppressed of the devil (see Acts 10:38). Jesus was at the synagogue on the Sabbath when he came upon a woman. Talk about being in the right place at the right time. There is no evidence that she attempted to reach out to Him, but He called out to her, "Woman, you are loosed from your infirmity" (see Luke 13:11–12).

The spirit of infirmity had oppressed the woman for eighteen years, and she was bent over so that she could not raise herself up. Jesus laid his hands on her, and immediately she stood up straight and praised God. It comes as no surprise that the ruler of the synagogue objected because Jesus had healed on a Sabbath. Jesus replied, "So ought not this woman, being a daughter of Abraham, whom Satan has bound in these eighteen years, be loosed from this bond" (Luke 13:16 KJV).

Luke specifically made note that the spirit of infirmity uses sickness to oppress and lock someone in bondage, thus revealing Satan as the source of some infirmity. However, through Jesus' death and resurrection on the cross, we know He has disarmed principalities and powers, and made a public spectacle of them, triumphing over them in it (see Colossians 2:15).

Demons Under the Spirit of Infirmity

Spirit of Oppression: The spirit of oppression attacks from the outside by suppressing, controlling, and dominating its target. One of its primary ways of oppressing is through various kinds of illnesses. This oppressive spirit works hand in hand with the spirit of heaviness. Together, they weigh the person down until they become inactive in their affliction. The spirit seeks to rob their freedom and keep them in its bondage. Acts 10:38: "God anointed Jesus of Nazareth with the Holy Spirit and with power, who went about doing good and healing all who were oppressed by the devil, for God was with Him."

Crippling or Disabling Spirit: The crippling spirit disables its recipient, significantly affecting their ability to move and function normally. This debilitating condition can result from an injury or affliction, either of which can result from this demonic spirit, and the work of Satan. Again, I mention the woman crippled by a spirit for eighteen years. Her condition forced her to hunch over so she could not stand erect. Luke 13:11–16 (ESV): "When Jesus saw her, He called her over and said, 'Woman, you are set free from your disability.' Then He placed His hands on her, and immediately she straightened up and began to glorify God."

Manifestations: Physical ailments, mental anguish, physical disabilities, emotional distress, asthma, arthritis, allergies, fever, viruses, lameness, lingering disorders, lung problems, breathing issues, sinus problems, seizures, convulsions, foaming at the mouth, inability to speak.

Strongman: Deaf and Dumb Spirit

Blind Spirit, Deaf and Dumb Spirit, Epileptic Spirit

Cast out: Deaf and dumb spirit (and any lesser demons discerned)

Pray for: Love of God

The deaf and dumb spirit may seem to be a quiet spirit, but it is anything but quiet. In reality, it draws the most attention and is quite the spectacle to viewers. When it manifests, it will exhibit a showcase event, complete with throwing its victim down, foaming at the mouth, and verbal sounds. For the undiscerning, it can be quite unsettling. This spirit mainly attacks a person's ability to hear, speak, or see. It also dulls their thinking, thus creating a lackluster approach to life. The deaf and dumb spirit overlaps with the spirit of infirmity, and brings forth additional demonic spirits, including the spirit of suicide, the spirit of mental illness, and the epileptic spirit.

In Mark 1:29-34, Jesus was in the synagogue on the Sabbath teaching when a man with an unclean spirit cried out, "What have you to do with us, Jesus of Nazareth? Have you come to destroy us? I know who you are—the Holy One of God." But Jesus rebuked and silenced him. The unclean spirit convulsing him cried out in a loud voice, and came out of him.

Demons Under the Deaf and Dumb Spirit

Dumb (Mute) Spirit: The dumb spirit silences a person and renders them speechless. Its attack deprives the person of the freedom to express themselves verbally including their ability to talk about Jesus and God's love for them. A deaf and dumb spirit afflicts a person twofold, through inability to hear and to speak. Luke 11:14: "And He was casting out a demon, and it was mute; when the demon had gone out, the mute man spoke; and the crowds were amazed."

Deaf Spirit: The deaf spirit causes a person to lose their hearing. A person born deaf may be under this affliction because of demonic influence, likely because of a generational curse. A believer can break the curse by using their God-given authority in the name of Jesus by saying, "In the name of Jesus, I break the inherited curse of deafness."

A deaf spirit can also afflict its host at any point in their life. Hearing loss can vary, and those born deaf are many times struck with a dumb spirit, losing both their ability to hear and speak. Mark 9:25-26: "When Jesus saw that the people came running together, He rebuked the unclean spirit, saying to it, "Deaf and dumb spirit, I command you, come out of him and enter him no more!"

Blindness: The blind spirit strikes its victim's sight, with the result ranging from a slight blur to a total loss of vision. It causes the person to struggle with daily activities that most take for granted. It was a common and much sought-after cure in ancient times. In Mark 10:46, Jesus and his disciples came to Jericho where a blind man named Bartimaeus sat begging. When he heard Jesus was there, he began crying out, asking Jesus to have mercy on him. Jesus asked what he wanted, and Bartimaeus said he wanted to receive his sight. Jesus said, "Go your way; your faith has made you well" (v. 52). The man immediately received his sight.

Epileptic Spirit: The word *epilepsy* is from a Greek word meaning "a seizure." The epileptic spirit afflicts its victim with what's called a "petit mal" (light seizure) or a "grand mal" seizure, which causes convulsions, loss of consciousness, biting one's tongue, and foaming from the mouth. During the seizure, the spirit forcefully takes control of the person and instills fear of reoccurrence (bondage). Matthew 17:14–18: "'Lord, have mercy on my son,' he said. 'He has seizures and is suffering greatly. He often falls into the fire or into the water'" (NIV).

Asthmatic Spirit: Asthma, a chronic respiratory disease, results in episodes of wheezing, coughing, chest tightness, and shortness of breath. The New Living Translation translates Job 34:14–15 as, "If God were to take back His Spirit and withdraw His breath, all life would cease and humanity would turn again to dust." In severe attacks, the bronchial tubes can close altogether, resulting in prolonged shortness of breath, causing death—one of the enemy's goals.

Manifestations: Blindness, burns, bruising, convulsions, deafness, dumbness, drowning, epilepsy, eye diseases, asthma, foaming at the mouth, gnashing teeth, inner ear disease, insanity, lunacy, mental illness, muteness, motionless stupor, prostration, suicidal tendencies, seizures, schizophrenia.

Strongman: Spirit of Pride

Leviathan, Spirit of Arrogance, Spirit of Ego

Cast out: Spirit of pride (Leviathan, and any lesser demons discerned)

Pray for: Humble and contrite Spirit: (Psalm 51:1–19)

The spirit of pride first appeared in the heavens when Lucifer took on his glorious persona as something he himself had accomplished, rather than recognizing he resulted from God's workmanship, and all glory belonged to the Lord God who had created him. Since that time, Satan has used the same spirit to influence mankind to entrap us. He did so in the garden of Eden when he encouraged Eve to eat the forbidden fruit so that she would be "like God" and know good from evil. It's the same spirit at work when we give credit to ourselves for the good, we accomplished, rather than realizing we have nothing apart from God.

James 4:6 tells us, "God resists the proud, but gives grace to the humble." Believers in bondage to the spirit of pride, which attaches to the heart, do what they believe is "the work of the kingdom" when in fact they are doing it of their own accord, and in their own strength. This causes them to seek recognition, or glory, for their work. Psalm 147:6 tells us, "The Lord lifts the humble; He casts the wicked down to the ground." The late C. S. Lewis, in his book *Mere Christianity*, says, "According to Christian teachers, the essential vice, the utmost evil, is Pride. Unchastity, anger, greed, drunkenness, and all that, are mere fleabites in comparison: it was through pride that the devil became the devil."[23]

Demons Under the Spirit of Pride

Leviathan Spirit: The Bible describes the Leviathan spirit as a serpent-like sea creature, associated with pride and control. This ancient high-ruling demonic prince, or principality is one of the most powerful and destructive spirits. Many times, rejection becomes the catalyst for which the spirit gains access. It is within this same prideful spirit that Lucifer succumbed to in the heavens before being cast out, a puffed-up, arrogant image of oneself that leads to self-worship. Job 41:34 says, "He beholds every high thing." He *is* king over all the children of pride." Those falling under the influence of the Leviathan spirit have opened themselves up not only to the spirit of pride and self-righteousness but

---

[23] Thomas A. Tarrants, "Pride and Humility," C. S. Lewis Institute, December 4, 2011, https://www.cslewisinstitute.org/resources/pride-and-humility/.

to the principality over these spirits. Job 41:34: "[Satan] beholds every high thing."

Spirit of Arrogance: The spirit of arrogance imposes an overload of pride that boasts of its superiority to all around it. It exalts its self-importance to an undue degree, making claims of excellence in an undue proportion. It causes people to be condescending and is demeaning to those it considers of lesser importance. Psalm 94:4: "They pour forth words, they speak arrogantly."

Spirit of Ego: The spirit of ego attaches itself to the mind, influencing it with an inflated ego that can lead to self-centeredness and a false sense of self-assurance. It imposes a distorted view of one's self-worth, and views self as superior to those around it, thus hindering one's ability to see a need for dependence on God. John 5:31: "If I bear witness of Myself, My witness is not true."

Manifestations: Pride, self-deception, scornful, idleness, arrogance, obstinance, strife, contentiousness, rejection of God, self-righteousness, rebellion, desire to control, mockery, vanity, twisting God's Word, breaking covenants, self-importance.

Strongman: Lying Spirit

Deceitful Spirits, Doctrines of Demons, (see Spirit of Error)

Cast out: Lying spirit (and any lesser demons discerned)

Pray for: The spirit of truth

The lying spirit leads its victim astray into various deceptions and falsehoods. It opposes God's truth and rather spreads the devil's lies. It has two principal methods to accomplish its given task. One way is through the mind; it whispers lies into our thoughts that, if unguarded, will take root. This happened to me once, and I believed the enemy's lie that God had abandoned me. The enemy gained a foothold when my faith was wavering and quickly planted its roots. From there it dug deeper and deeper until it became a stronghold and opened the door for the lying strongman to take hold. At that point, there was no telling me otherwise, and in my mind, the evidence was all around. For years, this demon deceived me, separating me from God's truth and wreaking havoc in my life, while I falsely believed I was spiritually enlightened. Then one day, the binding of this spirit opened my eyes to God's presence in my life, and I realized He had never left me but had been there watching everything, every abomination, that I had done.

It was a humbling realization, and it shows how one little lie can keep a person bound for years.

The lying spirit's second other means of attack is through the tongue. These are the lies we tell to others through gossip, accusations, and slander. Under the spirit's influence, the person quickly becomes a compulsive liar. I know a man who was under a lying spirit's influence, which made it difficult to know when to believe him.

In some ways, you could say he told great fisherman tales—you know, the kind that entertain the audience with exaggerations and tall-tale events for the sake of amusement. However, he continued to lie in every aspect of his life: finances, relationships, and work. He even lied about things there was no need to lie about. The deception was alarming. You could catch him red-handed in the act, and yet he would look you straight in the eyes and lie without a flinch. This type of compulsive lying results from being controlled by lying demons. They not only deceive others, but they deceive the person under their influence into believing that no one would ever know the truth.

Eventually, I discovered the severe abuse this man had suffered as a child. Punishments were harsh. On one occasion, his father had yanked him off the garage roof by his hair with such force that he ripped the hair roots right out of his scalp, leaving a fist-size bald spot. In order to avoid the wrath of his father, he had opened himself up to a lying spirit, who then influenced him to master the art of the lie.

Demons Under the Lying Spirit

Deceitful Spirits: These are deceptive spirits who promote lies in order to lure people from the truth of God. They use many forms of deception, such as manipulation, seduction, slander, gossip, accusations, and exaggeration in order to lure their prey into their web of lies. 1 Timothy 4:1: "Now the Spirit expressly says that in latter times some will depart from the faith, giving heed to deceiving spirits and doctrines of demons."

Demonic Doctrines: Deceiving spirits also work under the guise of false prophets and teachers. They secretly slip in heresies that are contrary to Jesus' teachings, then by imposing controversy and quarreling among believers, they provoke slander, suspicions, and dissension within them. Their prophecies either add, take away, or entirely twist the Word of God. They preach an empty or watered-down gospel to an undiscerning body of believers. These deceiving spirits work hand in hand with the spirit of error.

Manifestations: Accusation, adultery, critical spirit, deception, superstition, esteem of self, exaggeration, false prophecy, false teaching, flattery, gossip, hypocrisy, vain imaginations, lies, "religious" spirit, slander.

Strongman: Spirit of Error *(see Lying Spirit)*

False Doctrines, New Age Teaching, Doctrine of Demons, (see Lying Spirit)

Cast out: Spirit of error (and any lesser demon discerned)

Pray for: The spirit of truth

The spirit of error is a demonic force behind every false teaching and prophecy. It distorts the truth, causing believers to either misunderstand or misinterpret the Bible, and then they believe a lie or fall for false doctrine. Many times, it uses scriptural half-truths, which is a more subtle form of misinterpretation and can keep one in error while believing they are in truth. There is nothing more deceiving than the mixture of truth and error, and that is its expertise. It offers its recipient a poisoned chalice that, if tasted, will lead to spiritual death.

Demons Under the Spirit of Error

New Age Teachings: One of the most active places we can see the spirit of error at work is in New Age spirituality. The New Age has been entrapping people with its esoteric experiences for quite some time. The allure of hidden wisdom and the promise of a new era may sound convincing, but it's just another scheme of Satan to lead mankind astray. New Age dresses itself in enlightenment, but its light is artificial and its source none other than Satan himself in the guise of the angel of light (see 1 Corinthians 11:14). It has no defined belief system yet sets self to be its god. Not surprisingly, it incorporates many occult practices such as channeling, crystals, astrology, tarot, Reiki, and herbal medicines. The kingdom of darkness handcrafted it, and it's basically a hodgepodge of Satan's strategies in attractive packaging, marketed as a universal gift.

Another place we can find the spirit of error at work is within the church. Yes, sadly, I said the church. Since the church began, a spirit of error has been at work (see 2 Timothy 2:16–17), intensifying dramatically in the past twenty years as some congregations have adopted occult practices. A corrupted gospel has affected some churches, with false miracles and witchcraft seeping into their practices. The enemy's cunning deception causes believers to seek answers in ungodly things rather than God, resulting in a spiritually paralyzed church.

As we near the end times, apostasy in the church will increase as believers will go after the doctrine of demons (see 1 Timothy 4:1). We must always test every spirit (see 1 John 4:1) to ensure it aligns with God's Word, and reject it if it doesn't. To not do so could subject us to false teachings and open us up to the spirit of error. Deception can affect any pastor, regardless of popularity or the size of the assembly that he leads.

The Spirit of Error: The spirit of error recently publicized itself at a Christian men's conference led by a megachurch.[24] This church stages rather outlandish openings for its events—ones that appear to appease the flesh—though this year they took it to a whole new bizarre level. The opening act was a pole performance by a male stripper and a sword swallower. The next day, one of the guest speakers identified the Jezebel spirit as the source of the opening act, bringing the event to unexpected attention. Silence fell over the room as the guest speaker identified and exposed the demon—until the head pastor at the conference interrupted, shockingly telling the speaker to stop and leave.

The attendees who heard the truth became quite disturbed by this action, as the head pastor stood before the audience and defended the opening act, claiming the man was a former stripper who was now married with children and had become a Christian. This later proved false, as the performer came forward and admitted he wasn't married, he didn't have any children, and his only involvement with the church was his infant baptism. And he was still stripping in clubs. Despite the truth being revealed, the head pastor continued to deny the deception that he had allowed into the conference, and committed false witness against the guest speaker who exposed it.

Then, it didn't end there. The pastor continued to call out the guest speaker days later, demanding for him to repent, claiming it was a sin against him and attempting to apply Matthew 18 out of context. The enemy was having a field day, and the deception there obviously runs deeper than what's seen on the surface. This is a good example of how the spirit of error, along with its companion demons, attempt to hijack the truth, silence prophetic words, and occupy the sanctuary's high place.

Manifestations: New Age teaching, argumentativeness, contentiousness, defensiveness, defilement, deceptive words, error, false doctrines, false teaching, being a servant of corruption, stubbornness, being unteachable.

---

24 Preach and Lead, "Mark Driscoll Kicked Off Stage at John Lindell's Men's Conference (Lessons for Pastors)," YouTube, April 15, 2024, https://www.youtube.com/watch?v=_4W_qOLb7xE.

Strongman: Spirit of the Antichrist

Unholy Trinity, Son of Perdition, False Prophet
Cast out: Spirit of the antichrist
Pray for: The spirit of truth

The spirit of the antichrist is already in the world (see 1 John 4:3). The antichrist's last days debut is a topic of much discussion. So, how will we know him? Let's break it down in simple terms so it will jolt our memory. He is the unholy trinity: Satan (the dragon), the antichrist (the beast), and the false prophet that "looks like a lamb, but talks like a dragon." It's a metaphor. For instance, the false prophet doesn't literally have the face of a lamb; the wording means people will see him as pure, innocent, gentle, and good—similar to Satan's disguise, but no matter how attractive he may look, when he speaks, we'll know where he came from. His words will be vile, blasphemous, and slanderous against the things of God. It's the devil's disguise. The discerning will know his is not the voice of the Good Shepherd. In that hour, we must hold tight to the sword of the Spirit, the Word of God.

But what about now? Though we may not see his physical presence yet, the spirit of the antichrist is moving among us. He's been at work preparing mankind for his coming, and grooming him to accept his unholy agenda. His goal is to be the source of their worship. Satan has a battle plan, and behind the scenes he is strategizing to set his plan in motion. The antichrist's spirit, part of Satan's plan, scouted the land and planted traps. Do you recognize his presence in the world? Let's take a look.

He is the spirit of lawlessness (see 2 Thessalonians 2:7). Do you recall our shock at hearing "defund the police"? Why do we have such disrespect for authority and the rule of law? Why are crime rates rising in our city streets, and why do convicted criminals serve little to no time? The enemy sews discord, injustice, and chaos within our lives. He comes to distract, mislead, and destroy, but our society appears to not want to address or hinder the very things that make the devil gloat, even to the point of the societal lack of empathy and concern for innocent victims. Some cities today are even offering no-bail releases for more serious crimes, and enabling and harboring possible criminal activity in sanctuary cities from federal law enforcement. As well, the judicial system fails to enforce adequate and solid jail sentences that will deter future or repeat offenders.

Sadly, the lack of godly accountability and the increase of anarchy characterize today's world. As the spirit of lawlessness takes to the offensive, so we too must rise to the occasion, positioning ourselves to take a stance against the enemy. We go forth into battle under the authority of Christ, actively ready to engage in warfare with the sword of the spirit in hand, targeting our prayers for divine intervention and with shouts of praise as our key offensive weapons. Because of the power behind the antichrist spirit, we use this coordinated approach as Spirit-led believers, being the most effective method to leverage the collective power of the body of Christ.

Demons Under the Antichrist

Son of Perdition: The son of perdition will deny Jesus as Messiah (Son of God; born of the flesh; lived, died, and rose again). To the Jews, who are still waiting for the Messiah to come, he will fulfill the prophecies that they have long waited for. Sadly, the church will have fallen into apostasy. But how can that be—a Christian church that denies Christ? We'll talk more about that in a bit, but having deflected from the truth and replacing it with error, the church will fall prey to the son of perdition (see 2 Thessalonians 2:3–4). He'll be the global leader that brings world peace, and he'll usher in the one-world religion that denies Jesus Christ. The anti-Jew, anti-Christian, and anti-God forces will then reveal the truth and sit "as god" in the Jerusalem temple. And he will demand that all men worship him.

The antichrist's true personality will emerge. His hate for God and his hate for God's people will plainly be clear. Those who resist him will face persecution. The false prophet (the lamb that talks like a dragon) will be behind everyone receiving the mark of the beast, and for those who refuse there will be no food or water, the basics to sustain life. This will weaken one's body.

If that's not enough, the attack will also be psychological, creating severe mental anguish and torment to wear people down mentally and bring them to their knees to worship the beast. What's alarming is that there are Christians today who don't know their faith (see the spirit of error). It appears as though a spell of biblical illiteracy has fallen upon them, causing a severe deficit in their ability to know truth from error, or half-truth from whole truth. Now is the time to ask God, in His mercy, to write His words upon our heart.

Spirit of Antichrist (Apostasy in the Church): As I write this chapter, an example of the state of the church is unfolding. In its annual convention, the United Methodist Church (UMC) sided with human ideology over the Word of God. The vote was to accommodate a cultural change in society and the denomination's concern over wavering membership, but this presents a spiritual crisis over the flesh. The vote to change the UMC book of discipline resulted in the following changes: 1) to remove the denominational stance that declares homosexuality to be "incompatible with Christian teaching"; 2) to affirm "marriage as a sacred, lifelong covenant that brings two people of faith (adult man and adult woman of consenting age or two adult persons of consenting age) into a union of one another and into deeper relationship with God and the religious community"; and 3) to eliminate the ban on "self-avowed practicing" gay clergy.[25]

The Word of God is a guiding light that reveals the path of righteousness so that we can follow in His ways. Man will not defile God, and God will not change His ways to accommodate humanity's sin. Despite man's efforts to reword, remove, and replace church doctrines, the Bible remains unchanged, and one day mankind will face judgment accordingly. We should not be unloving toward the gay population, but should treat them with

---

25   Joey Butler, "May 2 Wrap-up: Delegates Declare Homosexuality No Longer 'Incompatible,'" The New York Conference | United Methodist Church, accessed June 28, 2025, https://www.nyac.com/newsdetail/may-2-wrap-up-delegates-declare-homosexuality-no-longer-incompatible-18356260.

respect and dignity, because God desires their repentance and salvation as much as He desires the redemption of all His children. It is possible to hate the sin while loving the sinner and yet stand firm and unwavering in our faith.

The United Methodist Church isn't alone in changing its stance on biblical worldly views; rather, it joins with the United Church of Christ, the Episcopal Church, the Evangelical Lutheran Church, and the Presbyterian Church (USA) in affirming LGBTQ activity, including ordaining clergy and same-sex marriage. As believers we're called to be the salt of the earth, but clearly here the salt has lost its flavor (see Matthew 5:13–14). It seems it only took a little of leaven that Satan ingrained within to spoil the whole lump (church).

However, as disheartening as this may be, God has promised that though the devil seeks to destroy the church and will lead many astray in the end times, He will graciously preserve the remnant who uphold His commandments and hold to the testimony of Jesus (see Revelation 12:17). This is the spiritual warfare over the church. The outside pressure to compromise comes not just from Satan, but from the world's push for the church to confirm and endorse a global acceptance of sinful behavior within its leadership and walls.

We must remember this biblical truth: Jesus said, "I will build My church and the gates of hell will not prevail against it" (Matthew 16:18). Amen!

Manifestations: Apostasy, denying the deity of Christ, denying atonement, being anti-Christian, being anti-Jewish, false prophecy, blaspheming, having a controlling spirit, humanism, lawlessness, legalism, persecuting the saints, teaching heresies.

Strongman: Seducing Spirits

Jezebel Spirit, Deceitful Spirit (See Lying Spirit)

Cast out: Seducing spirits (and any lesser demons discerned)

Pray for: Holy Spirit, truth

Seducing spirits often accompany the spirit of error and, as the end times near, the spirit of the antichrist. The seducing spirit will use seduction to lure people away from the truth and down the slippery slope of false doctrines and religious deceptions. We often think of seduction as having a sexual component to it, and often it does, but any temptation that uses charm or personal charisma as an enticement also embodies the spirit of seduction. Its primary goal is to lead astray, and it will use whatever means possible to coerce people away from God and then paralyze their ability to return to Him.

Demons Under Seducing Spirits

Sampson and Delilah: In the biblical story of Sampson and Delilah, we see the seducing spirit in full operation. God set Sampson apart from birth, and Sampson was to live by a vow to never cut his hair or drink alcohol. He became a judge of Israel and had tremendous strength from God, which he used to fight the Philistines, who were the oppressors of the Israelites. Samson willingly allowed himself into situations that led to sin, yet God turned each circumstance around for His glory, despite Samson's failure to obey. Over time, Samson gained pride from his strength and forgot from whom it came, which was a big mistake. He then met and fell in love with Delilah, a Philistine woman. Unbeknownst to Samson, the Philistine rulers bribed Delilah to learn the secret of his strength.

Today, it is the rulers of darkness that send seducing spirits to entice believers, and how we respond to their deceptive, cunning words will determine our outcome. Samson surely recognized Delilah's power over him and resisted her advances three times, but she persistently wore him down, and he finally succumbed to his lust for her and revealed that his strength came from his uncut hair. The seducing spirit is the ultimate betrayer, and will gain a person's confidence and trust despite their resistance. It casts its spell and lures them off into their fantasy to feed their own desires. Then, just as Delilah did with Sampson, it betrays and turns on them. By then, it will have seared or numbed their conscience. This desensitizes their moral compass, so they can no longer distinguish good from evil. If we find we've succumbed to the advances of the seducing spirit, we mustn't give up.

The Philistines beat Sampson, gouged out his eyes, and imprisoned him. In a spiritual sense, the seducing spirit will leave a person beaten, spiritually blinded, and bound, but just as Sampson found it within himself to repent, we too can repent if we find ourselves in a similar fate. Once Sampson repented, God came in with the ultimate victory, and Sampson regained his strength and removed a pillar, which caused the entire building to collapse and wipe out his oppressors. Never underestimate the power of our God over the enemy, though it is far better to discern seducing spirits before they seduce to begin with.

Jezebel Spirit: You're probably familiar with the term *Jezebel spirit*, though if you were to search for it in the Bible, you wouldn't find it. That's because Jezebel is the name of a rather a wicked queen who was married to Ahab, the king of Israel (see 1 Kings; 2 Kings). Jezebel, who persuaded Ahab and the Israelites to worship the Canaanite god Ba'al instead of God, embodied evil and used false accusations to kill men in order to take possession of their vineyards, and she had the prophets of God murdered. She heavily opposed and threatened the one remaining prophet, Elijah, after he challenged the prophets of Ba'al to see which god would light the altar during a drought.

The attempts by the prophets of Ba'al were unsuccessful, but when Elijah called upon God, fire fell from heaven and consumed the entire altar. Elijah then fled to Horeb after Jezebel promised to kill him. During her life, she used manipulation, seduction, and control to gain power, influencing and corrupting others.

Now, what does the woman Jezebel have to do with a demonic spirit? If we move forward to the end times church, in Revelation 2:20 Jesus says, "Nevertheless, I have a few things against you, because you allow that woman Jezebel, who calls herself a prophetess, to teach and seduce My servants to commit sexual immorality and eat things sacrificed to idols." Jezebel, the woman, died thousands of years ago, so it is the spirit of Jezebel being referenced here. The same spirit that used Jezebel to commit such heinous acts was at work within the church of Thyatira.

This spirit is actually a group of demons working together within one body. Several ruling demonic spirits had taken up residence within the carnal woman named Jezebel; they were "her demons," so to speak. This in itself is not uncommon, as once a demon gains access, it usually brings along a few more of its cohorts or lesser demons. However, in some cases, several ruling spirits, along with a few of their lesser demons, occupy the same residential host, such as with Jezebel. I classify these as a demon group. In the church of Thyatira, this would mean that this specific group of demons was operating within the church. They housed the same characteristics within the guise of a self-proclaimed prophetess who taught and seduced believers into partaking of a pagan love feast, comprising sexual immorality and feasting.

The spirit of Jezebel is first and foremost a seducing spirit, which is a ruling spirit, only it shares its occupancy within a demon grouping. It is the combination that makes a Jezebel so toxic. The Jezebel spirit is active within the walls of many churches today, and its influence will increase in the latter days. A person operating with a Jezebel spirit will use charm to ingratiate themselves into church leadership. After establishing credibility, they gradually move to take control over church functions, advancing themselves as teachers and proclaiming to be self-prophets or prophetesses. The Jezebel spirit has an animosity toward the prophets of God, and will do anything to quiet them. Its allure is bewitching, as it subtly maneuvers throughout the congregation causing division within the church. It is another end times strategy the devil uses to lead the church astray. While Jezebel was the woman demonized by these spirits in the book of Judges, we understand demonic spirits aren't privy to gender, and the spirit of Jezebel will attach itself to either a male or female.

Demonic grouping: seducing spirit, perverse spirit, lying spirit, jealousy spirit, the spirit of whoredom, along with the spirits of price and arrogance.

Manifestations: Seduction, enticement, witchcraft, false signs and wonders, hypocritical lies, a seared conscience, wandering from the truth, fascination with evil, aligning with false prophets, doctrines of demons.

Strongman: Spirit of Divination

Spirit of Rebellion, Spirit of Fortune-Telling, Witchcraft/Sorcery

Cast out: Spirit of divination (and any lesser demons discerned)

Pray for: The Holy Spirit, spiritual gifts

Divination is any practice not ordained by Scripture that seeks to gain knowledge from any source other than God. The Bible strictly forbids its practice in Leviticus 19:26: "You shall eat nothing with the blood, nor shall you practice divination or soothsaying." The spirit of divination is a demonic source that diviners consult to inquire of knowledge or manipulate the future. It has many forms of operation, such as fortune-telling, palm reading, tarot card reading, rune casting, scrying, and astrology, all of which were obtained from the aid of demonic spirits. The divination spirit may give tidbits of truth in order to coerce a person into believing. It will manipulate future events to reinforce reliance on its ability to foresee the future. Next, it will convince the person to use it as their go-to source in everyday life. By seeking our life's answers using any method of divination, we are seeking answers from demons rather than God. This is how they lead us into sin and to rebel against God. This also leaves an open invitation for it, and other spirits, to co-inhabit with it. It's deception, but it works far more times than most people think.

Divination is Satan's counterfeit to the spirit of prophecy, in which the Holy Spirit speaks through man with an inspired word from God (see 2 Peter 1:21). As Christians, we who lack wisdom are to "ask God, who gives generously to all without reproach, and it will be given" (James 1:5).

Demons Under the Spirit of Divination

Fortune-Telling: In Acts 16:16, we read of Paul's encounter with a slave girl demonized by a spirit of divination, or a spirit of a python in the Greek translation. It is also a counterfeit of the Holy Spirit's gift of the "word of knowledge." The slave girl, who was being exploited by her owners, profited well through her fortune-telling abilities that resulted from her demonization by the python spirit, which was active in the Temple of Apollo in Delphi. Apollo's temple in Delphi housed the oracle, and they called its high priestess "Pythia" because the python spirit controlled her; therefore, the term *python* became widely used for a person who had a spirit of divination.

This likely explains why people said the slave girl had a python spirit. The Oracle of Delphi attracted visitors from all across the ancient world. Both great rulers and regular members of society sought the Pythia's prophecies. In the temple, the Pythia sat upon a tripod chair and inhaled toxic fumes from a crevice in the ground until, in a trancelike state, she babbled words that the priest would then interpret as an oracle. The description of the enslaved girl as having a python spirit suggests she may have served as one of Apollo's chosen oracles.

At the time of Paul's encounter with her, he was with Silas and Timothy in Phillipi, preaching the gospel. When the slave girl began following them and prophesying (see Acts v.16: 16). She spoke the truth, saying, "These men are the servants of the Most High God, who proclaim to us the way of salvation." At first, Paul ignored her. But after a few days, Paul, being grieved, turned and said to the spirit, "I command thee in the name of Jesus Christ to come out of her" (v. 18), and within the hour, the spirit left.

Losing income from her fortune- telling highly agitated the owners and caused a citywide uproar. Guards beat Paul and Silas and threw them into jail. Here, we see spiritual warfare at work. The thwarting of Satan's plan caused his kingdom to retaliate with physical force, inciting a riot that led to the beating and imprisonment of Paul and Silas. In the end, God used what Satan meant to harm for His good: as an earthquake caused the chains to fall off Paul and Silas, and the jailer and his household got saved.

Spirit of Rebellion: Rebellion is the rejection of God's established authority, or disobedience to either His written or spoken Word. God considers rebellion a serious sin comparable to witchcraft and idolatry. First Samuel 14:23 says, "For rebellion is as the sin of witchcraft, and stubbornness is as iniquity and idolatry. Because you have rejected the Word of the Lord, He also has rejected you from being king." The spirit of rebellion undermines authority. It influences its subject to rebel against God, and godly ways, resulting in a loss of values, morals, and godly principles. The individual believes they are in control; however, the spirit of rebellion is influencing the person's ways.

The rebellious spirit seeks to satisfy the flesh, and adheres to self-will rather than God's will. It will cause havoc in homes, families, and churches. It entraps by willful disobedience to the voice of God, knowing that God blinds the eyes of those who have hardened their hearts because of disobedience (see John 12:39–40). Once an individual is spiritually blind, the rebellious spirit has compromised their ability to resist and fight back.

If the spirit of rebellion isn't successful entrapping by disobedience, it will use its own theology. Through this, it attempts to replace God's legitimate authority in a person's life with the illegitimate authority of witchcraft. Of course, illegitimate authority has to be supported by illegitimate power, and that power is the spirit of rebellion. Witchcraft and rebellion are so closely linked that it would be rare to find one without the other. This is so because at its root, a rebellious spirit is willfully under the authority of another spirit rather than the Spirit of God. Witchcraft stems from pride, seeking a self-will that satisfies the soul apart from God's will. This is the perfect match and why they are referred to as twin spirits. But there's more. Scripture says that "stubbornness is as iniquity and idolatry" (1 Samuel 15:23), meaning one's own stubbornness will cause them to refuse correction, avoid repentance, and follow other gods, which is idolatry.

The story of Saul and the witch of Endor provides insight into how the spirit of rebellion interacts and comes under the spirit of necromancy, which is sorcery, a form of witchcraft.

The Philistines had mustered their troops and camped at Shunem. Saul had assembled all of Israel and camped at Gilboa. But when Saul saw the Philistine troops, he shook in his boots, scared to death. Saul prayed to God, but God didn't answer—neither by dream nor by sign nor by prophet. So, Saul ordered his officials, "Find me someone who can call up spirits so I may go and seek counsel from those spirits." His servants said, "There's a witch at Endor." (1 Samuel 28:4–7 MSG)

Here we see the spirit of rebellion at work in Saul as he rebels against God, choosing to seek "someone who can call up spirits," which is strictly prohibited by God (see Deuteronomy 18:10–12). Next, he puts his rebellion into action through disobedience as he disguises himself.

> Then, taking two men with him, he went under the cover of night to the woman and said, "I want you to consult a ghost for me. Call up the person I name."
>
> The woman said, "Just hold on now! You know what Saul did, how he swept the country clean of mediums. Why are you trying to trap me and get me killed?"
>
> Saul swore solemnly, "As God lives, you won't get in any trouble for this."
>
> The woman said, "So whom do you want me to bring up?"
>
> "Samuel. Bring me Samuel."
>
> When the woman saw Samuel, she cried out loudly to Saul, "Why did you lie to me? You're Saul!"
>
> The king told her, "You have nothing to fear . . . but what do you see?"
>
> "I see a spirit ascending from the underground."
>
> "And what does he look like?" Saul asked.
>
> "An old man ascending, robed like a priest."

Saul knew it was Samuel. He fell down, face to the ground, and worshipped.

Samuel said to Saul, "Why have you disturbed me by calling me up?"

"Because I'm in deep trouble," said Saul. "The Philistines are making war against me and God has deserted me—he doesn't answer me anymore, either by prophet or by dream. And so, I'm calling on you to tell me what to do."

"Why ask me?" said Samuel. "GOD has turned away from you and is now on the side of your neighbor. GOD has done exactly what he told you through me—ripped the kingdom right out of your hands and given it to your neighbor. It's because you did not obey GOD, refused to carry out his seething judgment on Amalek, that GOD does to you what he is doing today. Worse yet, GOD is turning Israel, along with you, over to the Philistines. Tomorrow, you and your sons will be with me. And, yes, indeed, God is giving Israel's army up to the Philistines." (vv. 8-19 MSG)

Saul proceeded into sin, as he not only consulted the witch to perform the necromancy ritual but also engaged in communication, and falling down to worship, with whom he thought was the spirit of Samuel. The spirit of rebellion co-inhabited with the spirit of sorcery by way of the necromancy ritual.

Sadly, Saul got what he asked for. A demonic spirit, in the guise of Samuel, led him straight to his death and eternal separation from God: "So Saul died for his unfaithfulness which he had committed against the LORD, because he did not keep the Word of the LORD, and also because he consulted a medium for guidance. But he did not inquire of the LORD; therefore, He turned the kingdom over to David the son of Jesse" (1 Chronicles 10:13-14).

Witchcraft: The spirit of witchcraft is a demonic power that opposes God's will and leads to harmful behaviors such as spells, incantations, potions, and invoking other spirits used to achieve selfishly motivated results. Pride and control define it, where individuals prioritize their own will and desires over God's. It can manifest as manipulation, control, and an unwillingness to submit to God's authority.

The spirit of witchcraft is part of a demonic grouping and will always be associated with a spirit of rebellion. Other demons most likely associated with this grouping are the spirit of divination, the spirit of whoredom, and the spirit of bondage. Also, a familiar spirit, a perverse spirit, a seducing spirit, or a Jezebel spirit may be present.

Manifestations: Divination, python, rebellion, fortune-telling, palm reading, tarot cards, rune casting, soothsaying, hypnosis, magick (all forms), horoscopes, Ouija boards, stargazing, Zodiac signs, witchcraft, Wicca, sorcery, scrying, Satanism, illicit drugs.

Strongman: Familiar Spirit

Familiar Spirit, Monitoring Spirit, Necromancy, Spirit Guide

Cast out: Familiar spirit (and any lesser demon discerned)

Pray for: Holy Spirit, gifts

Familiar spirits are deceiving entities that present themselves as spirits of the dead or false guides, to mislead people and draw them away from God. They are most often attached to witches or mediums, as these two commonly establish relationships with entities in the spirit world. Intent communication or contact is how the familiar gains access. The witch or medium develops a strong bond with their spirit companion, and may have more than one. Witches and mediums use these spirits for divination, spell work, and necromancy. While they may believe the spirits are offering aid according to their request, it is actually they who work under the spirit's influence.

Familiar spirits can be purely spiritual entities, such as spirit guides or spirit animals, or a witch may have a physical animal as their familiar. Here, the close bond is with the animal, whose characteristics or energy the witch will use to infuse in spell work and/or to deliver it to the person of intent. Their demonic counterpart can also control physical familiars, becoming demonized animals. The familiar spirit is also known as a monitoring spirit, as it's close connection privies it to knowing the comings and goings of its host.

Demons Under a Familiar Spirit

Necromancy: Familiar spirits are not the sole province of witches or mediums. In fact, many people have ended up with a familiar spirit unknowingly. A common way someone outside of the occult, even a Christian, becomes associated with a familiar spirit comes from their desire either to talk to or learn about a deceased loved one.

Any time one seeks answers from divination or spirit contact, they are conspiring with demons. If the answers they get are right on the mark, it's only because the spirit called upon is familiar with the loved one being sought. The Bible clearly says that once a person dies, they can no longer communicate with those who remain on earth (see Hebrews 9:17). A person may also open the door through any method of contact with the dead, such as the Ouija, angel or spirit boards, or séances. These are all methods of necromancy, which is strictly prohibited by God.

Spirit Guide (Imaginary Friend): It's possible that an individual may be innocent of any wrongdoing and still have a familiar spirit. Many times, the spirit gains access during childhood and develops a relationship with the child through an imaginary friend. As a child, I developed a relationship with a familiar spirit that appeared to me in my mother's vanity mirror. It appeared as a young girl with a dark countenance and daunting presence, which intrigued me. I'd spent hours with her each day, and my mom would search the house, unable to find me. While baffled by my disappearance, my parents were completely unaware that I was being indoctrinated by demons. It would be many years later, after I fully immersed in witchcraft, before I realized the this "friend" was my first spirit guide, or familiar spirit, who I had spent countless hours being entertained by as a young girl.

Monitoring Spirit: A monitoring spirit is basically a

manifestation of what the Bible calls a familiar spirit. A familiar spirit is intimately involved in one's life. Knowing a person's habits, it can predict their responses and target their weaknesses. It keeps close tabs on what they're praying for, and specifically where they lack in faith. It's sometimes called a hoverer because it hovers over every aspect of the person's life, knowing them inside and out, which enables it to manipulate areas of their life. It knows the time of day or night when they're most vulnerable, and can then subtly suggest things that, when at their best, they may reject. The story of Sampson and Delilah (Judges 16:4–5) is a good example of this. Driven by an evil spirit, Delilah probed Samson's life until she uncovered his secret and sold him out to the Philistines.

A word of caution here. While we may know a familiar spirit as a monitoring spirit, we must remember that all spirits are monitoring. Demonic spirits that are assigned to a person are always watching. They're looking for areas that the person has left open as an easy access, and they likely know the person's weaknesses better than they do. So, we must always be on guard, and keep in mind that someone doesn't have to have a familiar spirit in order to be subject to demonic monitoring.

Manifestations: Sorcery, necromancy, medium, spiritist, spirit guide, animal spirit, monitoring spirit, imaginary friend.

Strongman: Perverse Spirit

Sexual Perversion, Pornography, Lust, Abortion

Cast out: Perverse spirit (and any lesser demon discerned)

Pray for: God's Spirit, pureness, holiness

The perverse spirit, simply put, perverts what is pure and true. It has a complete disregard for godly principles and strives to corrupt them. One of its fundamental characteristics is the ability to twist truth. It takes something pure and perverts it into something evil. The perverse spirit is power hungry and obsessed with control. Once the door opens, it corrupts the mind with perverse thoughts. It is an addicting spirit with a hungry appetite that is never satisfied, working hand in hand with the spirit of bondage, which is what makes breaking its hold so difficult. In addition, it works closely with the spirit of whoredom and leads to sexual perversion.

Demons Under the Perverse Spirit

Sexual Perversion: Sexual perversion is the opposite of God's version of a holy union between a husband and wife. The spirit of perversion, at its least, will make fornication and adultery appear socially acceptable. Perversion leads to very twisted thinking, and in terms of sexual immorality, it introduces what Romans 1:26-27 calls vile passions of unnatural relations between women and with men burning with lust for other men or homosexuality. It continues to spiral down into sex trafficking of the young and vulnerable, and even down to bestiality. The perverse mind isolates its thoughts from those who would find its delicacy appalling, and only shares its despicable desires with other warped minds.

The pagan practice of sex magic is an obvious example of sexual perversion. Basically, it is a ritual involving tantric sex (Hindu and Buddhist origins) between partners who raise energy through sexual activity, directing it at climax for their magical intent.

Another perversion I observed was at festivals deep in the woods throughout the summer months, where hundreds of pagans gather for days, engaging in many perversions—from demonic teachings to perverse sexual acts. Most people were in various stages of undress, scantily clothed, or nude beneath body paint, taking on the persona of an animal (spirit). When the moon rose high, Skyclad (naked) dancers encircled the fire as drummers induced others into a trancelike state, and some couples disappeared into the night.

Pornography: Pornography has morphed from magazines hidden behind newsstands to hundreds of millions of illicit photos shared across the internet. It has become easily accessible for the young and old alike, and a hidden haven for many criminal activities. The same perversions found in the minds of those with perverse sexual addictions become the fantasies of the pornography industry. If looking wasn't horrifying enough, some move on to act out their perversions. It is extremely addictive behavior that ruins marriages, families, and other relationships.

I know of a man who, against Christian leadership's warnings, began reading the "Attorney General's Commission on Pornography Final Report." The warnings given were because some of the material in it could lure the reader into the sin of pornography and supply inroads of opportunity they likely were unaware existed. Of course, this Christian man believed he could handle it, and he began reading. Within a year, he had not only searched vast amounts of porn on the internet but also had a huge hard drive filled with photos. It began with nude photos of women, but he was soon downloading men and women in the act, women with women, men with men, and eventually child pornography. The obsession played a big part in his marriage break-up and his walking away from the faith. The work of the flesh progressed to a demonic stronghold, and eventually the perverse spirit took control.

Lust: Lust is like eye candy, and it can be sexual, but many people lust after things such as wealth, power, or extravagance. Eye candy is anything that has physical appeal. No matter the candy, the eye sends the image to the brain, which is where the mind takes over and the battle begins. Satan whispers sweet lies on the battlefield of our mind to entrap us. If we entertain them, then we open ourselves up to the spirit of lust.

The Bible doesn't tell us to resist this spirit. Rather it tells us, "Flee sexual immorality. Every sin that a man does is outside the body, but he who commits sexual immorality sins against his own body" (1 Corinthians 6:18–20). We can suspect the spirit of lust in our life if we have an irresistible urge to indulge in lustful behavior. It leads to a downward spiral of fleeting pleasure and ultimate destruction.

Mark 6:22 recounts how lust overcame King Herod when

he saw a beautiful young girl (believed to be his stepdaughter) dancing. So much was his desire that he offered her anything she wanted. She asked for John the Baptist's head, and Herod, unable to resist, obliged. His lust spiraled down quickly, as he went from lust to murder, likely in the same hour.

Abortion: While abortion is a work of the flesh, the spirit of death and the perverse spirit accompany it. The perverse spirit reveals itself in the perverse actions of women who pridefully proclaim taking the life of their child. The twisted thinking that this spirit projects has caused many to accept the lie that "my body" is all that matters, when medically speaking we learn 1) The DNA of a baby in the womb differs from the mother's DNA. If the baby was "her body," their DNA would be identical. The mother is serving as a host to another distinct person created by God, and 2) The amniotic fluid acts as a barrier to prevent the mother's immune system from attacking the fetus, thus protecting its life. Here we see the baby is a separate individual, and the mother's natural response is to protect her child. This vile spirit attacks at the very heart of God's creation: humanity created in the image of God

Not surprisingly, The Satanic Temple (TST), an atheistic organization, has used abortion rituals to claim religious liberties. Adding insult to injury, *Cosmopolitan* published an article in its November/December 2023 issue that promoted the TST opening a telehealth abortion clinic in New Mexico, which provides a type of "abortion on demand by ritual."[26] According to the TSTHealth.org Satanic Abortion Ritual, it is a destructive ritual with the intent of "casting off notions of guilt, shame, and mental discomfort," freeing one of their God-given consciousness of sin.[27] Although the group denies worshipping a spiritual deity, the spirit of perversion drives this spiritual attack.

Manifestations: Sexual perversions, rebellion, contentious

---

26 I. M. Giatti, "Cosmopolitan defends abortion as satanic 'religious ritual,' calls satanism a 'nontheistic faith,' *The Christian Post*, December 5, 2023, https://www.christianpost.com/news/cosmopolitan-defends-abortion-as-satanic-religious-ritual.html.

27 The Satanic Temple, "TST Health – Satanic Abortion Ritual Flyer," Tsthealth.Org, 2023, static1.squarespace.com/static/63b68c961da991700b94e8b7/t/63eac53263f-3c063df3e1675/1676330291874/TST+Health+-+Satanic+Abortion+Ritual+Flyer-2.pdf.

spirit, doctrinal error, filthy mind, homosexuality, incest, lust, pornography, child abuse, abortion, twisted words, bestiality.

Strongman: Spirit of Whoredom

Sexual Immorality, Idolatry, Spiritual Adultery

Cast out: Spirit of whoredom, queen of heaven, Ba'al (and any lesser demon discerned)

Pray for: Spirit of God, pure spirit

The spirit of whoredom leads to more than just sexual immorality. It uses sexual immorality as a metaphor for spiritual adultery. We learn of Israel's idolatry in Hosea 4:12–13: "My people ask counsel from their wooden idols, and their staff informs them. For the spirit of harlotry has caused them to stray, and they have played the harlot against their God. They offer sacrifices on the mountaintops, and burn incense on the hills, under oaks, poplars, and terebinths, because their shade is good. Therefore, your daughters commit harlotry, and your brides commit adultery."

Israel was worshipping wooden idols and using a staff as a method of divination to seek answers that they should have been asking God for. We see the sin that Israel was committing against God, yet the depth of their idolatry was even greater because the spirit of harlotry (sexual immorality) was the root that led them astray. This suggests that the Israelites were engaging in common pagan practices of worship, which included sacred prostitution, or sexual acts committed during religious rituals. Therefore, in their unfaithfulness, they had committed spiritual adultery and opened themselves up to the spirit of whoredom. Being led further away from God, they "sacrificed on the mountaintops" to the unknown gods of pagans or demonic entities (Deuteronomy 32:17).

This example is not much different from many witchcraft rituals today, which comprise the worship of idols (many handcrafted from wood or created out of stone), engaging in various forms of divination, and either symbolically or physically engaging in sexual acts (the great rite), which is equivalent to spiritual harlotry. Satan still draws many into pagan practices today by tempting them to indulge in the acts of spiritual whoredom. These immoral acts cause people to disobey the will of God, and rather choose to satisfy the lust of the flesh. Though some will claim the act of spiritual power, the flesh meets its achievement. We must flee sexual immorality.

Demons Under the Spirit of Whoredom

Queen of Heaven (Inanna, Hecate, other pagan goddesses): The queen of heaven is another name for the Canaanite goddess Ashtoreth that we read about in Jeremiah 7 and 44. Depending on the culture, she was known by different names. She was revered as a goddess of love, fertility, and war, and was the mother and consort of Ba'al. Temple worship in her honor included ecstatic dance, orgasmic rites, men crossdressing as women, and temple prostitution. Once a year, her temple priestesses would prostitute themselves by accepting a coin tossed by the first foreigner coming into the city, in celebration of the goddess's sacred marriage.

It comes as no surprise that the prophet Jeremiah would chastise the Jewish people for the abominations they were committing to worship the queen of heaven. Worse yet, they defiantly rejected both the prophet and the word God had given him for them. Can you imagine having the audacity to argue that life was better for them during the time they worshipped the goddess of fertility? Yet that is what they did.

The queen of heaven is a demonic entity that works through lesser demons and pagan priestesses who carry out the orders of this ruling demonic entity. The queen of heaven spirit still influences people today in much the same way she did in days of old. Her main purpose is to deter mankind from worshipping the one true God, and to transfer their worship to herself. To entice humanity into the sin of idolatry, she uses charms, enchantments, seduction, and perversion as its tools of manipulation, which is witchcraft, to allure and validate its worship committed through acts of sexual immorality. We see her influences in much of today's society, where goddess worship is no longer frowned upon and sexuality is at a heightened awareness. Much of the world is in a state of sexual chaos, with transgenderism being the latest perversion to gain its grip. Her priestesses today still engage in ritualistic forms of ecstasy, as both demonic and human followers strive to spread her influence on earth.

Ba'al (Pan, Cernunnos, pagan gods): Ba'al was the Canaanite god of fertility, agriculture, and storms. His name meant master or lord, and depictions frequently showed him as a bull. Phoenician mythology often identified him as a god of the sky or heavens. He had Ashtoreth as his consort, and their fertility rituals showed many similarities. Temple prostitution was also the norm for Ba'al worship, as it was in the goddess's temple. Ba'al worship appealed to the flesh with seductive dancing, feasting, and music, which created the mood for fleshly pleasure. Often, the dances would lead to the worshippers retreating within Ba'al's temple for sexual gratification. People considered Ba'al the god of storms; therefore, they performed rituals to appease him, ensuring (they thought) pleasant weather and prosperity. Animal sacrifices were also a part of Ba'al's fertility rituals. The Israelites, while in the land of Cannon, fell into the worship of Ba'al, struggling to resist a religion that appeased the carnal man (see Numbers 25:1–3).

Eventually, many of the Old Testament gods, including Ba'al, disappeared, and other gods replaced them, at least in name. Greco-Roman and Celtic pantheons became more prominent in the world during the New Testament era. However, just as with the goddess, it's the same demonic entity working behind his many other names. They required many similar forms of worship. For instance, the Greek Pan's worship composed of drinking, sacrifices, and lustful ritualistic sex, much like Ba'al's rituals of old. The gods of today's witches are the Greek Pan and Celtic Cernunnos and similar ceremonies, including erotic drumming and dancing around the fire, ending with many couples running off into the shadows for sexual pleasures.

Conclusion of the gods: Jeremiah the prophet disclosed

how entire families were celebrating this goddess: "The children gather wood, the fathers kindle the fire, and the women knead dough, to make cakes for the queen of heaven; and they pour out drink offerings to other gods, that they may provoke Me to anger" (Jeremiah 7:18). I can see my former self doing the same, having my children gather wood and flowers that I used for crafting idols, and making goddess cakes in the shape of a crescent moon for rituals, then pouring the leftover wine on the earth as an offering. My opened eyes showed me how my actions broke my Father in heaven's heart, and it shattered mine.

It's important to note that when these people were engaging in the practices of evil, committing idolatry against the Lord, life seemed to be better for them. We falsely believe we suffer the consequences of our sin immediately, but that's not always the case. Even if we appear to prosper, and things go well for us, we cannot mock God. Galatians 6:7 says, "Don't be deceived. God is not mocked; whatever a man sows he will reap." Behind the deception of what appears good is the reality of what evil really brings. The people worshipping the queen of heaven believed their prosperity meant their actions were good; this was a deception. The devil is the god of this world, and he can allow us to prosper for a while.

It was like that for me. I believed my life was going well during the time I practiced witchcraft. It appeared I got whatever I wanted, though what I didn't realize was that my wants were not really what I needed. In fact, my desires were leading me down a path of destruction. Only I was blind to the truth. My soul's torment was inexplicable when I realized the extent of my iniquity after my eyes were opened. In fact, things were a lot worse. I can tell you that grace took on a whole new meaning.

Some people still work with the ancient gods and goddesses, but don't let that fool you; it's the same spiritual entity with different names. The same spirit working through the god or goddess by a different name or different culture may take on unique characteristics, which can make one question if they are in fact the same, but it is the same entity. When binding and casting out demonic pagan gods and goddesses, the stronghold of the queen of heaven (Ashtoreth) and sky king (Ba'al) should suffice. There is no reason to study or know all the names and characteristics of every pagan god and goddess. They are too numerous, to say the least, and unnecessary. However, if you are praying and the Holy Spirit reveals the name of a specific god or goddess, don't ignore it but bind it and cast it out.

Manifestations: Adultery, all sexual sin, fornication, homosexuality, idolatry, love of money, love of the world, prostitution (spirit, soul, and body), unclean spirit, unfaithfulness to God, worldliness.

Strongman: Spirit of Bondage

Spirit of Slavery, Addictions, Bondage to Sin

Cast out: Spirit of bondage (and any lesser demon discerned)

Pray for: Liberty, spirit of adoption

Perhaps one of the most visible demonic influences we can see with our physical eyes is the spirit of bondage. The effects of this unclean spirit are apparent in a range of addictions and its dominion over those it controls. Jesus came to free us from the bondage of sin and its consequences. In John 8:32 He says, "You will know the truth, and the truth will set you free." This verse makes a bold declaration about the liberating power of Jesus.

We do not have to live our lives enslaved by sin and the ungodly desires of our flesh. Still, many struggle with lifelong addictions to alcohol, drugs, nicotine, gambling, pornography, gluttony, and witchcraft, some of which may have roots from a generational curse. What satisfies the flesh becomes a foothold that leads to a personal slavery that entraps us in its deceptive allure of pleasure. At some point, we've lost the capacity of our will and it becomes a stronghold, or a fortress in which we can indulge uncontrollably in our pleasure. The spirit of bondage then has its grip, along with other spirits that work hand in hand with it, such as the spirit of fear, the perverse spirit, the seductive spirit, and the spirit of error. Irresistible temptations enslave us to their fleshly passions. Resisting at this point is next to impossible if we don't cast the spirit of bondage out so that it can no longer take advantage of us.

Demons Under the Spirit of Bondage

Spirit of Slavery: The spirit of slavery leads to fear and bondage (see Romans 8:15). It creates a false illusion that God is a distant, authoritative figure that we cannot trust and that we should be fearful of. In actuality, the spirit of fear is controlling us or causing external circumstances that imprison us. After it entraps us in a situation, it alludes to God as the captor, when in fact God is the one who will set us free.

Addictions: Alcohol addiction renders the mind vulnerable to demonic influences. It leads to impaired judgment, which can seriously hinder our ability to discern and resist temptations that we otherwise wouldn't give a second thought to. While the Bible doesn't condemn drinking alcohol, it condemns being drunk, even as far as saying that drunkards will not inherit the kingdom of God (see 1 Corinthians 6:10). The problem lies with one having the self-control to limit the amount imbibed. Soon they will find it "bites like a serpent, and stings like a viper" (Proverbs 23:31–32). How many times does one claim they're sober and yet cannot walk a straight line? Or claim they are only going to have one drink only to lose count of how many they drank? Beyond overindulgence, alcohol is also addictive, and this liquid spirit has caused many lives to be destroyed. The name "spirits," often used, stems from ancient alchemists' discovery and their claim that the vapor collected during distillation was "the spirit of the original material."[28]

Nicotine or Tobacco: This is another substance that is highly addictive and a major contributing factor to addiction in the world today. Its use alters the brain's reward system, which causes cravings and nicotine dependence fairly quickly. Although the Bible does not mention the substance, we know that smoking or

---

28 "Ancient Alchemy: The Secret History of Distilled Spirits," Wine and Spirits Journal, May 7, 2024, https://wineandspiritsjournal.com/2023/04/the-alchemy-of-distilled-spirits/.

vaping it causes sickness and disease. The Scriptures tell us that our body is the temple of the Holy Spirit and we are to respect and care for it (see 1 Corinthians 6:12). We cannot possibly keep our body healthy by filling it with such a highly addictive chemical that has proven health risk. This is yet another avenue the spirit of bondage uses to enslave through addiction.

Gluttony/Anorexia Nervosa: Gluttony and anorexia are opposites. Gluttony (overeating) is an indulgence of food, while anorexia nervosa (undereating) is withholding food despite a low body weight. One is often associated with laziness, the other often with compulsive exercise. Both disorders trend in those with low self-esteem, which results in either self-indulgence or self-denying. They both develop into addictive behaviors or manifestations of the spirit of bondage that hold them captive in an illusion of what their bodies are, compared to what they believe them to be. They rob the individual's true identity in Christ.

Religious Bondage: There are many manifestations of the spirit of bondage in the name of religion or a spiritual belief system. Some are through religious cults such as Jehovah's Witness, Mormonism, and the Church of Scientology, to name a few. We even find some cult characteristics in Christianity.

The spirit of religious bondage also manifests in Wicca and/or witchcraft. I experienced a high level of bondage beginning in the first few weeks of my endeavor into the craft. The addiction was mind-altering. Once I opened my mind to this spirit, it was like a massive computer download that overwhelmed my brain to the point I'd have to walk away. But no sooner did I walk away than I craved more. I just couldn't get enough of it despite the spirit of heaviness that weighed me down. The deception is that we're the one in control, and we determine our spiritual path, but we hunger for a desire that we'll do practically anything to reach.

Manifestations: Addictions, compulsive sins, alcohol, anguish of spirit, bondage to sin, captivity to Satan, nicotine, drugs, fear of death, gluttony, anorexia nervosa, religious spirit, servant of corruption, occultist practices, self-harm, suicide, premature death.

Strongman: Spirit of Death

Apollyon, Spirit of Suicide

Cast out: Spirit of death, strongman Apollyon (and any lesser demon discerned)

Pray for: Spirit of life (Genesis 2:7)

Apollyon, also called the angel of death, is a destroying spirit. He serves Satan from within his hellish domain, sending lesser demons into the world to cause accidents, sicknesses, and destruction on his behalf. For now, God holds Apollyon locked in the abyss, restraining him from destroying the earth until the appointed time. When humanity turns from God, God will unleash Apollyon and his demonic horde upon the earth, leaving him to his own devices. The Bible tells us his assault upon man will inflict such excessive pain that people will wish to die, but death will flee (see Revelation 9:11).

Demons Under the Spirit of Death

Spirit of Death: The spirit of untimely death has one agenda—to snuff the life out of God's children. It attempts to bring premature death upon a person before their appointed time to die. Usually, death comes in a violent or unnatural way, such as through a fatal accident, terminal illness, murder, or suicide. All forms of premature death in a family are suspect. It could also be the death of one's hopes and dreams for their life, which can provoke suicidal tendencies.

Spirit of Suicide: The spirit of suicide works hand in hand with the spirits of death and depression. It is a direct attack on the individual soul, bearing heavy on the will so to convince its host that the only way to peace is death. It can affect anyone with a history of abuse, severe depression, substance abuse, post-traumatic stress, or a generational predisposition.

Manifestations: Undiagnosed or rare disease, falling victim of violence or threat of violence, near accidents, severe sadness, hopelessness, withdrawal, dangerous behaviors, threatening suicide. (Note: If a spirit of suicide is at work in a person's life, we can bind the spirit but should seek immediate help from a licensed professional, such as a Christian counseling center that also works in deliverance ministry. In case of emergency, call a suicide or crisis hotline).

Legions of Demons: As we can see on our list, there are many demons. While this list describes eighteen demons, we understand that number only refers to the type of spirit. For instance, we can say there are approximately 340,710,121 Americans, but we could then break that number down into ethnicity and the specific characteristics common for that ethnicity. Each individual's upbringing in a different location gives them distinctive traits, and their unique personalities distinguish them. Therefore, while all these demons fall under the same ruling spirit, and most will exhibit most characteristics, they still have their own distinguishing personalities that may differ from another's, yet they are from the same rank.

As mentioned throughout our list, many demonic spirits work hand in hand with one another. Some do this like clockwork, so if we discern one, we'll likely discern the other. And there's a good chance many under the same ruling spirit will be involved. However, another ruling spirit may also have joined the fleet. In Mark 5:1–20, Jesus arrived at Gerasene, to be met with a possessed man who lived in the mountains among the tombs. He was unlike any other. No one was strong enough to subdue him despite their efforts of binding him with chains and shackles. Jesus asked his name, and he replied, "My name is Legion, for we are many" (Mark 5:9).

Demonization often includes more than one demon. With the demonized man, he had a legion, which can be up to six thousand Roman soldiers. No wonder the man manifested such physical strength. The important thing to remember is that Jesus cast out the entire legion, and He said we'll do even greater things than He did (see John 14:12).

This is the only place in Scripture where Jesus asked the

demon's name. Some scholars say he was asking the name of the man but the demon answered for him. Others believe He asked the demon. Either way, there are two points to make. First, the demon told a half-truth by replying "Legion" (or a multitude), not specific names. And second, that didn't matter. Jesus cast them out despite not knowing all their names. In all other instances, Jesus didn't ask names of demons, nor did he carry out lengthy conversations with them. Neither should we.

Now it's time to prepare for battle in Part III. We'll begin this next section by discovering the power and authority we have in Christ Jesus to tread over all the powers of the enemy.

Behind Enemy Lines

PART III

Preparing for Battle

Behind Enemy Lines

CHAPTER 10

Believers' Power And Authority

Before we engage in spiritual warfare, there are some things to take care of. One is to establish our assurance of salvation. This may seem simple or matter-of-fact, but it is the foundation on which we stand. Our salvation comes first by hearing the gospel message of Christ's birth, death, and resurrection, and is complete because of the finished work of the cross (see John 19:30). Romans 10:9 says, "If you confess with your mouth the Lord Jesus and believe in your heart that God has raised Him from the dead, you will be saved." The assurance of our salvation comes by "the Holy Spirit which bears witness to our spirit that we are a child of God" (Romans 8:16).

Our identity in Christ is important not only for our own confidence, but even more for when we stand against the devil. One area the enemy attacks is our identity. If he can convince us that we're not saved, or give us reason to doubt our salvation, we'll be standing on sinking sand and be out of the battle before we've even engaged in it. Another reason our identity is so important is because we won't want to engage in warfare against the kingdom of darkness if we aren't sure-footed in the kingdom of God.

In Ephesus, Paul, through the Holy Spirit's power and the authority of Jesus, healed the sick and expelled demons. The seven sons of Sceva, the Jewish high priest, were trying to exorcise a demon-oppressed man using Jesus' name. These men not only had no reverence for Christ, they weren't even followers of the disciples. They were exorcists by their own definition, doing fortune-telling, using spells for healing, and banishing demons. Seeing Paul's success in Jesus' name, they conspired and tried casting out demons similarly. However, after they swore by Jesus' name, the demon replied, "I recognize Jesus and Paul; but who are you?" Acts 19:15 recounts the possessed man's attack on the seven sons of Sceva, defeating them and driving them out of the house naked and injured. Evil spirits are not subject to the mere words "In Jesus' name" and are a force to be reckoned with. Many occultists have found this out the hard way. Evil spirits are subject to one name only; however, it's the power and authority behind the name that makes them obey, not the name itself.

Jesus' Authority

The New Testament Greek word for authority is "exousia," meaning power to act.[29] This is not just about having power, but about the right to exercise it. Matthew 28:18 reads, "And Jesus came and spoke to them, saying, "All authority has been given to Me in heaven and on earth."

Authority is the legal right to use power, and to be effective, the two concepts must work together. God's authority is supreme and absolute. He is the Creator and Sustainer of all things, and His authority is inherent in His nature. John 14:10 establishes Jesus' divine authority: "Do you not believe that I am in the Father, and the Father in Me?" "The words that I speak to you I do not speak on My own authority; but the Father who dwells in Me does the works."

The passage shows Jesus having all authority; thus, He can pass His authority onto us. Throughout His time on earth, Jesus showed His authority, in the following ways.

- Matthew 7:28–29 states, "the people were astonished at His

---

[29] "1849. exousia," Bible Hub, accessed June 20, 2025, https://biblehub.com/greek/1849.htm.

teaching, for He taught them as one having authority, and not as the scribes."

- Matthew 9:1-8 acknowledges His authority to forgive sin.
- Matthew 8:23-27 shows His power over creation; even the wind and sea obeyed Him.
- He possessed authority over healing and expelling demons wherever He went.

God gave Jesus, the Son of God, power over creation, and He exercises it. However, holding all authority, He showed kingdom authority differs from worldly authority (Matthew 20:20-28): kingdom authority is serving, not overpowering, others. John 13:4-17 shows Jesus' humble, servant nature by describing when he washed his apostles' feet. No wonder Peter at first objected. Can you imagine the King of the Universe stooping before you to wash your feet? Of course, His demonstration was a lesson to the twelve and all future followers of the role of servanthood expected in His kingdom.

Authority to Tread on Serpents and Scorpions

Luke 10:1-16 describes Jesus sending out seventy of his disciples with specific instructions to preach and prepare the way for His coming arrival. Jesus instructed them to travel lightly, or basically not to bring anything; to heal the sick; and to announce His kingdom's nearness if the city welcomed them. But if the people didn't receive them, they were to warn that "it would be more tolerable in that Day for Sodom than for their city" (v. 12). They returned with great joy, especially in their ability to cast out unclean spirits. The seventy excitedly exclaimed to Jesus, "Lord, even demons obey us in your name!" (v. 17). Jesus explained their sending out by saying, "Behold, I give you the authority to trample on serpents and scorpions, and over all the power of the enemy, and nothing shall by any means hurt you" (v. 19). He told them that rejoicing over their names being written in heaven was far greater than the miracles of their mission. For even Judas cast out demons and yet fell alongside the devil. To have one's name written in the Lamb's Book of Life—now that is worth rejoicing over.

Matthew Henry's Commentary provides interesting insight, confirming what the seventy said through Jesus' own observation: "(Luke 10:18): 'My heart and eye went along with you; I took notice of the success you had, and I *saw Satan fall as lightning from heaven*.' Note, Satan and his kingdom fell before the preaching of the gospel. 'I see how it is,' saith Christ, 'as you get ground the devil loseth ground.' He falls *as lightning falls from heaven*, so suddenly, so irrecoverably, so visibly, that all may perceive it, and say, 'See how Satan's kingdom totters, see how it tumbles.'"[30]

How encouraging it is to gain insight into what actually took place in the spiritual realm, "as the disciples went on their journey performing miracles, Jesus, by His divine omniscience, saw (His heart and eye went with them) the powers of darkness falling before their ministry and miracles; as He also foresaw how Satan would fall before the preaching of His Gospel by the apostles,"[31] and as He had seen Satan fall like lightning from heaven. Always remember that amid the battles we face, our power and authority come not from within ourselves but through an all-powerful Jesus.

It is these evil influences that Christians are called to contend with, be they principalities, powers, rulers of darkness, or spiritual wickedness. We are to stand our ground and war against any spiritual conflict we face. Our enemies may be powerful, but no one and nothing can stand against the power of our God (see 2 Chronicles 20:6).

Our Delegated Authority

We see Jesus sends us forth with "authority" to do the work that He has given to us, and we see the results of using that authority. But to move forward in our calling, we need to understand the authority that He has delegated to us. Authority is the right to command, act, or exercise. He is King Jesus, the one who holds authority, our Commander-in-Chief. *Delegated* means Jesus has given us a portion of His own authority. When He sends us, his

---

[30] "Luke 10:17–24," *Matthew Henry's Commentary* on Bible Gateway, accessed June 20, 2025, https://www.biblegateway.com/resources/matthew-henry/Luke.10.17-Luke.10.24.
[31] Ibid.

delegated authority goes with us. We act on His behalf, not of our own accord. His authority casts out demons and illnesses. Remember the story of the centurion who asked Jesus to heal his servant? Jesus said he would go to the man, but the centurion responded that he was unworthy of Jesus coming to his house and that if Jesus merely spoke a word, his servant would be healed. He explained that being a man under authority, and having soldiers under him, he understood Jesus needed only to speak a word and it would be done (see Matthew 8:5–13). He acknowledged Jesus' rulership and authority over the things of this earth.

Demons also understand authority since they adhere to a hierarchy within Satan's kingdom. They recognize they must submit to God's and Jesus' authority, as they know God has supreme authority over all things. We see evidence of this in Matthew 8:29, where the demons ask Jesus if He will torment them before the appointed time. Notice, they also are aware of the predetermined torture awaiting them. In addition, they are aware of the authority that Jesus has delegated to believers, and know that they must submit to those who exercise the authority they have in Christ. With the sons of Sceva, they knew these men were acting without divine authorization, so they did not submit and turned on them.

What, then, is the criteria for being delegated authority? Authority is a by-product of relationship. Upon their rebirth, God grants believers' authority and enlists them in the army of God. However, the more intimate the believer's relationship with God, the greater the authority given. I compare it to a relationship with one's spouse. After years of spending an enormous amount of time together, listening attentively and observing their comings and goings, we come to a place of knowing them so well that we can often finish their sentences. That's the closeness we should strive for, that when we open our mouths, we speak what's in the heart and mind of our heavenly Father. Having received delegated authority from Him, we receive the right to exercise His power, which comes to us through the Holy Spirit. The Holy Spirit is the "power from on high" (Luke 24:49) that Jesus promised to His disciples once He left this earth. It empowers us to go forth into the world, spreading the gospel, healing the sick, and setting captives free.

Holy Spirit Power

In chapter seven, we read the story from Acts 8 of Simon the Sorcerer, who tried to buy the anointing of the Holy Spirit from the apostles. Let's look at that same passage again, this time focusing on the people of Samaria. In Acts 8:14–25, Philip preached the kingdom of God to the Samaritans, healing and delivering many. Witnessing these events, the Samaritans believed, were baptized, and filled the city with joy. We might think they had it all: salvation, healing, and deliverance. What else is there aside from walking out of your salvation—right? Well, not exactly. The apostles in Jerusalem, having heard that Samaria had received the Word of God, thought it important enough that they sent Peter and John to them so the new converts might receive the Holy Spirit. Peter and John laid hands on them, and they too received the Holy Spirit (see Acts 8:17).

I find it interesting that when the church in Jerusalem heard the Samaritans hadn't yet received the Holy Spirit, they felt the necessity to immediately send the apostles to lay hands on them.

A similar scenario unfolds for each new Christian: they hear the Word, believe, confess Jesus as Lord and Savior, and are baptized. For many, it ends there. And while they certainly have the Holy Spirit within them, which infills them at salvation, they lack the outpouring of the Holy Spirit and fire, or the power imparted through the laying on of hands. It's very difficult to navigate through our world plagued with darkness while lacking the power that is readily available for every believer. When coming against the enemy of our soul, we cannot stand on our own strength. We need all the help we can get, and God has supplied the ultimate power source through the Holy Spirit.

Greater Works Will You Do

In John 14:12–14, Jesus says, "Most assuredly, I say to you, he who believes in Me, the works that I do he will do also; and greater *works* than these he will do, because I go to My Father. And whatever you ask in My name, that I will do, that the Father may be glorified in the Son. If you ask anything in My name, I will do it." Jesus assured His followers that though He would no longer be with them physically, He was interceding for them before His Father in heaven, and all they had to do was ask Him in order to receive. Since He has *all power*, in His name they too would have power in heaven and on earth, just like He did.

That being said, we're told that His followers would receive even greater victories than Jesus Himself received while on earth (John 14:12). Jesus encouraged His followers that if they loved Him, they would keep His commandments, and in return, they would receive a Helper who would remain with them forever. The Helper is the Holy Spirit, who would fall upon them shortly after Jesus ascended to heaven. The gift of tongues evidenced this outpouring of the Holy Spirit, which would serve as a sign of God's presence as they went forth to the nations.

Regarding the release the power and authority of the indwelling Spirit of Jesus (the Holy Spirit), Jesus said in John 14:16-18, "And I will pray the Father, and He will give you another Helper, that He may abide with you forever—the Spirit of truth, whom the world cannot receive, because it neither sees Him nor knows Him, but you know Him for He dwells with you and will be in you. I will not leave you orphans; I will come to you." Therefore, the Spirit of Jesus is the Holy Spirit. Scriptures teach that to receive the Holy Spirit's power, believers need to receive the baptism of the Holy Spirit from Jesus (see Matthew 3:11 and Luke 3:16).

Truth be told, we are witness to this today as we've seen how far and wide the gospel has spread, and how many have experienced, even today, the miracle of healing and deliverance across the world. As followers of Christ, we too are recipients of the same power and authority, in order that we may continue the work Jesus began, and the mission passed onto us.

Our Power and Authority

Believers have received both power and authority to preach

the gospel, drive out demons, and cure diseases. Besides having the authority, we also possess power. The Holy Spirit is the power from on high, available to every believer who asks for it. Power is the force that's exerted, such as the mighty wind that ushered in the flaming tongues on Pentecost. Authority and power work hand in hand with one another. Authority gives us the right to trample (exert power) over the powers of the enemy.

Our confession of faith, water baptism, and infilling of the Holy Spirit secure our identity, and we are almost ready for deployment. But first we must change into our battle gear and learn the proper maintenance and upkeep to keep battle ready at a moment's notice.

CHAPTER 11

Armor Up

Before my feet touched the floor, I already had the belt of truth buckled around my waist and had covered my chest with the breastplate of righteousness. I slid my feet into the gospel boots of peace and then got to my feet with the shield of faith at my side. I placed the helmet of salvation on my head and took the sword of the Spirit in my hand. Before I put on any physical clothes, I felt dressed and ready to face the world—or so I thought.

Millions of Christians perform the same ritual around the globe each morning, as most churches teach the importance of putting on the armor as part of our daily routine. What I didn't realize at the time was that not only wasn't my armor secure, but it also had many gaps that left me vulnerable to the enemy's advances. In fact, the only thing I really accomplished was memorizing Scripture.

Now, memorizing Scripture is a good thing, but a repetitious prayer, or vain repetitions, is something the Bible warns against (see Matthew 6:7). I believe that is one reason God heals by various means. Jesus, for instance, applied mud to the blind man's eyes, and He also healed the woman with the bleeding condition when she touched his garment. Through this, we learn that repetitious actions, or a "magic formula," will not produce our desired results. Rather, it is our total reliance on and faith in God that releases the Holy Spirit's power. Psalm 65:6 tells us, "God who is our strength clothes us in power." We don't suit up in the armor by a recited prayer, but by the power of the Holy Spirit, which was released in the baptism of the Holy Spirit.

The daily donning of armor implies its removal at night, thus requiring its replacement each morning, much like changing from street clothes to pajamas and back again. But what does put on the armor really mean? The Greek word ενδύω translates to mean sink into or put on. As important as the translation of the word is the tense that it is in. In this case, it is in aorist tense, which means it is a onetime action.[32] Consider a soldier who's smack in the middle of a war zone. When night comes, does he remove his armor and put it aside until morning? Absolutely not. That would be dangerous in enemy territory. Rather, he nods off in his battle gear and keeps his hand on his weapon, ready in the event of an attack.

That being said, why are we stripping off our armor and setting our weapons aside each night? Doing so leaves us unprotected during the witching hour. Night is a prime time for works of darkness. As a former witch, I can tell you that many cast spells in the wee hours, while most people are asleep and unguarded. It's considered the time when spell-casting powers are at their fullest. We mustn't think we're clear in the daylight, though, since the timing of spell casting depends on the practitioner's intent. However, banishing and other negative spells most often take place in the middle of the night.

Knowing this, remember the soldier on the battlefield. As long as we're in this world, we are in a spiritual battle; therefore, we need to stay aware, sober, armed, and ready 24/7.

The Armor of Light

God has not left us defenseless but has provided the armor of light—the protective attire that covers our soul. Romans 13:12

---

[32] "Language Studies – Greek Thoughts – Histemi," Study Light, accessed August 6, 2025, https://www.studylight.org/language-studies/greek-thoughts.html?article=529.

says, "Therefore let us cast off the works of darkness, and let us put on the armor of light." What does it mean to cast off the works of darkness? The works of darkness, or the works of the flesh, refer to the sinful age in which we live, a world that is plagued by all that opposes God. Paul tells us to cast off our old clothes, such as superstitions, immorality, and perversion, that we may have hidden in our lives. He instructs us to exchange our old filthy rags for the armor of light—but how can we put on light?

Paul is not suggesting we put on a literal garment made of light. Rather, he uses a metaphor to show a truth to us. The world is a spiritual battlefield, and our protection lies in being clothed in Christ. We clothe ourselves in Christ when we have nailed our old ways to the cross, and His grace and forgiveness envelop our new selves (see Ephesians 4:24). In John 8:12, Jesus told the people, "I am the light of the world. Whoever follows Me will never walk in the darkness, but will have the light of life." This verse establishes that Jesus is the light, and also shows that His followers also have the light of life.

And how do we wear Christ? Psalm 104:1–2 says, "O LORD my God . . . you are clothed with splendor and majesty. He wraps himself in light as with a garment." We can reasonably say that when we put on the armor of light, we are wrapping ourselves in the garment of Christ, who is the radiance of God's glory (see Hebrews 1:3). To get a better understanding, let's look at Romans 13:14: "Let the Lord Jesus Christ be as near to you as the clothes you wear" (CEV). The closest thing to our skin is our undergarments, so we need to be that close with Jesus. "To them God willed to make known what are the riches of the glory of this mystery among the Gentiles: which is Christ in you, the hope of glory." "Christ in you" is salvation," Colossians 1:27.

We have to *know* Him intimately, to the point that His thoughts and His actions are second nature to us. In fact, perhaps the best way to explain it is that it's like wearing a second skin. Its tight fit prevents its removal and leaves no space for evil to take hold. Putting on the armor of light is taking on the character of Christ, or to live as children of light (see 1 Thessalonians

5:5) in faith, hope, and humility. We do this by spending time with Him and by abiding in Him as He abides in us (see John 15:4). The armor of light is our best defense in the struggles we face against spiritual wickedness, and is how we gain victory in the battle against the powers of darkness (see Ephesians 6:10–18; 1 Thessalonians 5:8).

Putting on the armor of light isn't something we prayerfully hurry through to start our day. By wearing Christ, we are under His covering of protection night and day. His covering is vacuum sealed around us and prevents any devices of the enemy's advance against us. Not only that, but because of Him, we have heavenly instruments of war at our disposal. The meaning of *armor* is "instruments of war," and in the New Testament it's described as our means of defense in spiritual warfare, and the instruments by which we gain victory (Ephesians 6:13–17). Remember, our spiritual armor is not only exclusively defensive (as stated here) but is also offensive--- we take up the sword of the word, and pray in tongues, which by inclusion with the armor of God in Ephesians is a weapon for offensive warfare.

The Belt of Truth

The belt is a metaphor for the Bible's truth, which brings and sustains life. A belt may seem insignificant to us. After all, what could a lone belt do in battle other than to keep our pants from falling down? The Bible tells us to gird our loins with truth, which is actually an entire system designed to support other pieces of armor and hold them in place. I compare it to a carpenter's belt that holds his tools. It's the multipurpose pouch that holds and supports our ultimate power tools—or in our case, the weapons of our warfare. The belt may seem irrelevant compared to our arsenal, but it is actually the foundation that holds all the pieces of our armor together. I would compare it to core strength in the physical, providing balance and stability for us to carry our weapons and walk in obedience to God.

The cornerstone of the gospel is Jesus Christ. Jesus describes Himself as "the way, the truth, and the life" in John 14:6. He reinforces the truth of God's Word in John 17:17, which says, "Your word is truth." Not only is God's Word our truth, but it also serves as our foundation. We ground our faith and hope in it. A belt worn securely provides support in the same way that His truth is our infrastructure. It's what provides our steadfastness and confidence in a changing, frantic, and uncertain world. We may ask, "How do we buckle down in truth?" We wrap the truth of His Word around us to stand upright, making a personal commitment to live according to God's Word.

Securing our armor in place prevents us from falling prey to the enemy's lies and false doctrines (see John 8:44). A loose belt allows for a wavering faith to be tossed about like the waves of the sea and causes us to become an easy target of the deceitful schemes of the devil (see Ephesians 4:14). The enemy whispers half-truths in our ears (Genesis 3) and twists the Word of God just enough to cause us to stumble and fall away. An insecure belt will cause our armor to shift out of position and alignment with God's Word, leaving us in a vulnerable place. What if, when we try to lift the sword of the Spirit to ward off the enemy's attack, we discover we have dropped it, or that our vital organs are exposed to the flaming darts aimed at us? We would be defenseless against the enemy's attack as he bore down on us.

Having the belt secured around our waist provides the strength and support we need to carry the weight of our full armor and enables us to discern the enemy's lies. We can stand confidently in Christ's victory, proclaiming His death and resurrection. Through Him, we have become reconciled to the Father. In Psalm 24:8, we see Him as the Divine Warrior who has defeated the enemy: "Who *is* this King of glory? The Lord strong and mighty, The Lord mighty in battle." Our mighty warrior girds himself with righteousness and faithfulness (see Isaiah 11:5); we wear a battle dress like His, but His righteousness is what we put on. The best defense we have is that Jesus has already defeated the serpent of old. By securing the belt of truth around our waist, we stand confidently in the knowledge of Christ's victory.

Satan works tirelessly to manipulate and challenge the gospel message. One of his ambushes is by distorting the truth of God's Word. This was how my belt cracked under demonic pressure. I listened to the subliminal lies of the enemy, which led to my unbelief. I believed God's truth worked for others but was blind to it in my own life. Think about that. The very core or foundation of our salvation and hope is in the truth of God's Word. With that being compromised, the entire system collapses.

How did I end up so unprepared? My armor had become so misconstrued. My doubt in God's Word as truth gradually eroded my faith. The connection between the misaligned breastplate of righteousness and the belt of truth caused its displacement, enabling the enemy's fiery arrow to pierce my spiritual heart and paralyze my faith.

I share the breakdown of my armor with the hope of helping others avoid the same pitfall. Their path toward destruction may not be witchcraft, as mine was; it could be alcohol, drug addiction, pornography, or even the love of money. There are many roads that lead to destruction, but there is only one that leads to God. Jesus is the way, the truth, and the life. Doubt and unbelief are indicators that our armor has malfunctioned and our protection is seriously lacking. We must not let the enemy take us off the straight and narrow path (see Matthew 7:13). Rather, we must tightly secure the belt of truth around our waist, put on the breastplate of righteousness, and not give the enemy an inch to gain a foothold (see Ephesians 4:27). We stand firm in the Word of God, from which the power to defeat the enemy comes.

The Breastplate of Righteousness

Secured in place by the belt of truth, our next piece of armor is the breastplate of righteousness. It shields our heart and other vital organs, stopping any deadly blow against us in its tracks. A wound here could be fatal, spiritually destroying the soul. It is the piece of body armor that takes the deadly blows of the enemy—the ammunition against us, such as guilt, shame, deception and oppression.

Through Jesus' death and resurrection, we received God's

righteousness. Jesus' endurance of our sin on the cross offers us a covering of righteousness to protect our heart and soul from the enemy's evil and deception. Second Corinthians 5:21 says, "He who knew no sin became sin for us that we might become the righteousness of God." Isaiah 61:10 tells us that God clothes His people with the "garments of salvation" and a "robe of righteousness." God provided our salvation through the sacrifice of His Son. Though we once stood condemned in filthy rags, we now stand clothed in the garments of salvation. He has covered us in a robe of righteousness. *Barnes' Notes* explains that the word *robe* signifies a mantle that covered one's dress and provides protection.[33] God's righteousness delivers us from sin and demonic influences and enables us to live righteously.

Righteousness is not achieved through man's works; rather it is a free gift from God imputed to believers based on Christ's sacrifice. The breastplate of righteousness shields us from self-righteousness, a cause of judgmentalism and arrogance. Thus, we are made righteous before God through faith in Christ's righteousness, not our own actions. His righteousness sanctifies us, so the enemy's accusations can no longer affect us.

Being obedient to God keeps our breastplate strong. As we wear our breastplate, we develop purity of heart, which leads to conforming our life to His likeness. As we become more like Him, we make godly choices that protect us from deception. However, if we lack obedience, we risk our armor becoming deficient, and it may not withstand the attack. When we tolerate sin, are unforgiving, and concern ourselves with earthly things rather than being heavenly minded, we leave little room for an intimate relationship with God and, in effect, jeopardize the protection our breastplate provides.

Gospel Boots of Peace

In Romans 10, Paul quotes Isaiah 52:7: "How beautiful are the feet of those who preach the gospel of peace, who bring glad

---

33   "Isaiah 61," *Barnes' Notes* on Bible Hub, accessed June 28, 2025, https://biblehub.com/commentaries/barnes/isaiah/61.htm.

tidings of good things!" Now we may question the beauty of one's feet, but this passage isn't referring to God's craftsmanship of the foot, though that may be amazing. Isaiah describes a vision of the long-anticipated herald running down the mountainside, bringing good news to the oppressed and afflicted. He came to declare that their captivity was over and that peace and joy were being restored to their land. The beautiful sight is this man running to deliver the historical message of the Jews' release from captivity. However, in Romans 10:14–15, Paul broadens this application to the preachers of the gospel, who are the bearers of the good news of the redemption and salvation of mankind through Jesus Christ.

Before ascending to heaven, Jesus, standing on the Mount of Olives, commanded His disciples, "Go therefore and make disciples of all nations, baptizing them in the name of the Father and of the Son and of the Holy Spirit, teaching them to observe all things I commanded you" (Matthew 28:19). But treading off into a world that is against Christ, and therefore against us, can be quite the challenge. Especially in a world that is under the influence of evil and darkness. Still, we have received the weapon needed for this task. In Ephesians 6:15, this piece of armor is described: "having your feet shod with the preparation of the gospel of peace."

What exactly does it mean to have our feet shod with the gospel? I like to think of it as an all-terrain running shoe designed for use anywhere from rocky hillsides to concrete sidewalks. The perfect footwear provides maximum support, stability, and protection for urban, suburban, or rural runs. As soldiers for Christ, we wear the shoes of peace to help us maneuver the roads and share the good news of the gospel. We will traverse the earth's highways and byways, so we must protect our feet and enable them to adapt to diverse environments.

From a spiritual perspective, we're to be ready to share the good news of Jesus at all times, even in the far places of the earth. While we may go in peace, we trek into and through the enemy's turf, and he will do anything to stop the spread of the gospel.

Our journey is treacherous, but God has enabled us to run the distance. The gospel shoes protect us on the spiritual battlefield and help to keep our feet firmly planted so we remain on course. Despite enemy sabotage, we, equipped for the task, advance through the harsh demonic terrain and deliver the message of salvation and freedom.

Looking back on my life, I now realize I had not firmly planted my feet for the long haul. Short or long, battles require firm footing to withstand them. The Roman warriors would travel great distances to go to war, then stand in place for days at a time to defeat their foe. A warrior of Christ needs to stand their ground on the battlefield until the end, and therefore needs strength and endurance and firm footing. In my life, I started out standing on God's Word but lacked the perseverance. Over time, I grew tired and my feet weakened under the pressure until I began slipping. To make matters worse, I had failed to replenish my soul, and so my boots had no grip to protect me from falling.

Not everyone breaks over the long haul. Life events distract some people, preventing them from developing a firm footing. Sin or worldly things divert others, preventing them from ever becoming rooted. If only I had my feet firmly planted when the enemy set up his sabotage, I would have been able to trample the snakes and scorpions to keep on course. But over time, and because of the neglect of my shoes, the soles had worn thin and were no match for the slippery slope I attempted to climb.

The enemy sets all kinds of traps, and if we're not rooted firmly in our relationship with Jesus, we have nothing to anchor to when the devil's mudslide hits us.

In what way are we called to share the gospel of peace? Ironically, I received my call for sharing the good news while I was being drawn out of paganism. The Holy Spirit impressed Isaiah 61 upon my heart through a song. The message of preaching the good news, healing the brokenhearted, and setting the captives free from spiritual darkness was clear. Many times, the Lord will use our testimony as a light to those bound in the darkness that He rescued us from. We all have been called to share the good news—whether through writing, music, preaching, trekking to a foreign mission field, or another way—as we stand firm, fitted with the gospel boots of peace.

Shield of Faith

Our faith is a powerful shield that protects us from the fiery darts of the evil one. It's our first barrier of defense against Satan's ambush and what we hunker down behind when the barrage of arrows rains down on us. It deflects the attack and not only prevents a direct hit, but can also be effective as an offensive weapon to push the enemy back as we take back ground. According to *Strong's Exhaustive Concordance: Greek,* the *thureos* or shield was like a sturdy gate or door; the shield would be like an iron gate between the attacker and the warrior. It's further described as a "full-body-shield" that covered the whole person in spiritual warfare.[34] Besides protecting the whole body, it also covered all weaponry.

The Bible tells us to "take up" the shield of faith, which requires us to have an active part in our protection. Taking up the shield requires lifting it up into position. But how do we hold up the shield of faith? The more we believe God's Word and stand on the promises He has made, the stronger our shield and the more effective it becomes. It's interesting that the Roman shield (for which the shield of faith is a metaphor) required a daily supply of oil. The soldier arose each morning and anointed his shield to prevent it from drying out. Before battle, he would dip it in water before rubbing oil into each layer of wood.

There is wisdom for our spiritual shield as well. Our faith will dry out if not anointed with the Holy Spirit. We need to pray for an anointing of God's Spirit to fall afresh upon us each day. Not anointing our shield leaves our faith brittle and liable to go up in flames when the enemy's darts fly in. Before we enter spiritual warfare, the Holy Spirit should cleanse and anoint our faith. A sprinkling is not enough. We need a full saturation deep into the

---

[34] "2375. θυρεός (thureos)," *Strong's Exhaustive Concordance: Greek* on Bible Hub, accessed June 21, 2025, https://biblehub.com/greek/2375.htm.

layers of our faith. When properly cared for, the shield of faith remains intact when smote by the enemy's tricks or temptations, and quenches the flaming arrows he launches.

The Romans used advanced arrows, with some having tips of fire that ignited their target, and others piercing the skin with tips of poison that spread throughout the body. The evil one hurls deadly darts at us that are poisoned with doubt, distractions, and double-mindedness. He shoots flaming arrows meant to burn us with the lust of the flesh, the lust of the eyes, and the pride of life. I took on one of those burning arrows, which delivered a dose of wicked poison that attacked my faith at the core. It caused me to question God and the promises He had made. My faith was waning. The shield that would have protected me was down and the enemy knew it. His intent was not only to wound me, but to distract me from advancing in the kingdom of God. The attack came quickly and without warning. That's why avoiding a surprise assault is so crucial. If hit, we suffer the repercussions of pain and destruction it brings into our life.

The Roman soldiers carried two shields, one small round shield designed to reach their sword around in hand-to-hand combat, and one large rectangular shield used in tactical maneuvers. One particular method was to interlock the large shields creating a formation called a tortoise, in which they would form a tight square with soldiers on all four sides. Those on the inside raised their shields overhead to protect from above. By joining forces, they could create a protective barrier around themselves, making it nearly impossible to penetrate from all angles and enabling them to maneuver to the enemy's fortified walls. Once there, they grabbed their small shields and climbed the ladders to breach the walls.

Likewise, believers have the advantage of linking shields in the body of Christ for greater protection. Hebrews 10:25 tells us, "Do not forsake assembling." The assembly allows us to exhort one another and strengthen one another's faith, but it also does more. We read in Ecclesiastes 4:9–12 that "two are better than one." Basically, it's difficult to overpower two, and nearly impossible to break three. When the enemy attacks, believers can ward off the attack by linking arms and standing together. A lone warrior is an easy target, but a group will often keep the enemy at bay. We are stronger in numbers.

Looking back, I see how the enemy carefully strategized his plan to separate my family from the church body. The attack was on my marriage. From the day of my wedding, I had declared God to be glorified in our marriage, which we know is something Satan hates. So, not surprisingly, that's exactly where he attacked. The bombardment was continuous, from lack of finances, to mental and physical health, to a slew of events that drove a wedge between us and some of the church body. At a time when we needed to come under the protection of multiple shields, we stood solo, lone targets on the battlefield. For a while we stood our ground, but over time we failed to replenish our faith, leaving our shields un-oiled, dry, brittle, and susceptible to the enemy's advances. First Corinthians 16:13 says, "Watch, stand fast in the faith, be brave, be strong." We must always keep our focus on the faith of the gospel and never give up or back down. By doing so, we will stand our ground in the hour of temptation.

Helmet of Salvation

Have you ever had reoccurring thoughts that made you wish you could just put a cap on your head and block them out? They seem to pop into your brain out of nowhere, reminding you of past failures that provoke feelings of inadequacy. Perhaps it's a quick flashback of a past sin, followed by a lie that God can never use you, or even forgive you, because of what you've done. Even worse, it could be a Scripture verse twisted ever so slightly that causes you to doubt you're even saved.

These thoughts come at us from all angles. It could be fear that stifles our movement, anxiety that hinders our ability, or criticism that discourages us from moving forward. Let's not forget lustful thoughts that subconsciously cause us to succumb to guilt, or the temptation to act on them. These destructive thoughts derail us from God's purpose in our life and leave us depressed. Eventually, if we don't take these thoughts captive, they influence our behavior to the point of defeat.

Paul describes these thoughts as the flaming arrows that Satan targets our minds with. The good news is that God has provided the protection that deflects the fiery arrows from penetrating. But we need to take up the helmet of salvation and place it on our head.

Taking a direct hit on the head can be fatal. At the least, it can make us feel dizzy (confused) and unstable. It diminishes our decision-making ability and slows our reaction time. If the first hit doesn't take us out, it sets us up for the next blow. Just as a physical helmet protects one's head against blunt-force trauma, so the helmet of salvation protects our mind against the impact of the enemy's lies.

In Ephesians 6, the helmet and the sword are the last two pieces of armor a soldier puts on. The helmet of salvation is a metaphor for the spiritual covering that protects our mind. One might easily question the helmet's link to salvation, as it surely doesn't imply a need for salvation before each battle. The word for *salvation* used in this verse is the Greek word *solterion*, meaning deliverance, preservation, safety, or salvation.[35] Our mind is one battlefield of the enemy; therefore, we need protection or deliverance from his attacks in this area. Remembering what God has done for us in the past can counteract the enemy's attacking thoughts and is part of the operation of the helmet of salvation.

That's why it's so important that we are careful with what we allow into our mind. The world is full of the enemy's subtle but often flamboyant lies. It comes down to what we've opened our mind up to, such as through reading, watching TV, or scrolling social media. If we're not vigilant about what we allow in, our thought life becomes bombarded with various lies and deceptive tactics from the enemy. Paul warns us to "beware lest anyone cheat you through philosophy and empty deceit, according to the tradition of men, according to the basic principles of the

---

35 "Soteria," Bible Study Tools, accessed June 28, 2025, https://www.biblestudytools.com/lexicons/greek/kjv/soteria.html.

world, and not according to Christ. For in Him dwells all the fullness of the Godhead bodily; and you are complete in Him, who is the head of all principality and power" (Colossians 2:8–10).

Coming back to Jesus after backsliding, I found my mind under heavy attack. The enemy hurled temptation upon temptation at me. It was a struggle to resist the sins of my past and overcome the guilt I felt for committing them. I had a continuing battle being played out in my head for some time as the enemy attempted to bring me down. But God was the strength of my salvation. I couldn't have done it without Him. He covered my head on the day of battle (see Psalm 14:7).

Paul urges us, "And do not be conformed to this world, but be transformed by the renewing of your mind, that you may prove what is that good and acceptable and perfect will of God" (Romans 12:2). By renewing our minds according to God's Word, we learn how to know His thoughts and can live according to His ways. In 2 Corinthians 10:5, we are to "take every thought captive to obey Christ." Our active part is to examine every thought that enters our mind and quickly dispose of any that are ungodly comparing it to the Word of God.

We prepare for the battlefield of the mind by focusing on godly things, memorizing Scripture, and knowing how to apply the Word against every battle tactic the enemy throws our way. The helmet protects our mind, assuring our salvation through Jesus' sacrifice for our sins on the cross. In Him, we have victory over the enemy's attack on our mind.

Sword of the Spirit

"The Word of God is living and powerful, and sharper than any two-edged sword, piercing even to the division of soul and spirit, and of joints and marrow, and is a discerner of the thoughts and intents of the heart" (Hebrews 4:12). I can testify that, spoken in the correct context, God's Word cut through every argument and lofty opinion I held during my witchcraft years, penetrating straight to my heart.

With that said, I emphasize "spoken in correct context," as

I've also seen the Word used out of context (it did not have the same impact). In my early Christian life, I interpreted Psalm 37:4, "Delight yourself in the Lord, and He will give you the desires of your heart," as my having the perfect marriage and the blessings thereof. I failed to acknowledge John 16:33, where Jesus tells His disciples—and us—"In this life you will have trouble. But take heart! I have overcome the world."

It's a common Scripture that Satan twists and uses as bait. Psalm 37, in its context, addresses the prosperity of the wicked and the affliction of the righteous. In his commentary, Matthew Henry cautions us against discontent over the prosperity and success of evildoers.[36] In verse 4, Henry explains the desire of a good man's heart is "to know, and love, and live to God, to please him and to be pleased in him." Taken out of context, we easily fall into the trap of believing that Psalm 37:4 means that God will give us whatever our heart desires.

Remember, even the enemy knows Scripture and quotes his own interpretation of it. Going back to the garden of Eden, we find Satan using Scripture to tempt Eve. He took God's words out of context by telling Eve she would be "like God" if she ate the forbidden fruit. Eve listened to the lie, and the fall of mankind was underway. Ironically, Satan used what God spoke and twisted it, attempting to justify the temptation he offered to Eve. It's important that we treat God's Word with respect and study the Scriptures to show ourselves approved unto God, rightly dividing the word of truth (see 2 Timothy 2:5).

Ephesians 6:17 tells us to "take up the sword of the Spirit, which is the Word of God." The Greek for *word* in this verse is *rhema*, which refers to the spoken Word by God, the word written in the Scriptures, or the word through the voice of the Holy Spirit. In 1 Timothy 1:18, Paul instructs Timothy to fight the Lord's battles with the prophetic words he received. In other words, to recall the words spoken over his life and speak them out loud. The word referred to as the sword of the Spirit, then, can be the

---

36 5. "Verses 1–6," *Matthew Henry's Commentary* on Bible Gateway, accessed June 28, 2025, https://www.biblegateway.com/resources/matthew-henry/Ps.37.1-Ps.37.6.

God-inspired written Word, the voice of the Holy Spirit, or a word of knowledge spoken through a human vessel.

The sword serves as both an offensive and defensive weapon. Spiritual warriors use it offensively to silence and defeat the enemy, and defensively to block an incoming assault. Matthew 4:1–11 best exemplifies effectively wielding the spiritual sword against the enemy. The Holy Spirit has led Jesus into the wilderness, the battlefield where He will face off with the devil. Satan first tested Jesus with the *lust of the flesh*, or our carnal and physical appetites: "If You are the Son of God, command that these stones become bread" (v. 3). When Jesus responded with the Word, Satan changed his tactic to the *pride of life* (arrogance, self-pride, and self-reliance): "Then the devil took Him up into the Holy City, set Him on the pinnacle of the temple, and said to Him, 'If You are the Son of God, throw Yourself down. For it is written: "He shall give His angels charge over you"'" (vv. 5–6). Jesus again came back with the Word of God, and once again Satan changed his maneuver and made one last attempt through the *lust of the eyes* (coveting): "The devil took Him up on an exceedingly high mountain and showed Him all the kingdoms of the world and their glory. And he said to Him, 'All these things I will give You if You will fall down and worship me'" (vv. 8–9). At this, Jesus rebuked him and the devil left. Each time Satan tested Jesus, He responded with the truth of the Word. Jesus stood firm on the Word of God and overcame Satan and his tactics. So too are we to stand firm and let His sword come forth from our mouths to overcome the devil and his plot against us.

One thing my pastor shared was an "alliterative" way to remember the attacks we all face. An alliterative aspect was the use of the consonant "S" to start the word used for the attack. The first test was for Sustenance, or the enemy will tell us we wouldn't have enough food to eat and survive. The second was Safety. The enemy tempts us in pride to do "daredevil" things which are very unsafe! (Ever wonder why they are called daredevil things?) The third test was Significance, where our feelings of insecurity or importance, or a poor identity can lead us to strive for prominent positions or powers. Matthew 6:33 says, "But seek first the

Kingdom of God and His righteousness, and all these things shall be added to you."

Taking up the sword of the Spirit is more than just raising a sword. We have to know the Word, which requires us to memorize it, so the Holy Spirit can bring it to mind when the need arises. We must study the Scriptures to prevent taking them out of context. This requires delving into the Word consistently and researching passages in Bible commentaries to have a greater understanding of their meaning. Finally, we want to cover our study of Scripture with prayer so that we can fully activate this weapon at our disposal. As we spend time in the living Word, we come to know Jesus in a deeper, more intimate way.

Godfidence

With our armor fitted and orders in hand (see Ephesians 6:10-13), we're ready to wage war against the devil. But not so fast. Our deployment orders for us to "be strong in the Lord and in the power of His might" (Ephesians 6:10). We are not strong enough of our own accord to wage war against the devil. When faced with a spirit that was created with (great) power and influence that far exceeds our natural strength, all the courage that we can muster up seems minuscule. Even the strongest human is frail and weak compared to the enemy we face. But we mustn't fret. We just need to think about David when he stood before Goliath. He was small, yet bold compared to the heavily armed giant. Yet, height and weight are insignificant; the battle is fought not with flesh and blood, but with the Spirit. David's stature may have been that of a shepherd boy, but he had something far greater: he relied on the Spirit of God, which provided him enough strength to subdue a lion and a bear when protecting the sheep placed in his care (see 1 Samuel 17:34-36). To him, this giant was no more or less than another ravenous beast to bring down with divine help through his bare hands. He gave glory to God and did not cower at the intimidation of the raucous threat that provoked him. He merely slung a stone and trusted God to lay the giant flat. Oh, may it be so that we would know the courage of trusting God to deliver on His promises, and hold fast to our faith to see it manifest before our very eyes.

Our sufficiency is not of our own accord, but from God alone. Ephesians 3:16 says, "That He would grant you, according to the riches of His glory, to be strengthened with might through His Spirit in the inner man." The strength imparted to our inner man by the Spirit of God is the sufficient strength needed for our souls. It provides strength to our faith, strength to serve God, strength for long suffering, and strength to persevere on the battlefield.

Standing Firm

So, now that we're empowered by the Holy Spirit, are we ready to advance? Not exactly. Our instruction tells us to *stand*. Yes, before we can advance, we must first learn how to stand in a posture of readiness. We are not always on his radar, but the enemy strikes at inopportune times. In fact, his best strategy is to catch us off guard. Therefore, we must always remain armored and maintain our position. We must be able to resist the enemy's allurements and assaults. In order to do so, your feet need to be planted firmly on the solid rock of our faith.

That way, when the enemy strikes, and he surely will, we will be ready to withstand his advances. This first position on the battlefield will be for holding ground. An armored warrior standing firm will sometimes be enough to deter lesser demons to be persuaded into finding an easier target (unless they are specifically assigned). We may be called to take a position on the battlefield to secure and hold the ground. It's critical, therefore, that we learn how to hold our position by standing firm.

When the enemy pushes against us, we cannot back down. We must position ourselves firmly. The armor of God fully equips us to stand against the enemy, but it requires discipline on our part as we commit to being obedient to the Word and resisting the enemy's advances.

Resisting

Next, we need to learn to resist the enemy and all the deceptive lies he sends our way. We must have perseverance and stamina, and make sure our armor is secure. The slightest opening can be the means by which the enemy gains an advantage. Just when we're most vulnerable, the wicked whisper enters that gap between our helmet and ear, such as, "Aren't you jealous of Billy being chosen as the assistant pastor? You've served in the church much longer than he. You deserve that position!"

The critical moment has arrived. It's true, you felt slighted over the pastor choosing Billy over you. Worse yet, there's still some envy you haven't resolved to completely let go of. Then comes the actual blow: "Why defend a faith that is against you? You'll never be more than a pew hog. What makes you think you'll even inherit the kingdom of God? Give it up!" But oh no, never give up. Tighten that strap around your chin to secure our helmet and prevent the enemy's lies from whizzing through your mind. Jesus' death and resurrection secured our salvation, making you a child of the Living God. Reposition that breastplate so it snaps snugly in with the rest of your armor, allowing no gaps in between. Then silence. The voice inside your head is gone. Congratulations, you're still standing, and aside from a few garment mishaps you've resisted the devil, who has fled.

This is why it's important that we crucify our flesh and walk in the Spirit. The enemy will use anything that we've not surrendered to Christ as ammunition against us. The more uncovered sin we have in our life, the more he has to hold against us. Remember, we're saved, but still sinners. Philippians 2:12 tells us that we all must "work out our salvation with fear and trembling." Therefore, God allows for a gradual process in consideration of our humanity and in His mercy. Realizing our weaknesses or sins can surprise some believers, but really, it's the first step in God's process of "sanctification" of our soul, which could take a lifetime. We must resolve not to yield to Satan, but stand our ground and resist his advances. He has no choice but to flee when we hold strong to our faith in God and refuse to back down.

Now, having been equipped with our armor, we'll advance to the next chapter and discover the weapons of our warfare.

Behind Enemy Lines

CHAPTER 12

Weapons Of Warfare

Prayer: A Weapon of Warfare

In Ephesians 6:18, Paul transitions directly from his illustrations of the armor, to prayer: "Praying always with all prayer and supplication in the Spirit, being watchful with all perseverance and supplication for all the saints." We know prayer as our method of communication with God, but it is so much more. We can use prayer as a powerful weapon alongside the double-edged sword of the Spirit. Prayer lifts our needs to the throne of God, and He in return empowers our requests. Here, it releases the Holy Spirit's anointing on all pieces of the armor, which enables us to stand against the kingdom of darkness.

Jesus illustrated the need and effectiveness of prayer in Luke 22:31-32: "Simon, Simon! Indeed, Satan has asked for you, that he may sift *you* as wheat. But I have prayed for you." Jesus is giving us insight beyond our earthly vision. Satan, the accuser of the brethren, actually petitions God against us, but Jesus, our mediator, prays for us (see 1 Timothy 2:5). The accuser doesn't just bring accusations before God's throne; he wants more. He did this with Job and continues the same attack on believers today. The battle is real, and the enemy seeks to destroy our faith in order to devour our soul.

While Satan may request us from God, remember Jesus' response regarding Peter: "But I have prayed for you." Here, Jesus gives us insight into the power of prayer. It is at our disposal to use when the enemy attacks. Notice, though, what Jesus prayed for. He prayed for Peter's faith to endure, not for him to escape temptation. Now consider Job 1:6–12. Satan asked God for permission to attack Job's faith, and God granted him access to everything except Job himself. Job's ordeal wasn't exactly looking victorious when he lost everything, but he never lost his faith.

In the prologue of my memoir, *A Witch's Encounter With God*, I open with a personal experience. I found myself engaged in a spiritual conversation while my body lay at the bottom of a staircase. There were three beings beside me engaging in a supernatural debate. A voice warned me that if I stayed, I'd be in enemy territory but my salvation would be safe. I chose to remain for my children's sake and awoke to the phone ringing and a horrible headache. I was sold out for Jesus, and the thought of going to the enemy's camp was absurd. Yet, years later, I had fallen from grace and was practicing witchcraft. My faith had suffered a major blow. I relate it to the trials of Job, only I had failed miserably.

How could this have happened? Remember, Peter also failed the test of faith, but Jesus restored his faith after interceding for him. I came very close to losing mine, but thank God, He positioned prayer warriors to intercede on my behalf and Jesus rescued me from the kingdom of darkness. Never underestimate the power of prayer as you're interceding on behalf of someone, despite how dark the situation may seem.

Ephesians 6:18 instructs us to pray always. It's not enough to be clothed in the armor as we engage in warfare. We need prayer covering as we stand against the wiles of the enemy, both from prayer warriors who support us in battle and from ourselves as we lift our request up to the throne of God. We need to have an open dialogue with our heavenly Father that keeps our lines of communication active 24/7. Ephesians 6:18 says, "Praying always with *all prayer* and supplication in the Spirit, being watchful to this end with all perseverance and supplication for all the saints." The words "all prayer" emphasize that our focus should be on every kind of prayer, such as adoration, confession, thanksgiving, petition, and intercession, on each occasion and in every situation.

Supplication is a specific request we ask on our behalf or the behalf of another in the Spirit. Many believe that praying in the Spirit is speaking in tongues, and while it is a method of praying in the Spirit, it's not the only Spirit-led prayer. Jesus' prayer for Peter is an example. He didn't pray that temptation would cease, which is earthly minded, but that Peter's faith would not fail, which is eternally minded. His prayer was Spirit led, though it does not show that He spoke in tongues of angels. According to 1 Corinthians 6:17, he who is joined to the Lord is one spirit with Him. This does not do away with speaking in tongues, for we are told to use all prayer. So, if we have the ability to speak in tongues, by all means we should use our prayer language. Those who don't can still pray led by His Spirit. The point is not to limit the type of prayer that we use. The Spirit enables us to pray more adequately while being watchful in the end. As intercessors, we are watchmen on the wall, which requires us to be alert and on guard, praying with all perseverance and supplication for all the saints.

We read in 1 Corinthians 14:2 that "he who speaks in a tongue does not speak to men but to God." Verse 4 also states, "He who speaks in a tongue edifies himself." The Greek word translated as "edifies" is *oikodomeo*, and it means "to build, to construct, or to build up." Combining these verses reveals a pattern for praying most effectively. When needing to pray, one might express desires, feelings, or quote a relevant verse. Or, they could follow Jesus' model. How? In John 5:19, Jesus said, "I only do what the Father shows Me," and in John 12:50, referring to what the Father tells him, "Therefore, whatever I speak, just as the Father has told Me, so I speak." If Jesus turned to His Father, shouldn't we speak to God in tongues so that God can build up our souls in understanding and direction? Thus, ask the Lord for instruction on how to pray and pray in tongues, and your soul shall receive understanding on what to release to them.

Prayer is a powerful weapon, as it is interaction with Jesus. We also want all who take part in prayer to truly believe that God still hears our cries and performs miracles today. If they do not believe this, why do we pray at all? This lack of faith hinders our prayers. It reminds me of when Jesus called only three disciples to join him in raising a dead girl (Mark 5:35–42). Jesus overheard someone idly say, "Your daughter is dead. Why bother the teacher anymore?" Jesus replied, "Don't be afraid, just believe," and then (as I see it) chose three disciples to follow Him to the home of Jairus, the synagogue leader whose daughter had died.

When they arrived, crying and wailing greeted them, and when Jesus said, "The child is not dead but asleep," they laughed at him. With this display of lack of belief, not only did Jesus clear out the home except for the parents, but He also invited only the three chosen disciples who had the faith, to witness the miraculous—the raising of a little girl from the dead.

Praise: A Weapon of Warfare

When we think of praise, the first thing that usually comes to mind is exalting God through songs and music proclaiming His wondrous works. He is worthy and for that alone we lift our voices, but the results are far greater than many realize. Our praise joins with the worship of heaven and becomes a powerful weapon against the enemy of our soul.

Psalm 22:3 tells us that God dwells in the praises of His people, so when we praise Him, His presence falls upon us and pushes the darkness away. In that instant, the accuser of the brethren is silenced and we are no longer subject to his lies or condemnation. Psalm 8:2 says, "Out of the mouth of babes and nursing infants You have ordained strength, because of Your enemies, that You may silence the enemy and the avenger." The New International Version words it, "You have established a stronghold against your enemies, to silence the foe and the avenger." Praise literally creates a spiritual "no attack" zone and places us in a position of victory.

In 2 Chronicles 20, we see several armies joining forces to make war against King Jehoshaphat of Southern Judah. He became alarmed when several men approached him with the news that a vast army was fast approaching. Jehoshaphat proclaimed a fast, gathering all the people throughout Judah to seek the Lord. Jahaziel, a prophet and Levite, spoke to the king and the people and told them they need not fight this battle but should take up their positions, stand firm, and see the salvation of the Lord on their behalf.

Upon hearing this, the Levites and all those gathered stood up to praise the Lord God of Israel with a loud voice. Early the next morning, King Jehoshaphat and his men arose and set out to take their positions. He appointed singers unto the Lord, to praise the beauty of holiness as they went out before the army. As King Jehoshaphat and his men surveyed the land, they found only corpses, leaving no war to fight. Upon hearing this, all those gathered came to Jerusalem with songs, harps, and trumpets to the house of the Lord.

From this example in Scripture, we see how God inhabits the praises of His people. Amid preparing for battle, Jehoshaphat sent singers out to the battlefield, trusting what God had spoken through the prophet. In response, God confused the enemy to the point of their self-destruction. When we engage in spiritual warfare, praise becomes an essential part of our arsenal. Remember the battle is not ours but the Lord's.

Shouts of Praise

Joshua 6:20 tells how the walls of Jericho fell with the shout of praise and the blowing of trumpets (shofars)—hardly what one would expect God to use in order to bring victory to His people. In my life, praise broke down spiritual barriers, freeing me and bringing me to my place of victory. At the time, as a practicing witch, I had reluctantly accepted an invitation to church. When worship began, my prison walls fell down, leaving me exposed and defenseless to an all-loving God. I was spiritually blind for a long time because of my sin and rebellion. (John 12:40 says, "He blinded their eyes and hardened their hearts, lest they should see with their eyes, lest they should understand with their hearts and turn, so that I should heal them."), but as I stood among the praise and worship, the enemy was silenced, and for the first time in many years, I could see. God's grace restored my spiritual sight.

It's interesting to note that God sent the Levites behind the soldiers but before the ark of the covenant, marching while blowing their shofars around the walls of Jericho for six days. On the seventh day, they marched as they sounded the shofars, the people shouted, and the walls of Jericho came down. Levite Priests were appointed to inspire troops heading to war by blowing shofars, which symbolized God's remembrance in battle. Thus, God's ministers, by sounding the Jubilee trumpet of the everlasting gospel, which proclaims liberty and victory, encourage the good soldiers of Jesus Christ in their spiritual warfare.[37]

God breaks down the strongholds, and trains our hands for war and anoints our fingers for battle (see Psalm 144:1), but before we grab for our AK-47, we must take a deep breath, because physical weapons cannot prevail against the gates of hell. Our first line of defense is simple: we should let God arise, scattering His enemies. God going before us in battle diminishes our fight, leaving only a few skirmishes as we reclaim our territory.

Using Praise as a Weapon

How then do we use the weapon of praise? Besides the method used in the verses above, we can put into action Psalm 149:3: "Let them praise His name with the dance; let them sing praises to Him with the timbrel and harp." In 2 Samuel 6:14, King David danced with all his might as he brought the ark of the covenant, or the very presence of God, into Jerusalem. So, too, should we joyfully and mightily usher in the presence of God through song, dance, and with musical instruments. As a powerful form of worship and praise, dance expresses joy, gratitude,

---

[37] "Verses 6–16," *Matthew Henry's Commentary* on Bible Gateway, accessed August 6, 2025, https://www.biblegateway.com/resources/matthew-henry/Josh.6.6-Josh.6.16.

and love for God—things the enemy detests.

Psalm 149: 6 says, "Let the high praises of God be in their mouth, and a two-edged sword in their hand." The two-edged sword, or God's Word spoken or sung, becomes a powerful weapon of warfare. The entire book of Psalms is a compilation of songs and prayers. King David authored 73 of the 150 psalms and was called a man after God's heart (see 1 Samuel 13:14). We can follow his example and use the psalms to make our requests known to God. Using the same principle as praying the Scriptures, we can sing the verse or chapter instead of speaking the words.

Praise in Deliverance

A powerful biblical example of the effectiveness of praise in deliverance is found in Acts 16:16-33. At midnight, Paul and Silas, despite being imprisoned, bound, and in pain, prayed and sang hymns to God. The other prisoners, surprised by this, listened to them. Suddenly, a violent earthquake shook the prison, miraculously opening all the cell doors and freeing the prisoners from their chains

The experience of Paul and Silas in prison metaphorically represents liberation from both physical and spiritual captivity. God's deliverance, symbolized by this event, frees believers from physical slavery and spiritual bondage; this sets believers free from the chains of sin and its consequences.

Praise is an instrument to use in deliverance, either our own or someone else's. Praise clears the atmosphere of demonic influences in both the spiritual and natural realms. This reduces demonic resistance, if not easing it altogether, making the battle much easier since we're driving out demons even before our prayer for deliverance has begun. The reason praise is such an effective weapon is because God had created Satan for worship and instead, he desired the worship for himself, which caused his rebellion and fall. Satan and his demons absolutely hate it when Christians praise God, as it is a constant reminder of their own demise and expulsion from heaven.

If you're still questioning praise as a weapon of warfare,

consider the end times battle in Revelation 19, where Christ defeats the beast and his armies. We see Jesus' riding on a white horse with the redeemed following Him into battle, but if we look closely, we find something out of the ordinary.

Christ's followers wear no armor and carry no typical weapons of destruction. They are wearing white linen, similar to the garb of those who worship with the angels before the throne of God. That's because the battle is the Lord's, and the redeemed enter warfare with the weapon of praise.

Eternal Worship and Sound

The weapon of praise even penetrates into time and space. In a video "Worship and Sound," the executive director of Eagles Wings Ministries, Robert Stearns, offers insight that sound waves actually create a force in the atmosphere, and explains the physical theory that once sound is uttered, it is in a sense . . . eternal. Its waves may decrease to a place whereby we cannot physically hear it, but it still echoes in the universe.[38] With that in mind, we can envision the continuous flow of praise being carried throughout eternity. If sound influences the atmosphere, then praise is a never-ending bombardment on the enemy and his demons. With such worship, we not only cause confusion for demonic forces, but also offer an open invitation for God's presence to dwell in our midst.

Testimony: A Weapon of Warfare

Another way we overcome the accuser is by wielding the word of our testimony. A potent weapon at our disposal, it is the retelling of the very attack Satan intended to destroy us with—that is, until Jesus intervened and rescued us from the devil's destruction. Our spoken witness of the gospel message of redemption confirms God's Word through Jesus' shed blood. It tells of Christ's triumph over evil and all the powers of the enemy. When we testify, we expose the enemy's lies and reveal God's plan for salvation, thus overcoming the evil one (see Revelation 12:11). We

---

[38] extremeprophetic, "Patricia King: Worship and Sound (Robert Stearns)," YouTube, September 12, 2008, https://www.youtube.com/watch?v=DiI9z_s4WJI.

are the physical evidence in a world that is spiritually blind.

We first must understand that our testimony is actually testifying to what God has done in our life. It has nothing to do with us and everything to do with God. In Acts 1:8, Luke refers to Jesus' ascension and appointment of the church: "But you shall receive power when the Holy Spirit has come upon you; and you shall be witnesses to Me in Jerusalem, and in all Judea and Samaria, and to the end of the earth." That was Jesus' strategy for the gospel to reach the far ends of the earth. If we are Christ's servants in our generation, we also share the good news of salvation. We do this by sharing our faith and life experiences, or our testimony, which tears down the lies of the enemy and upholds the truth of God's Word. It also fortifies our faith and subdues the enemy with remembrance of Christ's victory.

Of course, we must remember who we are fighting against, and that there is nothing he will not use to defeat us, including our own testimony. This should not surprise us. After all, he attempts to twist the very Word of God, so he'll use anything at his disposal, including our testimony. But remember, God's story of our life consists of all the things that Satan once accused us of before the throne of God, that now stand as a testament against him. It declares the enemy is defeated, and in Christ is the victory.

Testimonial Attack

I regularly share my testimony of how Jesus graciously rescued me from eternal darkness and restored me to the kingdom of God. Ironically, while writing this section on our testimonial weapon of warfare, I received a response to a post I put on Facebook warning of the dangers of specific occult practices. The woman accused me of exposing and promoting occult practices via my Facebook page while cleverly disguising them in some type of backdoor exposure, citing Ephesians 5:8–13 as her source. Notice "the angel in light" coming forth as a messenger while *twisting* the Word of God to administer this message.

The first sign that the enemy was at work here was the

statement's hypocrisy—accusing me of both exposing and promoting the occult at the same time. What Ephesians 5:11 says is, "And have no fellowship with the unfruitful works of darkness, but expose them," which was exactly what I was doing. I rather think her emphasis may have been on verse 12: "For it is shameful even to speak of those things which are done by them in secret." This is a classic example of how the devil takes Scripture out of context for his own purpose.

As explained in Matthew Henry's commentary on Ephesians 5:12, "They are so filthy and abominable that it is a shame to mention them, *except in a way of reproof,* much more it be a shame to have any fellowship with them."[39] The verse is speaking of being in fellowship with those who are taking part in sinful wickedness so detestable that they are not even permitted to divulge it, and goes to say that good men should reprove such wickedness. In my Facebook post, I was not explicitly divulging acts of unknown wickedness, but rather common occult practices that the Bible speaks about, and I was doing so with reproof, as instructed.

And then came the attack on God's testimony of my life. These words lashed out at me straight from the devil, proclaiming that the Lord doesn't need my personal experience or books to expose what Scripture defines as evil. And there lay the root of the attack—my testimony. Revelation 12:11 says, "And they overcame him by the blood of the Lamb, and by the word of their testimony." Our testimony is a powerful weapon against Satan and his demons. We testify to God's forgiveness through the shed blood of His Son, our Savior Jesus Christ. So effective is His Spirit living in us, and testifying of God's love and power through us, that it destroys the very work the devil has set against us. In Mark 5:18, Jesus delivered a demonized man and said, "Go home to your own people and tell them how much the Lord has done for you, and how he has had mercy on you."

In Exodus 12, applying hyssop with lamb's blood to doorposts symbolizes Jesus' sacrifice—His shed blood cleanses and covers

---

39 "Verses 3–20," *Matthew Henry's Commentary* on Bible Gateway, accessed July 16, 2025, https://www.biblegateway.com/resources/matthew-henry/Eph.5.3-Eph.5.20.

our sins, granting us access to God. The comparison between Jesus' blood as a means of salvation and the Passover lamb's blood that saved the Israelites from the angel of death is clear. The Israelites slaughtered the lamb and its blood flowed into the basin. God instructed them to take a bunch of hyssop, dip it into the blood, and strike the doorpost. Similarly, our testimony is the hyssop with which we apply the blood of Jesus over our lives. It is, according to Revelation 12, how we as believers triumph over the devil.

Our personal accounts corroborate Scripture's description of the blood's actions. The word becomes effective in our life when we testify to it; otherwise, we remain like ancient Israel. The basin in Exodus contained blood yet offered no protection. While Jesus' sacrifice offers protection, we access it through our personal testimony, or our "hyssop." However, if we don't use the hyssop, if we refrain from testifying about what the Lord has done for us, and we allow the devil to silence us, then we diminish what the Word says the blood does for us. The hyssop is the means by which we get the blood from the basin to the door. It shows that the blood of Jesus and one's testimony of faith are both crucial components in overcoming evil.

Cloaked in Zeal

In Isaiah 59:15-17, we see God looking out across the land only to find evil and injustice. He searches for one intercessor who would cry out for mercy for their wickedness, or at the very least, ask for the avenging of the injuries of his people, but he finds no one. So, God takes up arms Himself, with the work of salvation as his helmet, fueled by his righteousness as his breastplate and with the cloak of zeal covering his shoulders.

In the Bible, a cloak or mantle is symbolic of authority. Therefore, the cloak of zeal draped across His shoulders displays His passionate authority, which He wears to war against his enemies. Not a warfare with blood and carnage, but with righteousness and zeal to secure the salvation of His people. The armor Paul speaks of in Ephesians 6, which God has provided for us, is the same armor that God Himself wore in battle. He then covers us with the cloak of zeal, giving us His authority to trample on serpents and scorpions, and over all the power of the enemy (see Luke 10:19). Notice that we don't go forth in our own authority, but He sends us forth under the covering of His (see Isaiah 41:10).

With the state of the world today, what does God see when He looks across our land? Violence, destruction, and lawlessness abound in our cities today. In our society, evil works have replaced many good works, and darkness covers the land. Even some churches are silent, while others defend the sins of our nation. Does God hear the cry of intercessors calling out against the injustice perpetrated on our children or the inequity that has come upon our nation? Where are those with a zeal for justice? The stories of teenagers whose bodies physicians have mutilated in the name of science should move us all as if we had any part in creation.

Apathy has seeped into the kingdom, and your devotion to God will be tested. Where are the watchmen on the wall? Not all have left their post, or surely the day of the Lord would be upon us. We, as believers, cannot sit idle as the enemy soils our land. God has equipped us with the armor needed to stand firm and resist the enemy and his forces. Do you lack zeal? If so, something is missing; you may be equipped, but you lack the final garment. Ask the Lord to wrap you with His cloak of passion, then lift your voice to the throne of God with prayers of repentance for the people, and prayers of intercession for those suffering injustice. Take your place and stand against the wickedness of this generation and the god of this age. To do so, you must love the Lord with all your heart, soul, and mind, which creates an environment where zeal thrives.

The zeal of the Lord comes with knowledge and a relationship with the Lord. God's Word and His love must temper this great enthusiasm. Zeal administered with knowledge produces grace that changes lives. Attempted without the Word of God, it can lead to legalism, which serves no purpose for the kingdom.

Here is one example of the zeal of God in my own life: After many long years of living in a backslidden state, most people who had originally been interceding for me had all but given up hope. I certainly can't blame them. Most who knew me believed my repentance and deliverance were unlikely after so many years of witnessing my defiance toward God and knowing my defense of the kingdom of darkness. Everyone, perhaps, except for my pastor who had received a word from the Lord to just love me. Despite the opposition he faced from others who advised he give up, he never did. And, on that glorious day it was as though God Himself had said, "Enough." Whisking the cloak of zeal over His shoulders, He came down and rescued me from the devil's domain.

Many have lost their zeal. For instance, many people have gotten the wind knocked out of them when the ministers they followed fell from grace. It's important that our zeal is based on our relationship with God, and not our respect of anyone else, even ministers of the gospel. Now that you have your arsenal at your disposal, you can counter the enemy's attacks. Possessing your weaponry alone is not enough, though; you must also know how to use it. In the next chapter, we'll look at a very important tactic to use in warfare. Spiritual discernment is the alert system that will warn of an impending ambush.

Behind Enemy Lines

CHAPTER 13

Spiritual Discernment

Spiritual discernment is a general ability to distinguish between right and wrong, truth and error, that believers develop through the Word of God and experience. It is not to be mistaken for the gift of discerning of spirits, which is a supernatural ability to distinguish the presence and nature of spirits, both good and evil. Paul, in 1 Corinthians 2, distinguishes between the natural and the spiritual man. The natural man cannot accept the things of the Spirit of God, instead considering them foolish and being unable to understand them because they are spiritually discerned.

Every believer receives the Holy Spirit, who comes and dwells within them, upon receiving salvation. Discernment enables believers to align their lives with God's will and purpose. As believers mature spiritually, their discernment increases. It's important for our spiritual growth that we're weaned off the milk of the Word, and progress to digesting the meat. We don't want to remain baby Christians any longer than necessary.

One reason for this is that we become a target of the enemy the moment we give our lives to Christ. His demons watch and study our tendencies, and make notes of both our strengths and weaknesses. This allows them to plot and scheme against us to steer us off track and prevent us from accomplishing God's purpose in our lives. Every believer can and should earnestly hone this ability.

The Bible urges believers to test the spirits to discern if they're from God, as many false prophets are in the world. This command instructs all Christians to be discerning and to examine the messages and teachings they encounter. The purpose of testing the spirits is to ensure that the teachings align with Scripture and to identify false prophets or teachings that can be misleading.

Now, how do we test the spirits? There are four ways:

1. Verify that alleged messages are from God's Spirit (in other words, are in line with all Scripture). The Bible is our guide, as any word spoken in truth will not be contrary to Scripture. Even a good pastor or teacher will tell us not to accept anything they have said without lining it up with the Word of God. Of course, for this to truly be effective, we have to study the Word. Second Timothy 2:15 says, "Be diligent to present yourself approved to God, a worker who does not need to be ashamed, rightly dividing the word of truth." As we read and meditate on Scripture, the Holy Spirit will automatically prompt us and reveal any error to us. The key is to be in tune with the Holy Spirit on a day-to-day basis.

2. Examine the fruit. Most often, false prophets appear in sheep's clothing. They look like Christians, but beneath the outer layer they are ravening wolves. They come from their father, the devil, in the guise of light, but by their fruit we will know them. Their fruit is either fleshly or of the kingdom of darkness. It's important for us to evaluate spiritual leaders and other people in our lives by their actions in order to determine whether they are exhibiting true doctrine. The enemy's fruit is poison and leads to deadly destruction. Beware of the evil that lurks within.

3. Examine the impact that the spirit has on the body of Christ. Prophets, evangelists, pastors, and teachers speaking under the guidance of the Holy Spirit will edify the body and encourage them to mature spiritually and participate in the great commission that Jesus assigned to the church. False prophets seek

division and destruction of the church. They come to devour and scatter the sheep, and drive them on crooked paths that lead them away from God. Grapes are not gathered from thornbushes, nor are figs from thistles (see Matthew 7:16). Their fruit does not edify the body, and if left in place, will spoil the bunch. So be on the lookout for wrong fruit or fruit showing decay.

4. Determine whether the spirit gives glory to God. Another telltale sign of a false spirit is when it doesn't give glory to God or to His Son, Jesus Christ. False prophets or teachers may honor God with lip service, but it is not genuine and distracts the focus away from God. Their actions show their pride and their hypocrisy... and ultimately, they promote themselves or their so-called ministry rather than doing the work of the Lord.

Let these be warning signs to avoid those who seek to deceive. We also must remember that, though we are living in a war zone, God has not left us unprepared and alone. The enemy is not the only one observing us, for our God is also watching over us. Psalm 121:8 says, "The LORD shall preserve your going out and your coming in from this time forth, and even forevermore." God not only watches but protects every aspect and every moment of our life. That doesn't mean the enemy won't attempt to dissuade us; make no mistake, he will make every attempt to stop our pursuit of God. We need to keep faith and trust God because no matter what Satan may throw our way, God will turn it around and use it for His plan for our life (see Genesis 50:20).

The Gift of Discernment of Spirits

The gift of discernment of spirits is one of the nine gifts listed in 1 Corinthians 12:4 that are bestowed upon some believers. This gift provides the ability to distinguish between divine spirits (God), satanic spirits (the devil), and human spirits (a person's inner self). God gave this supernatural gift "for the profit of all," not solely for the individual (see 1 Corinthians 12:7).

What benefit does having an ability to distinguish spirits provide to us in our earthly realm? We remember that while we currently live on earth, events in the heavenly realm do impact our daily life. Spiritual beings move back and forth across the earth, as well as in the heavenlies. Their activities in our earthly realm are highly significant, particularly when aimed at robbing individuals of their divine purpose. The gift of discerning spirits is beneficial where deliverance is concerned, as it identifies the spirit at work in one's life.

Four Purposes for Discerning Spirits

Here are four main purposes for the ability to discern spirits below:

1. It provides a glimpse into the hidden spiritual world. To be effective spiritually, we may need to see into the spiritual realm to gain insight into the impact heavenly warfare is having in our earthly environment.

2. It aids in deliverance ministry. Spiritual discernment allows the identification of the spirit affecting someone's life, so we can remove it and free them from its control.

3. It enables us to see the heart rather than the outward appearance of what it appears in the flesh. God's perspective differs from ours: We judge by appearances, but God sees the heart (1 Samuel 16:7).

4. It exposes the enemy in his guise as an angel of light. This gift safeguards us against the deception of Satan and his demons, who masquerade as good while being inherently evil. Their purpose is always destruction.

Four Types of Spirits

There are four types of spirits this ability allows us to identify.

The Spirit of God
(Also Called the Holy Spirit)

Primarily, discernment helps us recognize the Holy Spirit's work within individuals, the church, and the world. It enables us to hear and know what the Spirit of God is saying, and positions us to be co-laborers with Him.

John 1:32–34 recounts John's recognition of the Holy Spirit: "I saw the Spirit descending from heaven like a dove and resting on Him." He explains, "I did not know Him, but the one who sent me to baptize with water told me, 'Whoever you see the Spirit descending upon and remaining on, this is He who baptizes with the Holy Spirit.'"

To discern the voice of the Holy Spirit, we need to understand that the perfect alignment of the Holy Spirit and the Word of God means the Holy Spirit will never contradict Scripture. We can ask these questions:

- Does the inner witness of my spirit confirm what I am hearing (see Romans 8:11)?
- Does it bring a sense of peace (see Colossians 3:15)?
- Is there confirmation through prophets (1 Thessalonians 5:19–21), through visions (Acts 2:17–18), through dreams (Job 33:14–15), or through signs and wonders (Mark 16:20)?

Angelic Spirits

Discernment provides us with the ability to see or recognize angels. Angels are spiritual beings who serve various roles as protectors, offer guidance, and as divine messengers. The Scriptures describe them as "ministering spirits whom God sends forth to minister for those who will inherit salvation" (Hebrews 1:14).

While the Bible does not provide a detailed description of the appearance of angels, how angels often greet a person with "Fear not" supports their large and otherworldly appearance. At times, they take on human form, and writers often describe them as having a presence that is both awe-inspiring and comforting. Jesus also mentioned the concept of guardian angels, stating that "their angels in heaven always see the face of my Father in heaven" (Matthew 18:10).

Demonic Spirits

Spiritual discernment shows a sharp understanding of demonic presence affecting a person or place. The presence of unclean spirits leaves a heavy and oppressive atmosphere. Depending on the spirit, those gifted in this area can discern the demon associated with it. For instance, a spirit of fear may create anxiety or impending doom in the atmosphere.

In Acts 13:9–10, Paul encountered a magician by the name of Elymas who opposed his teaching. Recognizing Elymas's evil intentions, Paul, filled with the Holy Spirit, rebuked him, calling him a deceitful servant of the devil, who opposes righteousness and perverts God's ways.

The Spirit of Man (Human Spirit)

We use discernment to discern the condition of the human spirit. Luke 13:10 tells of Jesus' teaching in the synagogues and where a woman who had a spirit of infirmity and could not stand upright for eighteen years. He called to her, saying, "Woman, you are loosed from your infirmity." As he laid His hands on her, she immediately recovered. This example shows His ability to discern the spiritual condition of people.

A Lying Spirit in a Civil War Uniform

One Friday evening, my home church invited another local home church to worship with us. The living room was our sanctuary as we entered into worship. Our celebratory dance shook the wooden floor of the old country home, and then one of our guests, Elaine, interrupted mid-song, "Is this home built on a Civil War battlefield?" Not waiting for a response, she continued, "You should do research on your property. You might be amazed at what you discover." On her face was a foreboding smirk as she asked, "Can we stop the music?"

The visiting home church leader, Andy, cut in and asked that the music be stopped. My friend Bo paused the worship video, freezing the words on the screen's waterfall backdrop. "There's a heavyset man with a beard sitting on the couch," Elaine said. "He's wearing a Civil War uniform and hat, but don't be alarmed. He's a friendly spirit and wants to stay and chill."

This was bordering on the edge of comical and utterly

unbelievable. I felt a burning passion rise within me but remained silent. Andy started pacing and suggested that everyone pray about why this Civil War spirit had come and what message he had for us. Hebrews 9:27 says, "It is appointed for men to die once, but after this the judgment," so dead humans do not remain on this earth as ghosts. That meant Elaine's Civil War spirit was a demon masquerading as a nineteenth-century soldier.

We had no reason to determine the purpose of the demon, as any message would be purely demonic. I looked around, hoping that one of my home church members would speak up, and then it hit me: I was the one that the Holy Spirit was speaking to. This was my *kairos* (critical/right) moment! I stood and faced the group. "I'm sorry, but this is outright demonic," I said, then confronted the spirit. "I rebuke you, lying spirit, and cast you out of this place in Jesus' name!"

Elaine kept silent. At first, she scowled, but then the grimace lifted and her expression became peaceful. Andy stood still without uttering a word. The intense silence broke when Maggie, our home church member, exclaimed, "Amen! Thank you, Jesus!" Several others joined in.

Discerning Spirits and Deliverance Ministry

Within the church, discerning spirits is an essential function. It reveals the spirits' origins, protecting us from spiritual deception. This gift reveals good and exposes evil, and discerning the move of the Holy Spirit provides confirmation that the manifestations are an outpouring of the Holy Spirit and not from a false spirit.

Discerning spirits is crucial in deliverance ministry. Before casting out spirits, we use spiritual discernment to identify those at work in a person's life. Discerning spirits enables us to recognize the spiritual entities at play and release those held captive. This gift will become increasingly important as we continue to move closer to the end times, as deception will run rampant in that perilous time.

Discerning Manifestations

The Holy Spirit can make His Presence known through the visible changes in a person's face and body when God touches them. However, not every change comes from the Holy Spirit.

The enemy mimics the things of God, and sometimes the human spirit copies the experience for attention. Some manifestations may seem unusual to our natural eyes, but that in itself doesn't make them invalid. In all circumstances we are to test the spirit and not just assume it is from God.

Here are some examples of manifestations likely to be encountered.

1. **Laughter**: 1 Peter 1:8 shows the manifestation of joy or laughter, saying, "Rejoice with joy that is inexpressible and filled with glory" in believing in Jesus. Believers sometimes express this experience by laughing during church services; this laughter is contagious and often spreads to many others. Now, is this a genuine showing of the Holy Spirit? It can be (there is Scripture to substantiate it), and it has the potential to glorify God. It also can result from a demonic spirit or even a human spirit seeking attention. Here, we must exercise discernment. I once observed a worship leader's brief, unrestrained laughter that was a manifestation of the Holy Spirit's presence and joy. I've also witnessed a group of well-meaning ladies rolling on the floor of the church and laughing like hyenas; they were disruptive and drew attention to themselves, evidence of another spirit manifesting. Just remember, just because something happens in a church setting doesn't mean it is from God.

2. **Travailing or groaning**: This manifestation is a believer groaning or making inarticulate sounds conveying pain or despair, such as we find when Jesus was in the garden of Gethsemane (see Luke 22:44). It is the spirit of the person crying out in agony and burdened over the prayer going forth, which again can result from the Holy Spirit. Romans 8:26 describes intercessory prayer that transcends words, expressing itself in inexpressible groanings. Yet, when discerned, we sometimes find another spirit at

work. I once witnessed several women at a Woman's Advance who were lying on the floor, holding their legs up in a labor position while travailing as though giving birth. While we pray in anguish for a spiritual birthing in our lives, the physical manifestation of birthing a baby was not scriptural and drew attention to themselves rather than God.

3. Being Speechless: This is simply being unable to speak or communicate. It can be from being overcome by the Holy Spirit or receiving a vision that renders the believer speechless (such as in Luke 1:22 where Zechariah receives a vision foretelling of his future child in his and his wife's old age). Don't assume silence is from the Holy Spirit, though; we must test the spirit discerningly.

4. Trembling and Shaking: This can cause full or partial body shaking similar to being extremely fearful. In Daniel 10:7-11, Daniel has a vision that leaves him trembling. Seeing, or being in the presence of the Spirit of God or even an angel, can leave us fearful and trembling. I experienced this while receiving prayer at a conference (and others also experienced trembling in varied degrees). We approved the prayer because the Holy Spirit led it and glorified God. Likewise, I also have witnessed a woman at a different conference who rapidly shook her head left to right, and right to left while prophesying. The Holy Spirit is gentle, and a violent act shows another spirit. In some churches, this had become quite popular, but it neither edifies the body of Christ nor gives God glory.

5. Weeping: This is characterized by intense crying or tears running down the face, and is another way the Holy Spirit presents Himself. Revelation 5:4 describes John weeping because no one was worthy to open the seal, and there are many reasons we may weep because of the Holy Spirit's touch on our lives. When I first came back to the Lord, I wept throughout every worship service for the next six months. The Holy Spirit was moving upon my heart, and the result of realizing the horrors of my previous spiritual state was overwhelming. I felt myself drawn nearer to God, and to Jesus to Whom be all glory, honor, and praise for that. Every situation and manifestation requires discernment.

6. Traveling in the Spirit: In Acts 8:39–40, Philip is taken up by the Holy Spirit and placed in Azotus, where he traveled and preached the gospel until he reached Caesarea. There are many Scriptures that tell of those who God has taken up into the heavenlies or other places, though it always is by God's own doing and for His purpose. Many years ago, I went to hear a well-known prophet speak, and while there, he took the entire conference on a spiritual journey. He gave vivid details of the heavens as he escorted us through them. Though I began the journey with everyone else, I quickly broke the trance which I sensed was falling on his listeners upon discerning the spirit of astral travel. We always need to test the spirit, even when being led by prominent prophets and evangelists. Such self-induced or man-made guided trances are not biblical; thus, another demonic spirit is the tour guide.

In this chapter, we discussed a critical warfare tactic that will be increasingly necessary in the coming days. Spiritual discernment is the key in knowing whether a spirit is from God or the devil, and will aid us in discerning the manifestations that are being displayed. From here, we move on to setting the captive free. Our focus will be on healing the brokenhearted.

PART IV

Set the Captives Free

Behind Enemy Lines

CHAPTER 14

Healing The Brokenhearted

Every one of us has been brokenhearted at one time or another. Mankind was created with the ability to develop an emotional bond in order to maintain relationships with God and with others. However, this ability also makes heartbreak an inevitable human experience. In the Bible, the "heart" is a metaphor for human emotion, intellect, and spirit or in other words, feelings, thoughts and God-given desires - God's will. Luke 4:18 declares Jesus' mission to "heal the brokenhearted"; this implies that He will bring comfort, healing, and restoration to those who are emotionally and spiritually wounded.

Repeated rejection, abuse, or other harm creates emotional wounds that require healing. On the cross, Jesus bore our griefs and sorrows. His wounds atoned for our transgressions, His bruises for our iniquities, and He suffered the punishment that brought us peace. Isaiah 53:4-5 says that His stripes heal us. In addition, a wounded soul will often house unforgiveness, blaming their pain and suffering on the person they believe caused the offense. The sins of unforgiveness and blaming another provide the legal right for demons to operate, and they are all too ready to take advantage. The open wound becomes the access point where they gain entry into the person's life.

God commissioned the church to continue the work of Jesus—healing the brokenhearted, casting out demons, and preaching the kingdom of God throughout the world (see Luke 4:18–19). Deliverance is the means by which we cast out demons and set the captives free from oppression. Healing the brokenhearted is the administration of prayer for healing the heart and soul by the laying on of hands.

The Wounded Soul

The primary cause of a "wounded soul" is experiencing significant trauma or deeply disturbing events, such as rejection, betrayal, abuse, abandonment, injustice, or prolonged exposure to stressful situations that overwhelm an individual's ability to cope. Trauma can also have a significant impact on a person's thoughts and feelings, to the point of causing negative thought patterns and an overwhelming emotional response.

Emotional trauma can result from a physical incident such as being caught in the middle of a hurricane, getting in a serious car wreck, or being subjected to a home invasion. The person may sustain physical injury, but even if no physical harm is suffered, emotional trauma can still affect them. It can also result from an emotional experience, such as rejection or unproductive criticism. The emotional pain encountered with rejection alone can be debilitating.

Let's look at rejection as an example of why trauma has such a devastating impact on our life. God has created us with a desire for love and acceptance, which creates within us a desire for Him, as only He can fulfill our needs. The enemy takes advantage of how God made us, and tricks us into seeking the love and acceptance only achievable through God in another person. Once a person fails us—and they undoubtedly will, because of their own human imperfections and our expectations placed on them—our soul becomes wounded, and if we're not careful, rejection becomes the stronghold that oppresses our life.

The trauma of rejection can happen at any age, but it is even more damaging for a child who hasn't yet developed the ability to process complex emotions. The traumatic experience not only becomes long-lasting but also may play a major role in their childhood development. In a child's life, rejection is the bully on the playground, in the school room, and, sadly, even in Sunday school. Rejection can come as a direct insult, resulting in feelings of inferiority or the subtle offense of being the unwanted player on the team. Either way, the sting on our identity is severe. But even more devastating to a child is parental rejection, resulting in feelings of being unworthy and unlovable. Many who have painful experiences of rejection in childhood or parental criticism often develop avoidance behaviors that rob them of the ability to experience meaningful relationships later in life.

Consequences of Trauma

One consequence of emotional trauma is the soul wound, which lead to an array of upheavals, such as depression, repressed emotions, difficulty managing emotions, flashbacks (recurring negative memories), inflicting self-harm (cutting), insecurity, inferiority, mood swings, auditory hallucinations, suicidal thoughts, and post-traumatic stress disorder (PTSD).

There are also physical consequences of a wounded soul, as traumatic symptoms can have an adverse effect on the body causing a suppressed immune system. Included are such disorders as thyroid disease, digestive disorders, tendonitis, arthritis, chronic pain syndromes, hormonal imbalances, sleep disturbances, and an inability to maintain a healthy weight. When physical conditions result from soul wounds, prayer for emotional healing will often cause the body's restoration as well. Seek the Holy Spirit's guidance in diagnosing the source of the ailment, either spiritual or physical, before initiating healing prayer.

Emotional Reactions to Trauma

When we experience emotional pain, our body can respond with a wide range of emotional reactions because of our natural coping mechanism. It is our body's way of processing overwhelming stress and potential safety threats. However, emotional reactions usually resolve on their own. If they don't, they may result from soul wounds accompanied by other indicators, such as self-defense (putting up defenses around oneself), unpredictable emotions (unprovoked changes in mood, emotional state, or responses), flashbacks (reliving a past traumatic event), social withdrawal (the avoidance of social interactions), isolation (detachment from others), and self-blame (attributing the occurrence of a stressful event or outcome to themselves). Pray for each of these.

Spiritual Reactions to Trauma

Besides the emotional and physical reactions of trauma, we also experience spiritual reactions. Spiritual struggles that result from trauma often incite us to reevaluate our faith and, more importantly, our relationship with God. Because of our traumatic experience, we may question God's role in our suffering, or question why an all-powerful God would allow it to happen. Some may feel they are being punished for some wrong they have done. Or in the wake of being the recipient of an ungodly act, they may experience guilt in their innocence. This can lead to confusion or a spiritual identity crisis. To make matters worse, if the trauma occurred within the church setting, losing fellowship and support can be devastating.

Classifying Traumatic Experiences

Emotional trauma can occur because of a single event (called acute trauma), repeated and prolonged events (called chronic trauma), or exposure to multiple invasive events (called complex trauma). We can classify trauma into two categories: intentional and unintentional. An individual or a group of individuals who intentionally cause harm to another person often cause intentional trauma. These traumatic events include physical or emotional abuse, sexual abuse or molestation, and domestic violence or terrorism. Unintentional traumas occur without an intent to harm, such as accidents, natural disasters, or sicknesses. External factors like natural disasters and traffic accidents, as well as internal factors like medical emergencies and death, can all be causes.

The Root of the Problem

In order for us to engage in any intimate relationship, a certain level of vulnerability is necessary, which means we place ourselves at risk of being emotionally hurt, yet this vulnerability enables us to develop a deep connection with God and another person. The problem, then, is not that we have traumatic experiences, for God has designed a natural response mechanism for our bodies to react that will promote healing in such an event. Rather, it's when the enemy plays on our vulnerability, and uses trauma as a trigger to deceive us into reacting in unhealthy or ungodly ways that then open the door for the flesh, worldly influences, and eventually the enemy to gain a foothold in our lives. In time, his hold will increase, stunting our spiritual growth, hindering our God-given purpose in life, and stifling our relationship with God.

Isn't Deliverance Enough?

Once a person receives deliverance and has demonic influences cast out of their life, we often discover the underlying damage they left behind. Festering wounds often remain in the spaces they once occupied. If ignored, they can simulate the same symptoms as the previous demonization, leaving the person to believe the deliverance was unsuccessful when, in fact, the demons have gone. The wounds on the soul, which comprise the mind, the will, and emotions, need healing to close the offense to the soul and restore the person to wholeness. Having open wounds is also a means by which dislodged demons will return. Many times, it was the original source that gave access to them. Healing cleanses the defilement, promotes mending of the wounds, and resolves heart issues, thus strengthening the person's resistance.

However, sometimes, such as when a person going through deliverance cannot forgive, it's best to heal the soul first, as unforgiveness will hinder their deliverance. After we administer healing and the person forgives, we resume deliverance to set them free. I can't overemphasize the importance of discernment in every healing and deliverance session, because there is no set formula to follow. God moves by His Spirit and is all-knowing; therefore, He knows the best course of action we should take.

Healing the Wounded Soul

Isaiah 61:1 refers to "binding the brokenhearted," which describes God's desire that we bring healing and restoration to the lives of the emotionally distressed. In this context, "binding" applies to the act of wrapping or applying bandages to wounds to promote healing, implying God's ability to mend the emotional pain and suffering of those crushed in spirit and provide comfort for their souls. This verse was fulfilled by Jesus, the Great Physician. His healing comes to us by His blood, stripes, and wounds, or by applying pardoning grace to those in need. He binds up their wounds or their "griefs" to ease their pain and bring them peace.

There's an important point to make here. The Scriptures say Jesus will bind (or wrap to soothe and promote healing), proclaim liberty, and recover sight. It doesn't say He is going to erase memories or change the course of past events. Often, we're looking for an easy way out and expect some sort of magic wand to zap the source of our pain out of existence. That's not how healing works. There's no going back in time and undoing what has already been done. Rather, it's applying a healing balm to comfort and protect the injury from reoccurring friction that causes inflammation, which prevents healing from occurring. It's the forgiveness that He extends to us for our past transgressions that then enables us to forgive and release others for the offense they have caused us. This frees us from harboring bitterness, which otherwise holds us in bondage to the past.

We don't change our past; instead, we release it to God, who then restores our heart. He then does what He does best: transforms us into His likeness. Our wounds don't disappear. Rather, they become scars that have healed and testify to His goodness. Think of our resurrected Jesus revealing his nail-pierced hands to doubting Thomas. Even His resurrected body displayed a remnant of the suffering He had gone through, yet His once painful wounds had become scars of glory.

As believers, many of us have experienced Jesus' healing of our own broken heart. At the church I attended years ago, Carole, my pastor's wife, was my spiritual mom, and the Lord used her to administer healing to many. The prayer for healing and the instruction I received during my time at that church, along with the calling of Isaiah 61 over my life, is why I share what I've received today. As ex-wounded warriors, we've been sent forth to speak healing to the brokenhearted. By applying the "healing balm of Gilead" (or the blood of Jesus, for "by His stripes we are healed") we can pray to soothe wounds and, in Jesus' name, bind and restore broken hearts (see Psalm 147:3).

Healing the Brokenhearted

As believers, God has anointed us to share in Jesus' ministry; therefore, we pray and speak healing to the brokenhearted, release to the captive, sight to the blind, and liberty to the oppressed. We begin by lifting the name of Jesus, reading Scriptures, and offering thanksgiving. Then we submit ourselves to be an instrument of healing, and sing songs of praise, healing, and restoration. We pray for God's presence, and ask the Holy Spirit to work through us to bring healing to the soul held captive by oppression, to bind the brokenhearted, to break every stronghold, and to release them from the powers of darkness. We do this by praying for direction from the Holy Spirit and then using our own words.

According to the *Set The Captives Free* training workbook, an early resource I used, after prayer and forgiveness, we should petition the Holy Spirit for insight into the person's heart. Within it, my pastor explains his vision of heart damage in diverse states, including a stony (hardened) heart, a divided heart (God vs. mammon), and a non-beating heart (needing revival). He suggests in every case, we should pray that if the enemy attempts to bring back that hurtful memory, the person would instead remember how Jesus healed them and praise God for it. The enemy, knowing this result, would stop attacking. The testimonies from those receiving this kind of prayer are universally the same—no more memory, no more pain or sorrow from past wounds.[40]

Practical Steps for Healing a Broken Heart

Begin by assuring the prayer recipient of confidentiality throughout the session.

1. Pray for healing of the prayer recipient's heart, using the gift of discernment and the word of knowledge to reveal the source of emotional pain or brokenness. It may be a person who has hurt them or a situation that has caused them grief. These hurts can be recent, but they also could have occurred years before. The person may even believe they had already forgiven the person and moved on, but through prayer, the Holy Spirit reveals a deep wound that is still festering. As these incidents come to the surface, the person may relive the emotional pain to a degree. It's important to offer them emotional support as they share the burdens on their heart.

2. As the emotional pain is revealed, lead the person in prayer for forgiveness. They should name the person or event, acknowledge the offense, verbally forgive (or willingness to forgive) both the person(s) and offense, and release the offender to the Lord, ending any further blame. A quote from Max Lucado that comes to mind is "Forgiveness is unlocking the door to set someone free and realizing you were the prisoner."[41]

3. If the person receiving prayer can't forgive, ask if they're willing to forgive. This shows they recognize the importance of forgiveness and that, while the burden feels too heavy to bear, they desire the ability to forgive. Pray and ask the Lord to enable them with the help of the Holy Spirit to "let go" and "lay down" the person or event that has hurt them, at the feet of Jesus so He can carry those burdens away.

---

[40] Larry Arendas, *Set the Captives Free!: A Biblical Solution for Compulsive Behavior and Emotional Trauma* (Unpublished, 1980c), 6-3, 6-4.
[41] "All MAX LUCADO quotes about Forgiveness," Inspiring Quotes, accessed July 16, 2025, https://www.inspiringquotes.us/author/2271-max-lucado/about-forgiveness.

4. When injuries are significant enough to cause repressed memories, the prayer recipient may not remember what caused their hurt. In that case, bind the spirit of fear, and the spirit of heaviness as well as any lesser spirits of anxiety, and any torment and/or nightmares as revealed by the Holy Spirit, as these tend to manifest from repressed emotions. Pray for the Holy Spirit to expose the root of the hidden memory and guide you in addressing it. Allow time for the Holy Spirit to move.

5. Once the person prayed for has forgiven those who wronged them, it's crucial to remember that we often blame ourselves for the negative emotions we harbor. We may even blame ourselves for the actual offense. Even harder to admit, we may blame God for allowing the painful experience. After this is explained to the person receiving prayer, they may express and confirm any blame they hold toward themselves or God. These emotional responses are typical—so much so that we'll include them as part of our prayer.

6. Lead the person in prayer, asking for forgiveness for self-blame, for the negative effects of their hurt on themselves and others (including the offender), and for blaming God for the offense and its lasting impact.

7. Pray to break any stronghold or power of darkness that is holding the person in bondage through past trauma or unforgiveness, thus setting them free and enabling their healing.

8. Lay hands on the person being prayed for and anoint their head or forehead with healing oil. Begin praying as the Spirit leads, with this as a framework:
- Pray for (person's name) for (indicate wounded areas) and associated sorrow and pain.
- Pray against any hurt lingering in the heart, preventing healing and hindering its recovery.
- Pray for the release of healing and the closing of the wounds.

9. Ask the Holy Spirit to reveal the condition of the person's

heart, then pray according to His direction.

- For a hardened heart, ask the Lord to replace their stony heart with a compassionate one, as described in Ezekiel 36:26: "A new heart will I give you, and a new spirit will I put within you."
- For a devastated heart, pray God will restore their shattered heart and make them whole. Psalm 34:18 says, "The Lord is near to the brokenhearted and saves those who are crushed in spirit" (NASB).
- For a divided heart, pray against the heart being torn in two directions—between godliness and worldliness. Pray for undivided focus and for the heart to be unified. Psalm 86:11 says, "Teach me your way, O Lord, that I may walk in your truth; give me an undivided heart, that I may fear your name" (NASB).

10. Allow the Holy Spirit to flow through you, and pray for the healing of any other hurts or trauma revealed. Ask Jesus to

- Touch the wounds with His healing power.
- Anoint the wounds with (supernatural) healing balm to soothe the pain.
- Bind up all wounds to promote the healing process.
- Restore the heart to wholeness.

Closing Prayer

We then affirm the prayer recipient's true identity in Christ by sharing these biblical affirmations with them. They can also repeat them using "I" instead of "you," thus affirming and fully embracing them for themselves.

- You are His beloved (Romans 9:25), His chosen before the creation of the world (Ephesians 1:4–6).
- You are a child of God (1 John 3:1).
- God is for you, not against you (Romans 8:31), and He loves you as you are (Romans 5:8).

- God created you for good works (Colossians 3:12).
- You are a new creation (2 Corinthians 5:17).
- God forgave you (Colossians 1:14), and He is unashamed to call you His own (Hebrews 2:11).

Send the person who received prayer off with blessings and a psalm or song of healing. Many hearts find restoration through worshipping Him.

Suggested blessings include

- the garment of praise (anoint with the Holy Spirit's oil of gladness);
- God's Word to nourish their spirit (increase wisdom in the Word);
- increased faith and renewed vision for life;
- to be filled with peace (the peace that surpasses all understanding [Philippians 4:7]); and
- increase in strength (see Isaiah 40:29–31).

Personal Testimony of a Healed Broken Heart

In my Christian walk, I wanted nothing more than to glorify God in my life, my marriage, and my family. But about a year after the wedding, the happy marriage I had hoped for fell apart at the seams. In time, I no longer knew the man I had married, and life became a downhill battle filled with muck and mire ranging from undiagnosed mental illness to compulsive lying and poverty. After years of heartache and pain, I gave up all my hopes and dreams, fell for the enemy's lie, and ended up in a backslidden state. It would be many years before God rescued me from the claws of Satan.

Upon being restored in the faith, I tried to evaluate how I went from wanting nothing but to glorify God to degrading myself to the depths of darkness. Scripture says, "No temptation has overtaken you except such as is common to man; but God is faithful, who will not allow you to be tempted beyond what you are able, but with the temptation will also make the way of escape, that you may be able to bear it" (1 Corinthians 10:13). That verse confused me because the challenge seemed insurmountable; I didn't endure it, and I fell from grace. Years later, I still lacked understanding. And, I put my trust in God, believing I might never know the answer in this lifetime, resigned to the fact that He must have had a bigger plan or purpose.

While reviewing employee benefits online one afternoon, I discovered the name of an old acquaintance. We were colleagues when I was unmarried, and upon his hiring, I believed he was identical to the type of husband I had prayed for.

You can imagine my shock when we talked, and I found out he was a Christian, with a heart sold out to Jesus. I became really uncomfortable as we shared small talk and got acquainted in the office, so I put up a shield because I was in a relationship and we had discussed marriage. Looking back, I missed so many red flags, but I believed I was with the right person because even my pastor's wife thought our hearts were compatible. I got married, had a child, and left work.

The last I had heard about my office friend was years later when I ran into a mutual friend. I learned he had married a few years after I'd left, and had five children all attending a Christian school.

On that day, I learned that my office friend had just retired a few years earlier from an executive position with the same agency where we had worked at. He had an outstandingly successful career, and true blessings came his way. For a second, I questioned what my life would have been like if I had gone with my gut feeling years before and broken off the relationship I was in.

If nothing else, it would have saved years of heartache and a divorce. Perhaps it might have even prevented my fall from grace. That's what brought me to the question of "Why did God allow me to go through such turmoil?" Time had surely proved I hadn't had the ability to endure.

There in the quiet of my room, God spoke to my heart, "This was My plan for you. [My former coworker was on the computer screen in front of me.] But you chose not to take it." A well of emotion erupted within me, not because of regret but because it meant that my God hadn't set me up for a life full of pitfalls. No, what He had for me was good—very good—but I didn't take it. What I chose instead took me down a road I couldn't endure, but even there, God never left me, nor forsook me. And when He saved me from the mess that I had made, He gave me the desire of my heart from the beginning. He took my life and made it a testimony for *His* glory. He truly has been so good to me. And that is how God mended my broken heart and cause me to fall deeper in love with my first love—Him—all over again.

At that moment, the oil of gladness filled my heart, and it still brings joy to me today. Just knowing that God truly had a better plan for my life that was full of His goodness is more than enough. Psalm 30:5 says, "Weeping may endure for the night, but joy comes in the morning," and praise God, morning had dawned for me! Jesus came to heal the brokenhearted, and no matter what pain you may have endured, He will turn your sorrow into joy and set your feet to dancing (see Psalm 30:11). But that's not all, for you too are anointed to administer His healing to others in need. The next chapter will teach us how to break curses over ours and others' lives.

Behind Enemy Lines

CHAPTER 15

Breaking Curses

Are curses real? And if so, can they harm you? First, let's define that we're talking about words that supernaturally invoke a harmful or negative result. Being under a curse, a person suffers the repercussions of the evil spoken against them. Sickness, tragedy, or other dire circumstances can occur because of the curse.

Curses come in many forms. They can be God's curses, ancestral curses, or curses cast by others. Let's take a brief look at some of them.

The Earned Curse

With the fall of mankind (Genesis 3:14–22) comes the first known curse. We hear many arguments questioning how a loving God would create man and then put a curse upon him, but that assumption is unfair and is another twisted view from the devil who is continuing his attack today just as he did in the garden. We all know the garden story, and how Adam and Eve fell for Satan's temptation by partaking of the forbidden fruit from the tree of knowledge of good and evil.

This was more than just getting caught with your hand in the cookie jar. Genesis 3:22 reveals that this fruit caused mankind to be "like one of us" ("us" being the Trinity) and to know "good

~ 215

from evil." So captivating was the thought of receiving divine knowledge that Adam and Eve disobeyed God, as if they were fit to be gods. That same mindset caused Satan's ruin, and he still uses it to tempt mankind today. Adam and Eve's newfound knowledge revealed the evil that had befallen them, a result far different from what they expected. The result of their disobedience was their expulsion.

Yet, what might seem harsh in their expulsion was actually an act of love by our heavenly Father. For man, now having consumed knowledge to be "like God," became self-focused and self-sufficient, believing he had the knowledge to be independent of God and could make it on his own according to his own will. This truly was the curse of mankind, for he was no longer content with the will of his Creator; rather, he pridefully indulged in self-will. Had God permitted Adam and Eve to live forever under those conditions, having eaten from the tree of life, they would have lived forever in this cursed state. Instead, God prepared a way to break the curse of death and provide the means of forgiveness and life eternal through His Son, Jesus Christ.

The Broken Curse

Think of the same garden story. When Adam and Eve sinned, it exposed them to an evil that, until then, they had been unaware of. It enabled self-determination to replace their trust in God. They now had to contend with the sinful temptation that God had never intended for them, and even worse, they had to do so in an environment outside of the garden. Their children, and their children's children and ultimately the entire human race, were now born with the ability to see not only good but also evil. Thus, they would struggle between the will of their Maker and the self-will of their flesh while the curse lay teetering on the balance. The odds were against them, except for God's redemption.

God provided the means for mankind to be redeemed from the curse. Galatians 3:13 (KJV) tells us, "Christ hath redeemed us from the curse of the law, being made a curse for us: for it is written, Cursed is every one that hangeth on a tree" (see Deuteronomy

21:23). Jesus bore our sins upon the cross and became the curse so that we would be free from condemnation. For believers, faith can break the law's curse, releasing us from the curse of sin and death. It is imperative to break all curses if the believer exercises their authority in the name of Jesus and prays, *"In the name of Jesus I break the curses of _____ , _____."*

However, although God lifted the curse from us, and we broke the curses in the authority of Jesus' name, we still struggle with sin and rebellion against God (see Romans 7:14–25). Breaking curses won't stop temptation. One quick look around will tell us that the broken curse didn't immediately return our world to paradise. We still live in a fallen world, subject to its consequences because of mankind's sin (see Genesis 1–2). Our physical bodies still die and return to the dust of the earth; it is our spirits that are no longer subject to the curse of sin and death as our promise of eternal life awaits us in the heavenly kingdom. In other words, God provided a way out for us and we'll return to paradise in eternity.

Although God defeated Satan, He has not yet cast him into the lake of fire, which means he and his demons are still active on the earth and meddling in our lives (see Luke 9:1; Acts 10:38). Jesus' redemption did not eliminate evil spirits, but believers now possess authority over them (see Matthew 10:8; Luke 10:18). Remember the delegated authority we discussed in chapter ten? Those who do not walk in faith and obedience leave themselves subject to the law of sin and death (see James 4:7–8) and physical suffering (see Hebrews 12:1–3).

The analogy of a storehouse describes it well. The thief knows that he legally has no right to enter the storehouse, much less take anything, but if he can gain access, he'll enter anyway and take what he wants. He'll keep going back, taking more and causing havoc. You see, the thief doesn't care that he's doing something illegal, and as long as he has access, he'll continue freeloading from the storehouse. The moment someone in authority confronts him is the moment his freeloading stops. Of course, possessing authority is useless unless we exercise it.

The Modern-Day Abrahamic Curse

While the redeemed have escaped the law of sin and death and have the promise of eternal life, some mistakenly forget that the curse over the law of sin and death isn't the only curse that's been imposed. Many curses are still active today. Genesis 12:3 is one example: "I will bless those who bless you, and I will curse him who curses you; and in you all the families of the earth shall be blessed." God promised to make Abram a great nation, which was the beginning of the nation of Israel. Reviewing Israel's history reveals that those opposing the nation faced curses, while those blessing it received blessings. The United States of America is an extremely blessed nation, and we are also the nation that supports Israel most. This is the blessing of God fulfilled through the Abrahamic Covenant.

A modern-day example of the Abrahamic curse fell upon a member of the Turkish Parliament on December 14, 2023. He stood at a podium in front of the parliament, condemning Israel for defending itself against the terror of Hamas. Right after he concluded his speech by cursing Israel, he immediately died from a heart attack while still at the podium.[42]

Another such example of one who fell under this curse was Iranian president Ebrahim Raisi, ironically named after the father of the Jewish people, who became the first Iranian leader to launch a missile attack on Israel. Israel responded with restraint, yet President Raisi cursed Israel, saying that if Israel did anything, there would be nothing left of the "Zionist regime." He threatened to destroy Israel after sending death and destruction through the skies. One month later, on May 19, 2024, President Raisi met his own death when his helicopter mysteriously fell from the sky and crashed into a mountainside.[43]

These are just a few examples of the many curses that result

---

[42] Christians Hangout, "Turkish MP D#es | What you get for Cursing ISRAEL | Jonathan Cahn," YouTube, March 4, 2024, https://www.youtube.com/watch?v=15EoU-8JuGgQ.

[43] Jonathan Cahn Official, "The Curse That Struck Down the Iranian President | Jonathan Cahn," YouTube, June 7, 2024, https://www.youtube.com/watch?v=azJ-FgF-hWuk.

from our disobedience and rebellion. In addition, some curses result from people placing curses on one another. Noah cursed Canaan over the lewdness of his father, Ham (see Genesis 9:25). Elisha called down a curse on a threatening gang of youth who ended up mauled to death by a bear (see 2 Kings 2:23). And Saul cursed the Israelite troops if they ate before he avenged himself on his enemies (see 1 Samuel 14:24). Those curses had results that should caution us in the verbiage we use against one another.

The Generational Curse

A generational curse is a curse on a family that passes from generation to generation. People's cry against generational curses begins in much the same way as the cry against the Adamic curse: Why would a loving God curse children for the sins of their fathers and ancestors? Exodus 20:5 and Leviticus 26:40, are just two of the verses that speak of the iniquity of the fathers being visited upon the children, but neither scripture ends there.

If we read these passages in their entirety, we find the children who were being judged either persisted in rebellion against God or exhibited learned aggressive behavior, not inherited guilt. We now get a better understanding that God wasn't passing judgment on innocent children, but rather those who repeated the sins of their fathers. There's a big difference.

Still, while the weight of guilt doesn't fall on us for our ancestors' sins, we do still inherit a propensity to sin. Galatians 3:10–13 says that we still fall under the curse of the law for our own sins and we escape only because of our faith in Christ who "hath redeemed us from the curse of the law" (KJV). That's good news, considering ancestral sins pass down through a long list of generations. But does that mean we are exempt from generational curses? No, for curses result from the presence of sin on earth, and we are not exempt from the physical consequences of that sin. It means our faith in Jesus will keep us from eternal death, although we still suffer from our ancestors' past mistakes here on earth.

So, what exactly does a generational curse look like?

It could be verbal abuse or negative labeling within a family that is passed down through generations, which just goes to show that words are powerful. This type of abuse creates a cycle where children grow up and repeat the same behavior as their parents, creating a harmful dynamic that not only affects their self-esteem but also their mental and spiritual health.

Another example could be a father who is an alcoholic. His children grow up in an environment of substance abuse and are at least twice as likely to develop an alcohol or drug dependence as the general population.[44] So, does the spirit of addiction jump from clinging to the father's back to the child's back? Not exactly. It would be more the spiritual influence of addiction follows the family line—a presence that lingers, waiting for a foothold opportunity to invade (this is more commonly known as a predisposition). The child still has a choice to resist these tendencies, but their upbringing and environment play a role in the choice they make.

Then there is my example. My great-aunt was a bishop of a Spiritualist church. She engaged in divination and other occult practices, and so I had a family lineage of witchcraft. My mom was a Christian, and I was brought up in the Christian faith. In short, we avoided "that side of the family." I had a rebellious streak and was quite the disobedient child, and a look into my mom's past shows the source of that rebellion. For some time, my family had a spirit of rebellion influencing our behavior line.

Now, here's the interesting part. I became a Spirit-filled believer and willingly went through a deliverance session that cast out generational demonic influences in my life. This breaking of the generational curse removed the influence of the spirit of rebellion within me. But then years later, I got caught up in various circumstances that made me doubt God, and that rebellious spirit came right back. This time, it gained a foothold, which quickly became a stronghold of witchcraft. It was a generational spirit that once again had to be cast out of my life. So, two things to consider:

---

44   J. M. Solis, J. M. Shadur, A. R. Burns, and A. M. Hussong, "Understanding the Diverse Needs of Children Whose Parents Abuse Substances," Bentham Science, 2012, https://doi.org/10.2174/1874473711205020135.

First, spiritual influences do flow down family lineages, waiting for opportunities to invade, and second, just because they've been cast out once, doesn't mean they won't come back if the person doesn't keep their temple filled and their doors locked.

Interestingly, recent science has drawn the connection between heredity and a predisposition to certain behaviors. Research has shown that polygenic inheritance, or multiple gene factors, are what influence the transmission of addiction from one generation to the next.[45] But while genetics plays a valuable part, combined with epigenetics (environmental influence) that aid in the transition from use to abuse via neuroadaptations occurring within the brain, a generational curse surely links to addiction, and science is only beginning to understand the hereditary factor.[46] Still, this does not mean that every child born to an alcoholic will become one themselves. The predisposition of the curse lies dormant, and the child will come to a point of making their own choice to follow in their parent's footsteps or break the curse.

Curses Cast Against Us

For the rest of this chapter, we will refer to a curse as something spoken by one of Satan's servants. In witchcraft, a curse is when someone casts a spell with malicious intent on a person or family. With witchcraft out of the broom closet in the Western Hemisphere and visible to the public eye, people may not be as skeptical of its existence but may still disregard its power. Make no mistake, spells are often effective. Satan has limited power, and he'll use demonic influences and humans to disperse evil.

There are some who believe that a spell only appears to work because the person fears something bad will happen, and when something does, they attribute it to a spell that most likely had nothing to do with it. But I can tell you that I've seen many spells

---

45 "The Role of Genetics in Addiction," University of Pennsylvania Health System, accessed June 12, 2025, https://www.uphs.upenn.edu/addiction/berman/genetic/.
46 H. R. Krishnan, A. J. Sakharkar, T. L. Teppen, T. D. Berkel, and S. C. Pandey, "The epigenetic landscape of alcoholism," *International Review of Neurobiology*, 2014, 75–116, https://doi.org/10.1016/b978-0-12-801311-3.00003-2.

work, with or without the recipient's knowledge. One thing fear does is cause weakness in one's armor and provide easier access, which the magickal practitioner will take full advantage of.

Fear is one way a Christian can allow a spell to affect them. Fear is not of God, and when we allow fear in, we've opened the door and walked right into the line of a fiery dart. Fear is a stronghold that we must tear down immediately. If someone curses us in plain sight, we need to reject and rebuke it in Jesus' name. While we don't want to give in to fear, we also want to take it seriously. Let's examine the story of Balaam.

In Numbers 22:10-17, Balaam started out in the Spirit of the Lord, a prophet whom God confirmed. However, after making some bad choices, he became a false prophet who dabbled in witchcraft. Although Balaam was wicked, God used him to speak some prophecies. Then Balak, the king of Moab, driven by fear for his kingdom, sought to curse the Israelites as they journeyed toward Canaan. He employed Balaam to place a curse on the Israelites, prompting Balaam's departure.

As Balaam was traveling to Moab, an angel of God stopped him three times. His donkey refused to proceed and then collapsed. He then beat the donkey until God granted it speech. At that moment, God revealed to Balaam an angel on the road and commanded him to pronounce only blessings on the Israelites. Continuing on his journey, Balaam attempted to do as the king wanted, but upon seeing the Israelites, he blessed them rather than cursing them. Balak then fired him, resulting in Balaam cursing both Balak and his kingdom.

We can look at a story where a donkey talks, and a prophet cannot utter a curse against a nation as suspect and lacking any genuine power. However, God did not view these curses as empty, powerless words. Instead, He viewed them as a serious threat to Israel—so much so that He intervened and turned Balaam's curses into blessings. Therefore, if someone curses us, we must take the threat seriously and seek God's protection, and standing on the promise of Proverbs 26:2, trusting the Lord will intervene and bless us instead.

All too often, we stop reading the story here, content with the concept that we need not concern ourselves with Satan's or his servants' curses. But the story of Balaam and Israel doesn't end there, and we simply cannot put our guard down. Having failed to appease Balak by cursing Israel, Balaam resorted to his second tactic. He advised Balak to use the Moabite women to ensnare the Israelite men into sexual immorality and idolatry. This second tactic succeeded.

This left no need to curse the Israelites, for by breaking the first commandment of God, they brought God's own curse upon themselves. A plague broke out immediately and 24,000 perished (see Numbers 25). Satan cunningly used man's own selfish desires for their demise. Mankind so foolishly bit into a forbidden fruit that looked appealing to his eyes but was poison to his soul—and the same thing continues to happen today. We must remain vigilant because the devil plays dirty.

The story of Balaam provides a crucial warning for believers. Christians living in obedience to God and in harmony with one another can expect God's protection against curses spoken against them, but those who are disobedient to God, or engage in sinful behaviors, have stepped out from under God's protection, leaving themselves vulnerable to the enemy's attacks. Those who receive a curse spoken over them have provided the legal ground for the curse to come upon them. We must keep our gear intact and resist the enemy at every angle.

Symptoms of Curses

The following is a list of calamities that indicate a curse may be at work. Experiencing one symptom on this list doesn't mean a person is definitely cursed. However, a recurring calamity, or several occurring at once, certainly warrants a prayerful Spirit-led diagnosis.

- Mental or emotional breakdown
- Barrenness (infertility or menstrual problems)
- Sickness (chronic, undiagnosed, or hereditary)

- Addictions (alcohol, drugs, occultism, sex)
- Poverty (financial insufficiency)
- Marriage/family breakdown (divorce)
- Misfortunes (accident prone)
- Unnatural or untimely death (including suicide)

Breaking the Power of Curses

Once a curse has come upon us, it will not leave on its own. Therefore, to break its hold on our lives, we must first identify it. A curse is a curse, and breaking a curse is the same no matter how it came into our life. The first step in removing a curse is by the cross of Jesus, as His work upon the cross removes the legal ground of any curse placed upon us. If you haven't yet experienced salvation, professing your faith in Jesus is where you start. Romans 10:10 says, "For with the heart one believes unto righteousness, and with the mouth confession is made unto salvation." Both believers and those professing faith in Jesus for the first time begin at the foot of the cross. The following six steps for breaking curses are adapted from my pastor's *Set The Captives Free* training workbook.[47]

Break the Power of Curses Over You

Begin by assuring the prayer recipient of confidentiality throughout the session.

1. Pray acknowledging your belief that Jesus, the Son of God, died on the cross for forgiveness of your sins, and that He rose from the dead in fulfillment of the Scriptures so that you may have eternal life.

2. Repent and ask forgiveness for any sins, rebellion, disobedience, or idolatry, including any occult involvement or any other area you may have allowed the devil to gain a foothold.

3. Forgive those who have hurt you.

---

[47] Larry Arendas, *Set the Captives Free!: A Biblical Solution for Compulsive Behavior and Emotional Trauma.*

4. Renounce and break any curses written, spoken, or unspoken, and any symbols or objects with curses attached or transferred to you, whether through personal disobedience, generational lineage, or external forces, by the power of Jesus' shed blood and the fullness of His work on the cross, in Jesus' name: "In the name of Jesus, I break all (generational/self-inflicted/cultural/witchcraft) curses over me."

5. Command all demonic spirits that have gained access to you through curses to be removed from you and your household, in Jesus' name.

6. Pray a blessing over anyone who has cursed you, and claim every spiritual blessing that our heavenly Father has for you, to be restored unto you (see Ephesians 1:3).

In closing, pray Psalm 91 as your prayer:

He who dwells in the secret place of the Most High

Shall abide under the shadow of the Almighty.

I will say of the Lord, "He is my refuge and my fortress;

My God, in Him I will trust."

Surely He shall deliver you from the snare of the fowler

And from the perilous pestilence.

He shall cover you with His feathers,

And under His wings you shall take refuge;

His truth shall be your shield and buckler.

You shall not be afraid of the terror by night,

Nor of the arrow that flies by day,

Nor of the pestilence that walks in darkness,

Nor of the destruction that lays waste at noonday.

A thousand may fall at your side,

And ten thousand at your right hand;

But it shall not come near you.

Only with your eyes shall you look,
And see the reward of the wicked.
Because you have made the LORD, who is my refuge,
Even the Most High, your dwelling place,
No evil shall befall you,
Nor shall any plague come near your dwelling;
For He shall give His angels charge over you,
To keep you in all your ways.
In their hands they shall bear you up,
Lest you dash your foot against a stone.
You shall tread upon the lion and the cobra,
The young lion and the serpent you shall trample underfoot.
"Because he has set his love upon Me, therefore I will deliver him;
I will set him on high, because he has known My name.
He shall call upon Me, and I will answer him;
I will be with him in trouble;
I will deliver him and honor him.
With long life I will satisfy him,
And show him My salvation."

Three distinct types of curses exist: generational curses, cast curses, and earned curses. We have reviewed all three, including symptoms that indicate a potential curse may be at work in someone's life. Many people don't take curses seriously, but as we learned from the story of Balaam, God takes curses seriously, and so should we. The important thing is to recognize them and then break them. Now let's explore the ministry of deliverance.

CHAPTER 16

Deliver Us From Evil

Deliverance is a significant aspect of spiritual warfare that focuses on setting the captive free. Believers often consider it offensive spiritual warfare—breaking up legal grounds, tearing down strongholds, and casting out demonic spirits to free individuals from demonic bondage. It moves beyond preventive measures of spiritual warfare, such as guarding oneself against the strategies and schemes of the enemy, and engages in the direct conflict of casting out demons from an individual. In Matthew 10, Jesus commanded His disciples to heal the sick and cast out demons as part of their mission to preach the gospel. In most churches, this seems to be overlooked, and they don't preach healing and deliverance, let alone practice it. But by doing so, they deny the commandment of Jesus. Healing and deliverance are not negotiable; they're a command.

Atmospheric Attack

Luke 8:22–25 recounts Jesus casting out a legion of demons from the Gerasene demoniac man, but I want to direct your attention first to where Jesus and his disciples have stepped into the boat and are sailing across the lake where they will encounter the depraved man. On the way, Jesus falls asleep, and a windstorm comes upon them, filling the boat with water. The disciples (some of whom were fishermen) were terrified and woke Jesus, who rebuked the wind and raging water, causing the storm to cease, and there was sudden calm. This is an excellent example of the pre-deliverance harassment one may encounter when the demons realize their impending doom. Perhaps the boat would capsize, or at the very least Jesus and the disciples could return to shore, escaping the atmospheric attack. But even the wind and waves obeyed Jesus, and once He stepped foot on land, the Gerasene demoniac man fell on the ground before Him, begging not to be tormented.

The Demoniac of the Gadarenes

What better way to introduce deliverance than an example of Jesus casting out a legion of unclean spirits from the man known as the Gerasene demoniac, a name he acquired from the region in which he lived?

And when He stepped out on the land, they met a man from the city who had been demonized for a long time. He wore no clothes, nor did he live in a house but in the tombs. Upon seeing Jesus, he fell down before him, crying out, "What do I have to do with you, Jesus, Son of the Most High God? I beg You, do not torment me!" The impure spirit had often seized him, and people kept him under guard, bound with chains and shackles. Jesus asked him, saying, "What is your name?" And he said, "Legion," because many demons had entered him. And they begged Him, asking that He would not command them to go out into the abyss. Now a herd of swine was feeding there on the mountain. So, they then begged Him to permit them to enter the swine. And He permitted them. Then the demons went out of the man and entered the swine, and the herd ran violently down the steep place into the lake and drowned. (Luke 8:26–33)

There is one point I'd like to make first: The Gerasene demoniac man was not a follower of Jesus at the time Jesus stepped ashore. It was the power of Christ that restrained him as he came, fell at the feet of Jesus, and cried out to him. The power of the devil was instantly bound and his desire to follow Jesus showed a transformation of faith. Many people assert that only believers should receive deliverance. This belief is based on Matthew 12:43–45, where Jesus describes an unclean spirit leaving a person and, after returning to find an empty house, inviting seven even more wicked spirits to join it. That highlights the need for a Holy Spirit infilling post-deliverance, though it doesn't say deliverance is not for the unsaved.

With the Gerasene demoniac man, we observe a man who was not a follower of Jesus receiving deliverance and subsequently becoming one. Here's food for thought: Often, Satan's blindness prevents a conscious decision until deliverance; then, once the gospel's light reveals itself, the person is free to believe, and to receive the Holy Spirit.

The Miracle of Deliverance

Now let's look beyond his original state to his appearance after the demons were cast out. The men who owned the swine fled but later returned "and found the man from whom the demons had departed, sitting at the feet of Jesus, clothed and in his right mind" (Luke 8:35). Take note: While the man was under severe demonization, no one could reason with him. A logical conversation was out of the question. We may encounter the same when we come upon a demonized individual. However, when the devil's power breaks, the soul recovers, and the formerly demonized person returns to a right frame of mind.

Jesus denied the now-healed man's request to leave with him, instead sending him back to his community. In so doing, his testimony would do far more for the people who were more focused on the loss of their livestock than the miracle of deliverance that occurred on their shore. The power of one's living testimony is indeed a weapon of warfare that stands as a reminder of what our God is capable of.

Demon Oppression vs. Possession

Possession and oppression, though both are powers of Satan,

operate in different ways. Oppression means the person is under demonic influence, whereas possession is a misunderstood word because of its English translation. In the Greek, *daimonizomai* translates to possession, which means under the power of a demon. With possession, the person is under various degrees of demonic control, but unlike the English translation, it does not imply ownership. For this reason, unless it is a Scripture verse, I've replaced the word *possessed* with *demonized*, which refers to individuals who are under the influence or control of demons. There is a wide range of debate within the church over the word usage. One thing that most agree on is that a person cannot be owned by Satan. With that said, we'll move on to another widely controversial question: Can a Christian be demonized?

Sometimes, Christians can fall under some level of demonic influence. However, there are some cases, such as when a believer falls into habitual sin or leaves a door open to a demon, that warrant careful consideration. The argument against a Christian having a demon comes from the idea that light and darkness cannot coexist (see 2 Corinthians 6:14). This verse forbids believers from being unequally yoked with unbelievers. Paul gives several reasons to avoid this corrupt mixture, but the premise is that since we are temples of the living God, inviting in and communing with anything in opposition to God creates conflict within us.

But while this Scripture encourages the avoidance of coexisting, it doesn't say that it's impossible. How many Christians do you know who are married to an unbeliever? This only creates conflict within the relationship, and in doing so dishonors God; sadly, many who are unequally yoked still marry.[48]

We can also look at it in another way. In 2 Corinthians 7:1, Paul is addressing believers when he says, "Let us cleanse ourselves from everything that contaminates body and spirit." We see here that corruption can contaminate both the body and the spirit. *Matthew Henry's Commentary on the Whole Bible* further explains, "There are sins of the flesh, that are committed with the

---

48 "2 Corinthians 6," *Matthew Henry's Commentary on the Whole Bible* on Bible Hub, accessed July 16, 2025, https://biblehub.com/commentaries/mhcw/2_corinthians/6.htm.

body, and sins of the spirit, spiritual wickedness; and we must cleanse ourselves from the filthiness of both, for God is to be glorified both with body and soul."[49]

Think about this: If believers, filled with the Holy Spirit, can have spiritual wickedness corrupt their spirit, then sometimes both coexist. The late Derek Prince said this regarding whether a Christian can have a demon: "Mark 7 [lists] thirteen things that defile a man. One is pride, and one is foolishness." He says, "Good Lord, how many Christians would there be left if every time we got proud or foolish the Holy Spirit left us? So, the Holy Spirit dwells in vessels that are not totally pure."[50] Even with a defiled spirit, the Holy Spirit never leaves nor forsakes us. I understand it's a highly controversial topic, but I believe it explains my personal experience.

Having been a Spirit-filled Christian that backslid into spiritual wickedness, I prayerfully confronted this situation. It brings up the question of whether one can lose his or her salvation, which is another controversial subject. After much prayer and research, I don't believe it's a cookie-cutter answer, and each should prayerfully seek God if they've totally turned their back on Him. Personally, I realized how dangerously close I came, equivalent to hanging over a cliff by a hair strand. I was in total spiritual blindness, which kept me from seeing the truth that was right before me. Here, years later, the Lord opened my eyes to one practice I had done, invoking the goddess—which is, inviting the goddess [spirit entity] within. Back then, I denied the goddess as a demon, and I willfully submitted to what one can only describe as a severe case of demonic control. Considering that the Holy Spirit never leaves us, what a great dishonor it was to God for me to allow myself to be defiled in this way.

Rather than argue the levels of demonic oppression, verses

---

[49] "2 Corinthians 7:1," *Matthew Henry's Commentary on the Whole Bible* on Bible Hub, accessed June 23, 2025, https://biblehub.com/commentaries/mhcw/2_corinthians/7.htm.
[50] "Derek Prince – Is It Possible To Have The Holy Spirit And A Demon At The Same Time?," Sermons.Love, June 6, 2022, accessed July 16, 2025, https://sermons.love/derek-prince/11316-derek-prince-is-it-possible-to-have-the-holy-spirit-and-a-demon-at-the-same-time.html.

possession, let's just use spiritual discernment with each case scenario. The goal is to identify whether it involves oppression, or what degree of demonization. The only difference is that the greater control a demonic spirit (or spirits) has over a person, the stronger the hold will be. Regardless, it still must submit to the authority of Jesus Christ and leave.

Deliverance Options

Early in my Christian walk, I learned about deliverance from Pastor Larry and his wife Carole, whom God used to minister freedom far beyond our church walls and across the nations. It is from this foundation instilled within me, and built upon by spiritual insight and experience, that I share this knowledge with you today.[51]

There are three options when approaching deliverance: public, private, and self-deliverance. The primary focus is on spiritual liberation, freedom from sin and demonic spirits, and repentance and restoration to God. Believers can also experience deliverance upon salvation, through prayer and fasting, through renewing of the mind by the Word of God, or from a sovereign act of God. Let's look at these three options.

Public Deliverance

During His ministry, Jesus came upon many demonized people on the roads He traveled and simply cast the demons out. He often delivered people after teaching in the synagogue or on a hillside. He saw the need and dealt with it right there, whatever the setting. What we consider public deliverance seems to align most with Jesus' example. In these instances, churches or ministries will have a service teaching on deliverance and then set time aside to cast out demons, similar to what Jesus did. These deliverances happen spontaneously, led by the Spirit, without scheduled times for specific individuals. Either the demon manifests, or the spirit is discerned and cast out. The downside to this is that there often isn't time for prayer for an infilling of the Holy

---

[51] Larry Arendas, *Set the Captives Free!: A Biblical Solution for Compulsive Behavior and Emotional Trauma*.

Spirit, or follow-up with the person walking out the deliverance, especially if they're visiting from out of town.

On a personal note, I experienced deliverance from the occult within the church setting, which was not scheduled, on two separate occasions. The first time, I had accepted an invitation to church, if only to prove I was untouchable by God. After the service, the prayer team surrounded me in the back of the church and began praying. I fled once I felt demons leaving my body, and only returned to retrieve my car keys, which I'd left behind in my swift exit. I ended up recommitting my life to Jesus that day. And on another occasion, I went to an evening prayer service where Pastor Larry and Carole were supposed to be the prayer recipients. The Holy Spirit changed the direction of the service, and I ended up being the one to receive deliverance prayer that night.

Even though these deliverance sessions were in a public setting, they were also spontaneous events, as they provided no prior notice to any evil spirits, yet took place within a church with a healing and deliverance ministry. So, I wasn't just sent out after the deliverance, but received additional prayer and support in continuing my walk out from under demonic influences.

From my personal experience, I believe one benefit of this deliverance method is that it surprises demons, thus preventing pre-deliverance harassment, hiding, or temporary escape. However, I must stress that additional prayer and follow-up are necessary for long-term success.

Private Deliverance

Many deliverance ministries and ministers schedule private deliverance sessions. On a selected date and time, the person seeking deliverance comes usually to a home or church office. The session offers privacy and confidentiality, with only the individual, the deliverance minister, and the deliverance team present. The downside of a scheduled session is that the demons are aware of their pending expulsion and will often harass and cause havoc for their host to prevent them from getting delivered, sometimes preventing the person from going to the scheduled session altogether.

In my case, I had previously gone to a scheduled deliverance session when I was teetering on the fence. Even before the scheduled day, the demonic influences within me were attempting to pick the members of the deliverance team. Pastor Larry stood firm against it, and after almost not going, I reluctantly went, probably because of their pre-deliverance prayer. But the session didn't go as planned. I remember the ruling demon simply vacating temporarily before being cast out, then, as soon as the session was over, returning and whispering, "I'm still here."

We can and should use prayer against any pre-deliverance harassment, although I believe the best-case scenario involves surprising the demon(s). Matthew 10:16 says to "be as wise as serpents and as harmless as doves." We mustn't let other demonic influences manipulate us in their schemes, yet remain gentle and innocent toward the person receiving prayer. Private deliverance certainly has its place, as it is usually more involved and, for those in need of healing or personalized attention, provides the time and individualized focus necessary. Also, because of the preparation that precedes the session, it serves well for those cases, as Jesus told His disciples that "this kind does not go out except by prayer and fasting" (Matthew 17:21).

Self-Deliverance

Self-deliverance is the process by which a believer exercises authority, delegated by Jesus, over their life to cast out demonic spirits causing havoc in their lives. This usually happens without a deliverance minister present. It is not the preferred method of deliverance, as Jeremiah 17:9 says, "The heart is deceitful above all else."

A deceived heart leads us to deceive ourselves regarding our true condition. This self-deception hinders our capacity for self-deliverance, as we neglect our need for forgiveness and redemption. I've always been taught that people should avoid this method of deliverance. However, for those in areas where deliverance ministry is unavailable, an individual can resort to self-deliverance. Self-deliverance can also be beneficial when a person has already gone through deliverance and, at a later time, the Holy Spirit reveals an additional demonic influence that they can cast out at the Holy Spirit's direction.

Deliverance Basics

One of the first things we need to acknowledge is that no two deliverance experiences are identical. There is a wide range of variables that make each case unique. To begin with, deliverance ministers have different methods they prefer to use. Most spend time getting to know the person, their spiritual background, and their family history. The entire process is Spirit-led, or at least it should be. We begin with seeking the Holy Spirit's direction in how we should proceed and then continue to rely on His guidance as we move through the process. This deliverance section serves as a guide, not an absolute, and is likely to produce different results each time. We may sometimes need to break curses before casting out demons, or cast out demons before inner healing begins. We discern each case individually, and it may change or develop during the process, depending on the Holy Spirit's guidance. Spiritual discernment plays a key role in obtaining the information we will need.

It is crucial to avoid conversing with demons during the deliverance session. Demons will speak through their hosts when they are being challenged. We must remember they are liars and deceivers, and any imparted knowledge they reveal to us falls in line with the doctrine of demons. Avoid interrogating spirits to gain information. The Holy Spirit provides all the information we need through the ministry of discernment.

Battle Readiness

Prayer and Fasting

In the days preceding deliverance prayer, the deliverance team prepares for the upcoming session. Matthew 17:14–21 tells of a father who brought his son, an epileptic who often fell into the fire and the water, to Jesus. He explained that he had first brought him to the disciples, but they could not cure him. Jesus rebuked the demon, and then it left the boy, and the boy recovered within the hour. Then the disciples asked why they could not cast it out. Jesus responded, "Because of your unbelief; for assuredly, I say to you, if you have faith as a mustard seed, you will say to this mountain, 'Move from here to there,' and it will move" (vv. 19–20). Jesus first addressed their lack of faith, then added, "This kind does not go out except by prayer and fasting" (v. 21).

When we engage in spiritual warfare, it's important to have the faith to believe that when we say to a demon, "Come out," that it will indeed obey. If we waver in unbelief or doubt, then we risk an unsuccessful result, for surely the evil spirit will take advantage of our lack of faith. For this reason, it's important for us to have developed a mature level of faith. Yet, unbelief alone is not the only hindrance. "This kind" reveals that some spirits, as we already know, hold a higher-ranking or greater power over their victim. The words of exorcism spoken with little to no faith are not powerful enough to defeat some demons, so prayer along with fasting positions oneself to receive power from on high, along with the ability to cast out demons that otherwise would have resisted expulsion.

Mend Your Garment

One of the first things a person preparing for deliverance ministry must do is ensure that their armor is in good shape. Remember, the spiritual warrior likens their armor to a second skin and never removes it once donned. It's a life application, not a raincoat that is put on only in stormy weather. It does, however, require upkeep by the daily washing of the Word and the anointing of the Holy Spirit. If we have become lax in its upkeep, we certainly want to check for any tears or snares before entering the battlefield. If you find your armor weakened, stop, go home, and mend your garment before going to battle.

Pray for a Convenient Memory

Those on the deliverance team pray for a convenient memory, basically asking God to remove anything from within their minds that was revealed in the deliverance session that He does not want them to keep (and only remember that which He does). In this way, they can continue to interact with the person without condemnation operating against them.

Binding Bedevilment

While we'll be binding demons during the deliverance session, we can also use binding to prepare for deliverance, to reduce any pre-deliverance harassment on both the prayer recipient and the deliverance team. The person we're praying for does not have to be there or even be aware of the binding. This frees them from any demonic obstacles in the way of prayer. See the example below.

"In the name of Jesus, I bind all demons who would come against _____ to harass, cause confusion or attempt to prevent him/her from being set free."

Shortly after returning to Christ, a song about angels awakened me from a sound sleep, which was one such example in my life. I reached across the bed to my radio on the bureau, wondering how it had turned itself on in the middle of the night. When my fingers reached the button, I realized it was off and the song wasn't coming from the radio. Immediately after, I felt led to pray for warring angels, so I prayed to God for them until I felt God's peace and fell asleep. A few weeks later, God delivered me from witchcraft for the third and last time, and I believe the Lord sent His warrior angels to protect me from the demonic attack and harassment.

Opening Prayer for Deliverance

Begin by assuring the prayer recipient of confidentiality throughout the session.

Adoration for our Deliverer

We enter the battle through deliverance prayer. Using our own words, we begin by acknowledging Jesus as the name above all names (Ephesians 1:21). We place Him above all else in our lives and acknowledge His many roles and attributes, such as Jesus as the Healer (Luke 7:1–17). His healing power is limitless and holds no bounds in what He can accomplish. It reaches beyond the confines of physical healing to spiritual, social, and emotional healing, and reflects His divine nature. We recognize Jesus as our Deliverer (Luke 4:31–36). He came to set the captive free, liberating us from the bondage of sin, the curse, and demonic strongholds.

Raise the Banner of Praise

Create an environment of praise. Worship is instrumental in warfare, and I really can't stress that enough. When God's presence inhabits the praises of His people, the atmosphere changes within the space, causing demons to flee. Removing the demons minimizes, if not completely removes resistance before deliverance even starts.

So, raise the banner of praise! Strum guitars, strike the keyboard, sound the horn (shofar), and lift your voice exalting the King of Kings. Psalm 144:1 says He "trains my hands for war, and my fingers for battle," which is a preparation for spiritual combat using our spiritual fingers (i.e., strumming, striking, blowing, or belting) to wield the sword of the Spirit. The Holy Spirit may also lead you to sing rather than cast out demons, as happened occasionally during deliverance prayer in my former church. Many times, they simply sang in tongues, which totally freed and healed the person.

Pray as the Spirit leads. The battle is the Lord's, and we want to go forth in His name and under the authority He has granted us.

Reinforce Your Spiritual Armor

It's wise to reinforce our armor, reflecting on its purpose and protection amid the upcoming battle. Therefore, we recount Ephesians 6:11–20 as we reflect on the whole armor of God.

Pray and ask Jesus to cover the prayer recipient and all present with the protection of His precious blood.

Binding Demonic Manifestations

We want to bind up any manifestation of demons, and any harassment or confusion they may attempt during the deliverance session. We are not looking for demonic theatrics to glorify the works of the devil. Jesus has already made a public spectacle of principalities and powers by disarming them by His work on the cross (see Colossians 2:15). We're working toward keeping their exit as uneventful as possible. Matthew 12:29 says, "How can one enter a strongman's house and plunder his goods, unless he first binds the strongman?" The term *bind* means to restrain or overpower—in this case, the strongman. Here, Jesus' response to the Pharisees' accusations against Him reveals a valuable lesson in binding demons. Basically, the house is the unregenerate soul, where demons occupy, and in order to remove them, the strongman or ruling spirit needs to first be bound.

We do this by speaking out loud and declaring the demon bound and restrained "in Jesus' name" from causing any torment, confusion, and evil communication, or from calling on other spirits to aid them.

Manifestations During Deliverance

While binding demons before deliverance minimizes their manifestations, some manifestations are not uncommon. Mild manifestations can include coughing, burping, choking, gagging, spitting, crying, deep yawning, trances, distorted voices, or vomiting. Sometimes, demons may leave through the mouth, and in that case, we don't resist or bind the demon, as we want it to come out.

We should remain vigilant for signs of more violent manifestations so that we can deal with them appropriately. For instance, by observing the person's face, hands, and eyes (believed to reflect the soul) we can recognize violent manifestations and bind them before they occur. More severe cases of demonization may exhibit shaking or screaming, or the person may experience body pain. Although rare, you may witness supernatural or unnatural strength, or levitation, physical struggle with the ministry team, and demonic convulsions can sometimes manifest with demonization, especially during deliverance involving the occult or Satanism.

It's important to recognize that manifestations only prove a demonic presence. They don't necessarily mean the demon has left. Demons also hide, or temporarily leave their host and then return as soon as the deliverance ends. This is another time we rely on our gift of discerning spirits to determine whether the person is in fact demon-free.

Renouncing the Occult

Few people have not entertained some aspect of the occult, if only in reading one's horoscope. But regardless of the level of involvement, all occult involvement is an abomination to God and needs to be repented of and renounced by the prayer recipient. The renunciation should include every occult activity, such as

"In the name of Jesus, I repent of and renounce all occult activities in which I have taken part, specifically horoscopes, Ouija boards, tarot cards, etc."

Following the prayer recipient's occult renunciation, the deliverance team should bind and cast out any associated demons.

"I bind and cast out the spirit of _____, in Jesus' name."

To Set the Captive Free

Here are the steps to take for deliverance.

1. Identify the Strongman or Ruling Spirit: It's best to have someone with the gift of discerning of spirits to identify the spiritual entities influencing the person. This happens through a word of knowledge or observation, although conversation with the person receiving deliverance can also identify demons. Writing down the names of the identified spirits is helpful; chapter nine contains a list of ruling spirits and their manifestations and can be used as a reference. Having the person seeking deliverance reject every ruling spirit is exhausting and unnecessary. It's best to use the list created through the gift of discernment.

2. **Repent and Renounce**: The person receiving deliverance repents and renounces any sin in their life, confirming they will no longer engage in a lifestyle that feeds off the desires of the flesh.

3. **Reject Demonic Spirits**: The person receiving deliverance exercises their delegated spiritual authority and rejects demonic spirits that someone identified or discerned. In the case of a non-believer, the minister would be using their delegated authority.

4. **Cast Out Demons**: Identify ruling demons by name and cast them out in Jesus' name. (For example, say, "In the name of Jesus Christ, I command you, spirit of ____, to come out of him/her!") However, if the first step reveals a lesser demon, you should also cast it out. Reliance on the Holy Spirit is essential. Note: Bind to stop a spirit from manifesting in a person, or when the spirit attempts to prevent the person from speaking.

5. **Stop**: Deliverance ends when all identified demons are cast out and the Lord's peace descends. "When Satan's power is broken in the soul, the eyes are opened to see God's glory, and the lips opened to speak his praise" (Henry 1706).

Post-Deliverance Prayer

After the demons have been cast out, pray in this way.

1. **Anoint with the "healing balm of Gilead"**: Anointing is a biblical act involving pouring oil directly onto a person (usually the head or applying it with a finger to their forehead). This symbolizes God's protection and empowerment, breaking the yoke of bondage, setting the captive free, and bringing deliverance (see Isaiah 58:6). The true healing balm of Gilead is a rare, healing resin that comes from the region of Gilead. It symbolizes Jesus' power, and represents bringing back to a state of wholeness, signifying a complete restoration of the spirit.

2. **Pray for the Holy Spirit's Infilling**: After removal of the demonic influences that once occupied areas of someone's life, there will be empty spaces that need to be filled. Matthew 12:43-45 says that when a spirit leaves a man, it searches for a place of rest but, having none, returns to its house, bringing seven more spirits with it. We pray for a fresh infilling of the Holy Spirit to fill every area of the person's life so there is no place for unclean spirits to reoccupy. This requires the person's surrender to God in order for a genuine spiritual transformation to take place.

3. **Speak Prophetic Words**: We should share any prophetic words the Holy Spirit speaks through us and pray that the person receiving deliverance would have an open heart and willingness to receive the words spoken. It's a good practice to have one of the deliverance team write any prophecies for the person so they can later reflect on them for edification and encouragement.

4. **Pray Against Retaliation**: Pray for discernment of any weak areas that need reinforcing so the person can stand their ground when the day of evil comes. Also, pray against any demonic retaliation.

5. **Close with Scripture**: A good way to end deliverance is by reading a Scripture passage about deliverance, such as Galatians 5:1: "It is for freedom that Christ has set us free. Stand firm, then, and do not let yourselves be burdened again by a yoke of slavery" (NIV).

Deliverance plays a crucial role in spiritual warfare, focusing on freeing individuals from demonic bondage through direct confrontation, as exemplified by Jesus' teachings in Matthew 10. It involves casting out demons rather than merely defending against them. We'll complete the deliverance process with steps to walk out one's deliverance in the next chapter.

CHAPTER 17

Walking Out Deliverance

Once the temple (body) has been swept clean of any demonic influences, maintaining an infilling of the Holy Spirit is crucial to ensure ongoing victory. While I write this chapter with a focus on those who have experienced deliverance, the instructions are also helpful for those who are part of a deliverance team.

In my case, after the initial shock of being set free (my deliverance wasn't pre-planned), I found myself restless and unsure of what to do next. Fortunately, I received a call from my pastor and spiritual father early the next morning, and that was just the encouragement I needed. And during the next several months, it was as though the Lord lifted me up and held me in His divine presence, care, and protection. Truly, He had taken me under the shadow of His wings, (see Psalm 91).

During this time, I saturated myself with worship and praise. I filled my surrounding space with worship songs from Scripture. His Word was being poured into me nonstop. Sometimes I listened, other times I sang, and I shed a humongous number of tears, which cleansed my soul. Worship is the key to victory. It truly is a determining factor, because Satan flees and God dwells in our midst to provide our breakthrough from bondage. We lift our voice in song and/or instrumentals in "joyful noise" (see

Psalm 98:4)—an audible, energetic expression of praise to God for our salvation.

There are other things people can do as well, such as avoiding stumbling blocks and restoring and reclaiming.

Avoiding Stumbling Blocks

One of the most common stumbling blocks the enemy uses to hamper our deliverance is doubt. It's one of the oldest tricks in his battle plan, but by now we're likely to realize that all of Satan's strategies are the same old recycled junk. Doubt was the fundamental cause of the first sin in the garden, and it was also the sin that caused my falling away and the falling away of many others.

It can come as negative thoughts like "You can never stay free," "Delivered people always relapse," or, worst of all, "God says you're unworthy of freedom." We mustn't fall for the lies. Instead, we resist temptation by guarding our thoughts and blocking any lies (fiery darts) from penetrating our mind. Raise and recite the Word of God, as Jesus did on the mount of temptation: "Away with you, Satan!" (Matthew 4:10) and "But the Lord is faithful, who will establish you and guard you from the evil one" (2 Thessalonians 3:3).

Restoring and Reclaiming

Recurring thought patterns, once controlled by a stronghold, partly cause our struggle to maintain our deliverance. Many times, we've become so accustomed to their faulty thinking that it seems only natural to continue in the same thought patterns. We pulled down the strongholds, and we plundered the once demonically occupied house, taking it back (see Mark 3:27), but the destruction's aftermath remains. It will take time, and a conscious effort on our part, in sweeping away the residue they have left in our lives. Remember, the buildup has taken years, and we're likely to find hidden "skeletons in the closet" and dated debris from our former life in the least likely places.

Think of discovering that your house has termites. At first you probably didn't even know they were there, and may have overlooked a few squeaky floorboards. Eventually, you found a crumbling windowsill that caused suspicion, but it wasn't until you walked into your bathroom full of winged bugs scampering across the floor that you knew termites had made your house their home. It was time to call an exterminator. After eliminating the termites, you discovered the damage they had done and began restoring your home. To stop pests from returning, you fixed cracks in the foundation and sealed gaps around doors and windows. To complete the protective measures, you created a separation between the edge of the house and the mulch against the foundation.

Likewise, we must clean up after evicting demonic strongholds by renewing our mind with God's Word and receiving the Holy Spirit's infilling to strengthen our defenses against future attacks of evil.

Seven Steps to Walking Out Deliverance

1. **Read Scripture**: We must meditate on God's Word daily to keep our heart and mind focused on the things of God, thus ensuring a continued infilling of the Holy Spirit. Renewing our minds is vital for transformation. We remove false and negative thinking and replace it with things that are good, pure, and true. I was always taught that by thinking about things that are worthy of praise, and by embracing daily biblical affirmations, we counterbalance any negative thoughts—something especially important after deliverance. Perhaps even greater, the more we spend time in the Word, the more we develop a deeper intimacy with God. This requires that we seek His face with our whole heart, and that we intentionally and consistently read the Bible and pray for understanding. We must *know* Him.

2. **Pray in the Spirit**: First Corinthians 14:15–17 says that we should both pray and sing in the spirit and also with understanding. Paul explains we should pray with understanding in corporate worship so that others lacking knowledge can agree with our prayers. If one has a spiritual gift of speaking in tongues, they should only do so if someone with the gift of interpretation joins

in. Praying in the Spirit is praying with guidance and empowerment by the Holy Spirit, according to God's will and purpose. When we are in our alone time with God, or with others who also pray in their prayer language, then we are free to pray as the Spirit leads us. In times when we don't know what God wants us to pray, we pray in the Spirit, *or in tongues*, which is our spiritual prayer language that exceeds words, and may include groans, sighs, and other utterances or spiritual language unknown to man (see Romans 8:26–27). The Holy Spirit provides prayer in tongues to those who ask, either through a fiery baptism as at Pentecost or through the laying on of hands. "It is a valuable weapon to be used against demonic attacks, particularly when we are walking out of our deliverance. Ephesians 6:18: "Praying always with all prayer and supplications in the spirit." This means that praying in tongues should always be on our lips. If you've already received this gift, use it, and if not, consider asking for it.

3. Take Our Thoughts Captive: We renew our mind according to the Word of God (see 2 Corinthians 10:5). One of the main areas of spiritual attack is the battlefield of the mind. The enemy places land mines, such as vain imaginations, carnal reasoning, and conceited thoughts, which are strongholds, as arguments against the knowledge of God. By guarding our thought life, we filter out what comes into our mind through what we see, hear, and receive in our heart.

4. Guard Our Tongue: The tongue spews poison if not bridled or tamed. Luke 6:45 says, "The mouth speaks what the heart is full of!" Therefore, there is clearly a direct connection between taking our thoughts captive and guarding our tongue, for what we receive in our heart is what will come forth from our mouth. We should practice speaking words of life, which will also fill our heart and mind with the things of God. Ephesians 4:29 says, "Let no corrupt word proceed out of your mouth, but what is good for necessary edification, that it may impart grace to the hearers."

5. Fellowship with Believers: Engaging in corporate worship and fellowship with other believers provides mutual encouragement, spiritual growth, and a deeper infilling of the

Holy Spirit. Fellowship is of utmost importance when walking out of our deliverance. It can be as simple as sharing a meal or attending a Christian coffee house together. Spending time with other believers will provide the encouragement, support, and edification that will help our spiritual growth, lift us up in times of despair, or encourage us during times of struggle (see Acts 2:42–47).

6. Spiritual Disciplines: Engaging in healthy spiritual habits helps us develop, strengthen, and maintain a surrendered heart and faith in Christ. They are such things as Bible study, worship, fasting, journaling, and serving others.

- Bible study: This can be a weekly Bible study at church, followed up with further in-depth personal study during the week, or personal use of a solid Bible study book. It shouldn't replace daily Bible reading or meditation on Scripture, but it can encourage a more in-depth perspective to deepen our faith.

- Worship: We counteract the darkness by worship. When we worship, God's presence falls, darkness flees, healing flows, and our heart sings of His praise. We can sing a cappella, play an instrument, or sing along to worship music. Choose songs that are based on Scripture or the Psalms.

- Fasting: Fasting is either the reduction or elimination of food consumption for a specific time and purpose. An absolute fast, also known as a dry fast, is voluntary abstinence from both food and water for a short period. A full fast involves only consuming liquids, such as water or clear broth, for a limited time, while a partial fast involves omitting specific meals or certain foods, such as meat, caffeine, or sweets. Regardless of our choice of fast, we should combine it with prayer and keep it private between you and God (see Matthew 6:16–18).

- Journaling: There is no command to journal in the Bible, but many people find it helpful to record scriptural insights from Bible reading. Some Bibles have space specifically for this, or a blank journal can be used. We can also journal prophetic words we receive, or insights revealed to us throughout the day. Journaling can become a part of our regular prayer time, recording anything the Lord impresses upon our heart. This is also a great way to document our walk into total freedom. For this type of journaling, have a journal specifically for this purpose. (see Habakkuk 2:2 says, "Write the vision, and make it plain that he may run that readeth it").

- Serving Others: We are called to feed the hungry, give water to those who are thirsty, show hospitality to strangers, clothe the naked, and visit the sick and imprisoned. Many churches have opportunities to serve in these ways, or we can move as the Holy Spirit leads in helping those in need. Every believer possesses a gift for serving others (see Peter 4:10–11), so prayerfully seek your gift and how to be a faithful steward of it.

7. Remain Alert for the Enemy: We must stay vigilant and watchful "because your adversary the devil walks about like a roaring lion, seeking whom he may devour" (1 Peter 5:8). Actively watch out for potential threats or dangerous traps the enemy has set up. Keep your mind clear and focused, ready to react if needed. Resist and raise the sword (the Word of God) in response to any temptation.

- Resist: James 4:7 tells us, "Therefore submit to God. Resist the devil and he will flee from you." *Resist* means to exert force in opposition. We must avoid yielding to the devil's temptations, and stand strong in the armor *against* him. Then he will flee.

- Raise the Sword: Take up the sword of the Spirit to withstand the enemy's attacks. Our spiritual sword has the same power and authority as the written word, and we wield its influence to push back the enemy. Use your voice to skillfully and effectively quote relevant Scripture and take control.

John 8:36 tells us, "Therefore if the Son makes you free, you shall be free indeed." Hallelujah! My friend, after deliverance, the power of sin no longer binds you. He severed the demonic chains that held you captive, and you are now free. Jesus says, "Take My yoke upon you and learn from Me, for I am gentle and lowly in heart, and you will find rest for your souls" (Matthew 11:29). Jesus walks with you, and He makes His strength perfect in your weakness; therefore, you will no longer walk heavy and downtrodden.

The seven steps we just went through include a lot of information to help a person walk out deliverance, but don't become burdened by them. They are meant to be steps to guide you, not a burden you take on in exchange for another. Jesus offers you rest for your soul, that is to sit at His feet and hear His words. In His love, you will find peace and acceptance, so focus then on God's love. Draw near to Him, and He will draw near to you (see James 4:8).

Behind Enemy Lines

PART V

Reclamation of Supernaturalism

Behind Enemy Lines

CHAPTER 18

Waste Management

Another strategy of the enemy is to infiltrate our homes with objects that have demonic influences attached. Many of these objects appear innocent and fall under the guise of aesthetics, aromas, and cultural decor, but they are actually spiritual inroads into our living space. Believers need to be spiritually alert of what they allow into their homes, as they could decorate with objects that attract evil influences and succumb to a spirit of compromise.

Some objects bring more than character into our house. Rather, they act as open channels for spiritual entities, disrupting what should be our safe space. Deuteronomy 7:26 contains God's explicit command to avoid bringing detestable things into our home; otherwise, we will face the same destruction. We cannot be naive in believing that these objects sit idly on the shelf without repercussions. In the Bible, God used objects, such as the ark of the covenant, which carried His presence, for His purpose and glory. However, remember the counterfeiter; he also uses objects that attach spiritual influences. It's important to understand that whether carved in wood or chiseled out of stone, these objects cannot see, hear, or understand, and therefore lack power on their own. Association with spiritual entities is their source of empowerment.

An object in our home, dedicated to another spirit, certainly carries an evil presence. We may see it as a harmless decoration because of its outward appearance, but beware. The enemy is subtle, often cloaking evil as insignificant artifacts. And before we know it, our home becomes a catalyst for confusion, fear, and division. Something just feels off. We can't put our finger on it, but it's foreboding. The sanctity of our home should provide a reprieve from the evil and darkness of the world. What we bring into it determines whether we will experience the peace of God or the chaos of the demonic. The good news is that demons don't have to be permanent residents. Once discerned, we simply evict them and restore the peace of God in our home.

Common Open Doors

In order to discover any demonic influences within your home, you'll need total reliance on the Holy Spirit to help you discern any objects that your natural mind may look upon as destitute of power and, therefore, easily abandoned. (see 1 Corinthians 2:13--16). The Bible tells us that the heart is deceitful above all else (Jeremiah 17:9), and many times we develop an attachment to specific items that may be hard to let go of. Therefore, the first thing we need to do is pray and ask God to open our spiritual eyes and reveal any ungodly things we may have developed an attachment to. Then we pray to break the attachment in Jesus' name.

Next, it's time to sweep the house clean of any spiritual contaminants and discard anything we have no use for. If we're like most people, bits and pieces of memorabilia from our past clutters our home; all the things that we once brought in that reflect our former lifestyle occupies our living space. But what we possess reflects what we allow. There are probably books lining the bookshelves, jewelry in the bottom of the jewelry box, posters or wall hangings on the walls, clothing hanging in the closet, and statues on tables or objects hidden in secret places. They are everywhere, and just like we expelled such things from our spiritual temple, we need to evict them from our home as well.

Many deliverance ministries develop a list of demonic items

to dispose of. I caution against relying on a list, as that may act as legalism, and the enemy can even use it against you. If you must use a list, do so only as a guide, praying over it and asking the Holy Spirit to reveal the things you need to remove while being open to anything else the Spirit may reveal that's not on the list. We will review some of these things, but realize that no list can be complete for every individual and, by relying on one, we risk missing items that need to go. Let the Holy Spirit be your go-to source.

Cultural Items and Family Heirlooms

Families find it difficult to part with inherited idols, such as family heirlooms that have been passed down through the generations and remain in our homes for sentimental reasons. We need to be cautious of heirlooms that could carry more than family ties. Since we're most likely unfamiliar with how they came into the family, we need to pray to make sure they're not an accursed item. Accursed items can be anything, even costly items. Though they originally appeared harmless; a curse may have attached to them at some point.

In the Bible, we read the story of Rachel, who stole her father Laban's household idols, slipping them into her camel's saddlebags when she, her husband, and her family were departing her father's house for the land of Canaan. Her father followed them, confronting her husband Jacob for stealing his gods. Jacob, unaware of his wife's theft, swore an oath that whoever had taken the gods would not live. Laban searched but did not find the idols that Rachel concealed.

Rachel's reasons for stealing the idols remain unexplained, but a childhood connection to them could explain her strong emotional attachment. A few scholars suggest that she could also have used them to claim her family inheritance when the time came. Whatever the reason, stealing them soon endangered her life (see Genesis 31:22–42). Now, I'm not saying that every family heirloom is an accursed idol that comes with severe consequences. Many are indeed harmless and can be a blessing for generations to come, but to discern the difference, we need to rely on the Holy Spirit's guidance.

Accursed items extend beyond ancient artifacts. In fact, a modern-day accursed item that is given to you will probably be something you find appealing. Always pray before accepting anything you weren't expecting from someone.

Charms, Amulets, and Talismans

Charms, amulets, and talismans are small objects believed to possess magickal powers that bring good luck or protection, or enhance power or abilities to its owner, based on superstitious beliefs or pagan spirituality. Relying on them may get us more than we bargained for, as they serve as magnets that draw demonic influences into our life. These little trinkets or objects may even seem harmless. After all, many "Christian" (as well as pagan) symbols are made into charms, and while many claim to wear them for looks or as a symbol of faith, we must examine our heart carefully. For instance, a person may wear a Saint Christopher charm for safe travels, but that does not differ from wearing any other charm for protection. Avoid being deceived. Charms can charm us into compromise. Our faith is not in a religious charm, but in God alone.

People boldly use amulets and talismans as intended, as magickal charms that ward off negative energies or are created with a specific magickal purpose that directly opposes God. But, "This is what the Sovereign LORD says: Woe to the women who sew magic charms on all their wrists and make veils of various lengths for their heads in order to ensnare people. Will you ensnare the lives of my people but preserve your own? . . . I am against your magic charms with which you ensnare people like birds and I will tear them from your arms; I will set free the people that you ensnare like birds. I will tear off your veils and save my people from your hands, and they will no longer fall prey to your power" (Ezekiel 13:18, 20–21 NIV). These women were using charms to lure the people into believing their false prophecies. As Christians, we discern prophecy, discard anything that doesn't align with God's Word, and avoid charms or tokens of persuasion.

Symbols and Idols

A symbol is an object or visual icon that represents something else. A vast number of symbols exist throughout the world in various forms, each holding a unique meaning. The symbols we want to avoid are those that represent other gods, spirits, or rebellion, and there are many. Just as vast as the number of symbols is the number of places we can find them. We often find them on clothing, posters, candles, art, jewelry, and home decor. Some of the most common occult symbols are zodiac signs, Celtic symbols, the ankh, and the Neronic cross or peace sign. I remember walking into church one Sunday and, to my dismay, one of the young ladies was wearing a T-shirt with the words "I Am A Goddess" on it. We must be careful what label we put on ourselves. Yes, we are a child of God or a daughter of the King, but we are not gods or goddesses, and we do not want to identify as one. Other symbols to be avoided are those associated with Freemasonry, Wicca, Santeria, Satanism, and all branches of the occult.

An idol is anything that we put in place of God, or worship as if it were God. Idols can be objects, concepts, or even people. People often create idols that represent gods from foreign lands; for example, it's not uncommon to find Buddha or other Hindu statues when shopping for home decor. Perhaps even more alarming is finding the same goddess statues found on a witch's altar marketed as bookshelf decor in a retail home furnishing store. These items, once limited to specialty witchcraft shops, now appear in mainstream stores. The undiscerning may use these simply for aesthetic purposes, bringing them into their homes out of ignorance; however, what seems a harmless decoration may actually be a conduit for darkness.

The question often arises concerning Christian statues, since many adorn their homes with statues of Jesus, Mary, and the saints. Even these can become idols if we allow ourselves to reverence and worship the physical statue rather than God Himself. We have to be careful that we're not replacing a personal relationship with Jesus with an outward expression of our faith. We recognize a statue is only a man-made object, and any object that we direct our worship to becomes an idol.

Another place where idols may be located in the home can be as close as our own backyard. Many fountains and statues of foreign gods or goddesses line our walkways. Green Man plaques hang on shed doors, crystal balls enhance our gardens, and fairy and pentacle wind chimes hang from our porch roof eaves. We must leave no stone unturned in our search to uncover the unfruitful works of darkness.

Occult and Witchcraft Items

People may ask, "Can an object as small as a tumbled stone, stunning crystal, or votive candle be a big concern? What harm could they bring? The candle's package says 'Peace' and that it aids in relaxation." They may also question the harm in using a white sage smudge stick. Or even a vial of an essential oil that came from a Christian retailer who said it is holistic. But if we read the small print and do our research, we'll find out where it originated. What about the tarot reading at the Renaissance Faire? Your friends stopped by the tent and everybody got a reading. It was just for fun. The lady even gave you a tarot card to bring home! These are just some ways witchcraft items can end up in the home.

Remember, one little foothold is all the enemy looks for at first. He introduces these devices, which are deeply rooted in spiritual deception, unbeknownst to us. As in the cases above, the items brought into the home, though small, carried a heavy spiritual weight. These items open spiritual doorways, providing demonic forces with an entryway into the home. Keeping occult objects in our home aligns us with the forces of darkness. Deuteronomy 18:10 states that witchcraft in any form is detestable in God's sight.

Any items associated with the occult or witchcraft, such

as wands, athames, chalices, pentagrams, tarot cards, Ouija boards, and magickal mirrors, are tools of the devil. Even crystals, incense, and gemstones can carry demonic influences, as they are connected to occult practices. God warns against the practices of divination, sorcery, and necromancy, for they are an abomination to Him (see Isaiah 8:19). Witchcraft is a direct rebellion against God, and by resorting to the use of magick, people are choosing occult methods over godly methods (such as to pray and seek wisdom from God alone). Seeking answers by other means directly opposes His command. It doesn't matter whether or not we understood the spiritual significance in these objects when we bought them; the enemy has no problem using that ignorance against us.

The enemy is not oblivious to how knowledge and literature shape our life. Books are powerful tools that carry ideologies, spiritual principles, and demonic influence into hearts and homes. Occult practices used to be shrouded in secrecy, and only those initiated had access to their teachings. However, that has all changed and many books containing spells, rituals, and other practices are now widely available in local and online bookstores. These books lure readers into the world of occultism, often promising power, success, and supernatural knowledge, but they deliver spiritual bondage.

Entertainment and Media

The enemy has infiltrated the entertainment industry on a grand scale. Today, it can be hard to find anything admirable to be entertained by. Music and films are powerful mediums that have the potential to deliver good, wholesome entertainment or to invite spiritual darkness into the confines of our home. All too often, they glorify violence, sexuality, rebellion, and witchcraft. It's no longer subtle hints, but rather a blatant over-sensationalized demonic invasion. Some musicians and filmmakers admit to their own involvement, which they incorporate into their craft of filmmaking, lyrics, and stage performances.

These are spiritual declarations that are so easily downloaded into our home. It's no longer limited to tapes and CDs in our entertainment center. We must now do a thorough wipe on computers, tablets, and phones. All devices that house digital downloads are subject to this home invasion, and many saved items need to be deleted. Psalm 101:3 warns us to set our eyes on things that are right and good, not on any forbidden fruit.

Taking Out the Garbage

By now, you've likely felt the prompting of the Holy Spirit and have some idea of items that must go. But if this is the first time, you're doing a spiritual housecleaning, or you've noticed some accumulation of unwanted junk, you will want to be thorough. Go through each room of your home with prayerful eyes and, by using spiritual discernment, locate anything the Holy Spirit reveals as something that doesn't glorify God and needs to go. If you find yourself attempting to justify keeping any questionable item, keep in mind that ignorance is not innocence, and remember the heart is deceitful above all else (see Jeremiah 17:9). By practicing spiritual discernment, we strengthen our ability to align our lives with God's will and avoid future deception. Keep a prayerful attitude and compile all items revealed to you in a large sturdy garbage bag or trash can. Make sure you search with discerning eyes in every nook and cranny. Continue until you've prayed through the entire house.

In Acts 19:17-20, Ephesus was notorious for the use of magick. They furnished themselves with books on things such as astrology, telling fortunes, interpreting dreams, raising spirits, and predicting future events. They even sought tutors in the instruction of the black arts. Upon having their consciences awakened, they renounced their magick. They gathered all their books together and burned them in the sight of all men. Having counted up the value, the books were worth fifty thousand pieces of silver.

The above Scripture reference shows the Ephesians' fear, remorse, and desire to not give in to temptation or pass demonic influences onto others. Their bonfire should be an example to us, as upon having our own conscience sheared, we should bring forward the ungodly books and items that glorify the god of this world and dispose of them. We too, should want to remove any temptation, and demonic influences from our lives, while also preventing passing them on to anyone else. One way we can accomplish this is by having our own book-burning event. Be sure to find a safe place outdoors and a fireproof container to build your fire. An outside fire pit works well. Don't forget to adhere to city or township ordinance codes regarding fire pits and open burning to ensure compliance and safety.

Pray as you place the books and items into the flames, and repent from having them in your home and having any involvement with the works of darkness through them. Renounce and break any association, power, or hold over any book or accursed items by the blood of Jesus, then ask Jesus to cleanse you from any unrighteousness and close any doors you may have opened as an entryway. Then incorporate praise and worship; read Scripture, play praise music, and worship the Lord. You can also incorporate psalms in song. If you've been involved with the magick arts, please see the appendix for a sample prayer to use when disposing of magickal tools and items, as well as tools used in various initiations.

If you don't have the space or cannot build a fire, you can shred books, destroy objects or jewelry, etc. so that they are no longer usable. I threw all my occult and witchcraft books, items, and clothing into a firepit that Pastor Lyndon had set ablaze. Later, I took a sledgehammer to my stepdaughter's metal idols and ritualistic knives, then dumped the pieces into the river. Just be sure to make them unusable in case anyone else gets a hold of them.

Anointing the Home

Once the home has been spiritually cleansed and all spiritual garbage has been disposed of, it's time to reclaim the home for the Lord. In order to keep our home safe from any evil kickback, we'll want to activate our Holy Spirit Security System (HSSS) for our home protection. Psalm 91:10 says, "No evil shall befall you, nor shall any plague come near your dwelling." Therefore, not only are we under God's protection, but our dwelling (our home) is also under His divine protection. I suggest prayerfully anointing the home with oil to set it apart for the Lord and receive promised protection. Oil represents the power of the Holy Spirit, and is symbolic of being cleansed and made holy, so anointing is an act of symbolically consecrating our home unto Him.

We anoint our homes using the Passover as an example. In Exodus 12:22–28, God instructed the Israelites to anoint their doorposts with the blood of a sacrificial lamb, thus marking their homes for protection from the destroyer. Since Jesus became our sacrificial lamb, we no longer slaughter a lamb at Passover. However, we can symbolically anoint our doorframe to protect our home from the evil one. For this, we use anointing oil, since it is what Moses used when anointing the tabernacle (see Exodus 40:9). My choice is oil from Israel, but any olive oil will suffice. The oil itself doesn't hold any power; it is putting our faith in the finished work of Jesus on the cross that has power. Once you've selected the oil, pray to consecrate (set aside) it for anointing. You'll want to store it in a separate vial or jar and use it strictly for anointing.

Spiritual Housecleaning

Begin in the room where you enter your home. As worship music plays softly in the background (if possible), pray out loud and in the spirit:

1. Rebuke any evil still lingering in the room/home and any attempt by the enemy against your home or family.

2. Invite the Holy Spirit to come and dwell within the room and in your home. Reclaim and dedicate the room to the Lord. Pray God's will be accomplished in your household, and that He receives glory in it.

3. Anoint the doorframes of the room with the oil while praying for God's supernatural protection over your home and family through the blood of Jesus. Remember, Jesus is the Anointed One, who covers and protects you.

4. Let your heart and home be a place for His Holy Spirit to live and dwell within.

You can think of a spiritual housecleaning like spring cleaning. It's not a bad idea to schedule one once a year. I personally do mine near Passover, since it's the time of year when many typically do a physical spring cleaning. You can select another memorable day that serves as a reminder to go through the house and check for any items that may have crept into the home during the year. It's also good to clean house whenever you move into a new place or discern a spiritual disturbance within the home. Another time to do a spiritual housecleaning would be right after you or someone in your household has gone through deliverance.

In closing, a fitting proclamation is Joshua 24:15, which was a bold showing of loyalty and commitment to God after the battle of Israel turning away from their shameful behavior and the false gods they worshipped: "And if it seems evil to you to serve the LORD, choose for yourselves this day whom you will serve, whether the gods which your fathers served that *were* on the other side of the River, or the gods of the Amorites, in whose land you dwell. But as for me and my house, we will serve the LORD."

In the next chapter we'll reclaim our goods that the enem has stolen from us.

Behind Enemy Lines

CHAPTER 19

Taking Back Ground

This present darkness has permeated entire communities throughout the globe, leading to moral decay and societal decline. As we've discussed, many have fallen prey to the enemy's lies, and if that's not bad enough, they defend immoral acts and impious beliefs as though they hold the keys to life. The deception is smothering. Like an army of hornets at summer's end, they erratically swarm about, attacking anyone in their flight, and knowing that not only is their season over, but the end is on the horizon. Their time to inject a poisonous sting into the church body is now or never, and the more believers they can take out, the less they'll have to contend with.

As the church, we need to discern the times, as we know we are about to experience *kairos* or God's appointed time and we need to be busy doing the work the Lord has called us to do. We have a war to fight, and just as the enemy's camp is mobilizing for aggression, we need to be prepared to be on the offensive when necessary. Notice I said "when necessary." Ninety-nine percent of our warfare is defensive, as we stand strong and resist the enemy's attacks against us. We primarily use defensive weapons, although some have dual purposes and can also serve in offensive roles. As the days grow darker, and even now, there are times we actively tread on serpents and scorpions, crushing (ground captured by) our spiritual adversaries, otherwise known as Satan and his demons.

Going On the Offensive

We're on a mission, and sometimes our mission calls for offensive warfare, where we invade enemy territory to either reclaim or gain ground. Breaching enemy ground is not something we want to do haphazardly, but with expert intelligence and strategy based on our knowledge of the Word of God and spiritual discernment. The terrain we tread may call for clearing spiritual thorns and thistles, discerning and determining demonic landmines, and engaging demons that attempt to hinder our directive. This is another form of offensive warfare.

There are several ways to forge ahead in offensive warfare, such as evangelizing captives bound in the enemy's encampment, bringing freedom to the demonically oppressed, and advancing the kingdom (including taking back ground). We may find a dual purpose for warfare. For instance, deliverance for the demonized individual, and warfare to take back ground that the enemy stole during their demonization. We use the same weapons of warfare as used for defense, but with a different approach. We'll get into our weaponry in a bit; for now, let's delve into the reasons we take an offensive position.

Forging Ground Offense

As discussed in chapter eleven, we step into our gospel boots to advance through the harsh demonic terrain to deliver the gospel message of salvation and freedom to those held captive by the enemy. There are two major groups of people for whom we trek into this hostile territory.

The first is lost sheep who have gone astray (i.e., believers who have wandered from the truth and fallen into the enemy's trap). The god of this age blinds those who once saw. Jesus shares the parable of the lost sheep in Matthew 18:10–14, telling of the good shepherd who leaves the ninety-nine to find the one lost sheep and then shares the joy of the sheep being found and returned to the fold. The second is unbelievers whom the enemy has entrapped. The god of this age, Satan, has deceived them, so we must pray for their eyes to be opened, and for the truth of the gospel to be revealed.

In order to reach them, we navigate through inhospitable areas, removing obstacles in the way and engaging in warfare with demons blocking our path. Once we've reached these people, we pray that the veil of deception would be removed and their eyes would be opened. The light of the gospel shines in, overcoming the darkness, breaking through the prison doors, pulling down strongholds, breaking chains, and setting them free. The aim of engaging in offensive warfare is to bring restoration and liberation to those held in captivity.

Opening Prison Doors

Our mission to drive out demons from those being held captive is another form of offensive warfare. We don't sit on the sidelines waiting for demons to come out on their own; rather, we confront them here on earth, which God has given man the authority over. The demons have come onto our turf, so to speak, and are harassing our fellow human beings. In Luke 9:1, Jesus gave the disciples the power and authority to cast out demons; therefore, we have the jurisdiction to liberate those experiencing demonic oppression.

Taking Back Stolen Ground

Many times, particularly after deliverance, we realize what the enemy has stolen from us. Usually, we've left ourselves unguarded, giving the enemy an opportunity to ransack our home. We discover our goods plundered only after we become victims of theft. In 1 Samuel 30, we read about David, the man after God's own heart, and yet in his weariness and unbelief he stepped out of God's will. Operating in a spirit of fear and unbelief, he pledged his loyalty to the enemy of God's people. Unbelief is so very dangerous. It is one of the enemy's surest ways of causing our downfall, and we must avoid this pitfall at all costs.

God has given us free will, which enables us to make our own choices, including trading His truth for the lies the devil feeds us. But with that choice comes consequences. For those who fall to the enemy's schemes, destruction awaits. David finally did what he should have done at the get go: he encouraged himself in the Lord and asked God if he should pursue the Amalekites, who had plundered the homes of his men and taken their women and children captive. With God's direction, he led his men and found the Amalekites eating, drinking and dancing, unprepared for the fight. This made their conquest all the easier, and they recovered all that the enemy had taken and then some.

So, what are we to do if our house has been plundered? The devil may have stolen someone from our family, in particular our child. Maybe he's stolen our health or finances. He could have stolen our joy, or our sense of the Lord's calling in our life. The enemy can steal precious time and opportunities and keep us in deception. Do we pursue or let it go? We seek God, repenting of anything that needs repentance, and then if God directs us to pursue, we pray for the strategy to take back what the enemy has stolen. Many make declarations of going to take back what the enemy stole, but remember, David made a surprise attack, and his surprise attack on the enemy camp made his conquest easier. Do yourself a favor, and unless God tells you otherwise, let your repossession of your stolen goods be unexpected.

Remember, when we pray and bind the strongman, One stronger than he will come and overpower him by taking away all his possessions. He had no legal right to those stolen possessions. The enemy may have a hold on what's rightfully ours now, but Jesus is the stronger man who takes the stolen goods from the enemy's grip and restores them back to their rightful owner.

We're reclaiming our possessions by engaging in earthly warfare. We have authority over our home, family, inheritance, and possessions, and we're reclaiming what is rightfully ours. Some of the earthly demonic forces may be from the spiritual realm, but the battleground is here on the earth.

Restricted Air Space

Many times, believers will step into the heavenlies warfare unknowingly. This can happen when we decide to come against principalities in geographical regions. We can think of New York City as an epitome of evil, and while we're called to pray for the lost and share the gospel message on the streets, thus engaging in warfare on our earthly level, we'd step into a whole new level if we were to wage war against the principality over New York City. That would be engaging in warfare in the heavenlies, the abode of principalities we have not been given the authority over.

Remember, the angel delivering a message to Daniel struggled against the prince of Persia in the heavenlies for twenty-one days, causing a delay. Michael, one of the chief angels, had to help him overcome the resistance. Since even an angel required help from a higher-ranking angel, how much less capable are we beings, who are created a little lower than angels, of winning a battle in an unfamiliar and unauthorized territory? Not only do we want to avoid engaging principalities in warfare, but we also don't want to wrestle with Satan. Rather, we wrestle with his demonic infantry.

As another example, many years ago, the church I was attending often joined with a pro-life group in the area to protest at abortion clinics and pray for the unborn. Many from all over the country have diligently gone before the Lord for the innocent lives being discarded for many long years, and now, what a joy it was to see those prayers come to fruition at the beginning of this year. The battle is not over, but we've taken back a lot of the ground that was once lost, by praying for the women and rebuking the spirit of death and abortion over the lives of the unborn. This is spiritual warfare, within our earthly realm that we have the authority to engage in.

Even so, we don't have authority to rebuke a principality over abortion in specific cities or regional areas, as that would take warfare beyond our earthly realm. Principalities over cities, states, and countries have legal rights to those areas, as God placed them in positions of power over these regions. Mankind then exhorts them in these places by their evil hearts and actions. By far, the fight is not over, and we cannot become complacent, rather continuing to advance forward on the ground while leaving the angels to contend within the heavenly realm.

Advancing on Enemy Territory

So, is there nothing we can do to hinder the work of principalities and powers that release evil into our communities from their positions of power? No. We may not battle the rulers of darkness, but we are not powerless to affect the situation. Remember, prayer is one of our weapons of warfare, and we can pray by asking God to change the hearts and minds of the people who substantiate the right of the principalities we're up against. Godly powers and principalities replace evil principalities and powers in heavenly realms when we transform high places in our natural realm. Amos 3:6 tells us that when the city does right, God removes the evil, but when a city falls into sin, God allows evil to be in charge. Our hearts help determine what will rule in the heavenlies. In order to tear down the strongholds over regions, we have to tear it down within the hearts of mankind.

We can also contribute to heavenly realm warfare by praying and asking God to send His warring angels to wrestle with spiritual wickedness in high places to intervene for us, thus preventing an attack from the heavenly abode that would affect us on earth.

Spiritual Specialty Operations

Regardless of the above warnings, there are some who believe it is their mission to engage in warfare in the heavenlies. If you believe you are called to this type of warfare, I'd suggest you seriously and prayerfully reconsider. Principalities and ruling demons are not powerless beings to be taken lightly, especially in their domain. They are active agents of Satan working to annihilate you completely from the spiritual realm. Before you attempt such endeavors, check with your pastor or church elders, and at the very least be sure you have training, gifts in discerning of spirits, and proper spiritual covering. While my pastor encourages us to know our limits (2 Corinthians 10:13), he is one who addresses ruling spirits over cities or nations, but states that it requires a coordinated Spirit-filled group who move in discernment and who can come in agreement to focus on that spirit. Keep in mind that he has been in deliverance ministry for years. It's certainly not for the average believer.

Offensive Weaponry

For offensive maneuvers, we use the dual weaponry in our arsenal—the defensive weapons that can also be used offensively. The difference is how we wield them. In defensive positions, we're standing our ground and pushing back the enemy that comes against us. On the offense, we're moving forward into enemy territory, clearing a pathway and striking whatever stands in our way. We have a simple goal in focus, given to us by God; this is certainly not something we do just to flex our spiritual muscles. Much prayer precedes our specific task, and then we wait upon the Lord until we receive His command.

The territory may be the enemies, but the battleground is still on earth. It's an area demonic forces have taken over. We're not taking over a territorial principality; rather, we're rescuing one of our own who has is entangled in its zone. The goal is to reach them and get out together. We can also use offensive warfare when we're advancing the church into an enemy's hostile area. We are called to bring the gospel message into all the world, which means we may trample on scorpion tails that try to stop the spread of the gospel.

The Sword on the Offense

The Word of God is the sword of the Spirit, and people use it defensively and offensively. To take up the sword is to speak out a Scripture against our opposition. God's authority and power reside in the written Word, and speaking it releases that power into the battle. One difference in using the sword for defense versus offense is the Scriptures we speak. The Holy Spirit guides our choice of Scriptures, which we then speak with God's authority. Our tongue is like a sharp sword, being is a deadly weapon than can wield both life or death (see Proverbs 18:21). We must use it wisely and with caution.

Advancing in Faith

We use the shield of faith not only for defense but also as an offensive weapon. Using a shield to push forward is a technique that causes the enemy to back off, and can create an opening for us to strike with the sword of the Spirit. It is faith that forces our way in to move the mountains that stand in our way. Faith and the sword of the Spirit work to both defend and defeat the enemy. An example would be the previously discussed turtle formation, where believers lock shields, creating a tight protective shield that repels enemy's attack as they force their way into an area.

Praying on the Offensive

Prayer is a powerful weapon of warfare that reaches great lengths. When we engage in prayer on the offense, we enter the throne room of God, petitioning for the Lord to strengthen us and provide help in our time of need. At a moment's notice, we can call for backup through prayer support or for angels to assist us or intervene in the heavenlies that is spilling over onto earth. Praying in the Spirit and speaking in tongues are two amplified forms of prayer that touch the heart of God to move heaven and earth on our behalf. These forms of prayer change the spiritual atmosphere and unlock the power of God within us, disarming the power of the enemy. These are secret communications with God, in a language that prevents the enemy from comprehending our request, through the Holy Spirit making intercession through us.

Front-Line Praise

Our praise joins with the worship from heaven, which means we have the company of heaven joining us as we march into battle. We should always lead our battle with praise to God. When He rises, the enemy scatters, clearing our path. When we praise God, our words become like the double-edged sword, destroying the obstacles the enemy has placed in our path. The Levites are an excellent Old Testament example of this. They were musicians and worship leaders who would accompany the troops into battle with music, song, and praise, creating the atmosphere and seeking God's divine favor and protection.

Testifying to Victory

This weapon of our warfare is one that many believers overlook. It's often difficult to get people to share what the Lord has done in their life, perhaps because the enemy has done a good job of concealing from believers the enormous power it holds. If only we could convey the magnitude of this weapon, we'd have an endless stream of people testifying.

Testimony serves as an offensive weapon because when we testify, we overcome the enemy! That's it—he's done. The whole gospel in a nutshell. Testifying gives glory to God for what He has done in our life. This atmosphere enables God to work miracles in other people's lives as they hear how God touched someone else. It builds faith and gives hope to others for their own miracle. It breaks the chains of fear, doubt, and unbelief, and releases the hold over them. The blood of Jesus is a powerful weapon that destroyed the work of the devil. By His blood, we overcome the enemy, and by the word of our testimony, we find victory over Satan and the assurance of our salvation.

Next, we will establish why our preparedness for end times battles is essential.

Behind Enemy Lines

CHAPTER 20

Preparing For End Times Battles

As we navigate the end times, how do we prepare for what, according to the Bible, will be the worst time in history? The keyword is *prepare*. We must move hastily, for we do not know how much time we have. While the exact hour is unknown to us, we can discern the seasons.

Jesus used the fig tree as a metaphor to teach about the signs preceding His second coming (see Matthew 24:32–33): "When its branch has already become tender and puts forth leaves, you know that summer is near. So, you also, when you see all these things, know that [the day of the Lord] is near—at the doors." Although the exact day and hour of Jesus' return may not be known, the "seasons" are discernible. It's interesting to note that figs grow behind the leaves on the ripened branch, so unless we look for them, we miss them; therefore, we must be watchful and pay attention to their progression. When the time has come into fruition, and the figs have fulfilled their purpose, they will fall with the great shaking of the earth. At that moment, the final chapter comes to a dramatic end. Jesus said we would not know the day and hour, but He has also warned us of what to expect and advised that we be in a continual state of preparedness.

Preaching the Gospel to All Nations

I believe we're currently in a reprieve. We've had a foretaste of what our world will be like when the Lord lifts His hand of restraint of the wickedness on the earth. Although we breathe in fresh air, kick off our slippers, and relax in our recliner, we cannot simply lie back and savor the moment. We must seize the day and advance the kingdom of God. It is not the time to sit idle. As soon as our boots hit the ground, we must run, traversing the highways and byways across the earth, spreading the gospel message, casting out demons, and healing the sick. We go as lambs among wolves to bring the gospel of peace to those who will receive it, and we move on from those who don't. The internet has interconnected most of the globe, greatly advancing our ability to share the gospel; however, some places still lack internet service, and often hands-on ministry is necessary. This is our mission, Church.

Jesus told us that all nations will hate us for His name's sake (see Matthew 24:9-14). The disciples certainly endured their share of persecution, even unto death, as they went forth to preach the gospel. Yet, they did not see the end of days in their lifetime, and Jesus' words remain relevant today for the church at large. What befell the early disciples also foreshadows what believers may undergo at the hands of an antagonistic world. Today, millions of Christians globally face persecution and discrimination, which can be as slight as cultural hostility or insults or as extreme as violent attacks and governmental oppression. Even in the United States, the home of religious freedom, the persecution of Christians is a growing epidemic, an increase that we can expect as the end of days nears.

Our brother in the Lord, Ron Harnage, whose testimony appears in my second book, *From the Craft to Christ*,[52] suffered such a fate. Ron spent nearly ten years in outreach ministry and heeded God's call to evangelism all the way up into the mountains of India, where he witnessed the miraculous power of the

---

[52] S. A. Tower, From the *Craft to Christ: The Allure of Witchcraft and the Church's Response* (Dwell Publishing, 2014, 2019).

Holy Spirit at work. It comes as no surprise that as the gospel was spreading in this spiritually dry and thirsty land, the forces of darkness arose to hinder the work of the kingdom.

It is most likely that religious extremists got wind of Ron's evangelism and had someone set him up with an offer to pastor a church. Two weeks later, authorities discovered Ron's body in the hills near where he had preached and helped the orphan children. In the end, Ron paid the ultimate sacrifice, being persecuted and suffering for his witness to Christ. His testimony didn't end when he came out of the occult, but continued as he witnessed for Christ in the villages of the Himalayan Mountains and even now, continues to bring glory to God from his grave.

Wars and Rumors of Wars

We certainly have seen an increase in wars, and there is a rumor that World War III may be just over the horizon. Currently, Russia and Ukraine are at war, and Israel and Hamas are also at war. We should more closely observe the latter conflict for relevance in end times prophecy. Either of these wars could escalate into World War III, but use caution, because wars and rumors of them, in and of themselves, are not good predictors of the last days, and Jesus has said they are to be expected.

There is also unrest with a potential threat of China over Taiwan and Russia over those with historical or geographical ties. Certainly, we are witnessing an increase of conflicts on a global scale, but Jesus said they are a part of the ongoing human condition. He offers us assurance, telling us to keep our hearts from being troubled, and encourages us to put our trust in Him despite the rumors we hear (see John 16:33). Wars are an inevitable piece to our timetable, but they are not a *sign* of the end times. Rather, they are considered birthing pains. The end is not yet, so we expect that things will get much worse, for "nation shall rise against nation, and kingdom against kingdom" (Matthew 24:7).

False Prophets and False Christs

Jesus warned His disciples in Matthew 24:4-5, "Take heed that no one deceives you. For many will come in My name, saying, 'I am the Christ,' and will deceive many." Before we delve into false prophets, let's be sure we understand what a genuine prophet of God is.

God has certain requirements for a person to be a prophet. According to the Scriptures, a person is called to be a prophet (see Deuteronomy 18:15 NLT).

It's not something that we just decide we want to be, as it is a gift and not taught. The prophet's role is to communicate God's truth to an individual, a group, or the world. Sharing hard truth can create quite the stir, even within the church body. They are also called a "seer" because they see visions and dreams and interpret them into the message that God is conveying to the people. Many who claim to be prophets are not of God. These self-proclaimed prophets may be on the rise in the world, but as we've already established, a prophet must be called by God and must show a great deal of continual prophetic accuracy. To determine whether a message comes from God, we examine whether it aligns with God's Word and whether the prophecies are fulfilled. If neither of these exists, then we should disregard these prophecies.

One thing I believe is of the utmost importance is Luke 17:24: "For as the lightning that flashes out of one part under heaven shines to the other part under heaven, so also the Son of Man will be in His day." On that day, if anyone claims to be Christ—no matter how good the teaching, how many healings he has done or the signs and wonders that follow—we must not believe him. Jesus forewarned that many will come in His name (see Matthew 24:4-5) and said that even the elect will be deceived (Matthew 24:24). Jesus has already told us that when He returns, it won't be like His first coming (see Matthew 24:26-27). He will not be walking around preaching and healing the sick. So, anyone who says he is Jesus, isn't. When He returns, He will come as quick as a flash of light. He'll be here and gone in the twinkling of an eye and will have gathered His church with Him.

S.A. TOWER

Remember Lot's Wife

Jesus has provided an excellent visual of what the day will look like (how evil it will be) before His coming. We can use the story of Lot's wife as a barometer to weigh the corruptness of our current world and get an idea of where we fall on the scale of time. There are two important points here: 1) It is the outcry of grievous sin that provokes God to execute justice (as it was in the Days of Noah); and 2) Jesus emphasized that in that day, wherever one may be, "let him likewise not return back," but "remember Lot's wife" (Luke 17:31).

With a warning coming directly from Jesus, we as believers would be wise to take heed of this important instruction. And what can we learn from Lot's wife regarding His second coming? Let's look at Genesis 19, and the towns of Sodom and Gomorrah.

God blessed Abraham and his nephew Lot with prosperity. Each owned many livestock. However, their herd keepers constantly quarreled, forcing the two men to separate. Lot chose the town of Sodom as his home because of its well-watered plains in the Jordan Valley, which reminded him of the garden of the Lord, or the land of Egypt (see Genesis 13:10). The men of Sodom were wicked men who sinned greatly against the Lord (see Genesis 13:2–13); they dishonored God and His ways by practicing sexual perversions, pride, gluttony, and inhospitality. So wicked was this place that God told Abraham, who had been interceding on behalf of his nephew, that upon hearing the outcry of the grievous sin of Sodom and Gomorrah, He would execute justice.

Two angels, who appeared as men, visited Sodom to survey the wickedness. Upon seeing them, Lot hurried them out of the town square to the refuge of his home, but while they were eating, the townsmen came pounding on the door demanding Lot hand over his guests so they could engage in sexual relations with them.

Lot attempted to deter them, to no avail, even offering his own daughters to them, but they desired the two men. Just as the crowd turned on Lot, the angels pulled him back inside, shut the door, and struck the townsmen with blindness (Genesis 19:1–26), hindering their ability to pursue them. As dawn broke, Lot was awakened by the two angels, who urged him to escape the impending doom with his wife and daughters. When the family was outside the city gate, the angels instructed them to flee for their lives to the mountains, and warned them not to look back.

Lot and his family arrived in the small town of Zoar, and God's judgment fell as brimstone (sulfur) and fire rained down on Sodom and Gomorrah from out of the heavens. However, Lot's wife turned and looked back. The Hebrew word used here for "looked back" is to gaze or look intently at or regard with pleasure.[53] So Lot's wife is described as looking back from behind him, which may indicate she lingered behind gazing or desiring to go back. The text doesn't provide the details, but it's possible that she fell behind Lot and in the time, she spent longing for her home, she got caught in the fire and brimstone raining down from heaven, turning her into a pillar of salt.

God destroyed Sodom, Gomorrah, and three other nearby cities, leaving a wasteland uninhabitable to this day. It has, however, after many years of desolation been located. To really gain an understanding of the destruction of this once well-watered plush land full of vegetation, check out the video "Sulfur Balls of Sodom and Gomorrah," by Expedition Bible on YouTube.[54] It journeys to the ancient cities of Sodom and Gomorrah after four thousand years. You'll see the ashy burnt layer just beneath the surface of the entire site that is full of human bone fragments and pottery from the Bronze Age (the time of Genesis) as well as the burnt layer of destruction over the cemetery where over a half a million people's bones warped in their graves by heat, proving a natural disaster had occurred. I believe the most interesting evidence is the numerous white sulfur balls found around the site that, when lit in multitudes, would create burning sulfur raining down from the sky as described in the Bible.

---

53   "Genesis 19:26 Translation & Meaning," Quotes Cosmos, accessed June 23, 2025, https://www.quotescosmos.com/bible/bible-verses/Genesis-19-26.html.
54   Expedition Bible, "Sulfur Balls of Sodom and Gomorrah," YouTube, June 3, 2022, https://www.youtube.com/watch?v=jQl4KaRtef8.

What must this sin city have looked like in its heightened wickedness? It reminds me of an incident that took place in a small town that was the hub of witchcraft in my area. My Christian friend Bo had come up to meet with me one night and arrived early, giving him time to observe the town. When the ritual I was involved in ended, I went out to meet him, only to find him furious. He said, "As I sat outside tonight waiting for you, I watched gays and lesbians romantically embracing one another as if it were normal. The people coming out of the bars are wasted. Sin is blatantly acted upon without remorse, and even people coming out of the place you were in, laughed about engaging in sexual acts." He then shared that God had revealed to him that this whole town was like Sodom and Gomorrah, and warned me to get out. At the time, I wasn't at all receptive to his discernment, but years later, after looking back with a repentant heart, I saw a small-town model of Sodom with a big-town level of wickedness. I can only thank God that He rescued me before the end of days, because that is what Jesus was talking about.

Each of us is called to leave behind the sins of our past, including the places where we entertained them. Although I didn't have a dramatic falling out with my past pagan friends, I had to leave the town, the people, and my sinful activities behind because those friendships were rooted in wickedness. This is a heart issue, and there is no room for compromise. I needed to set my eyes above and follow the leading of the Holy Spirit to escape the destruction that will one day come upon that place.

Wherever our past sin may be lying—pride, greed, drug addiction, alcoholism, sexual immorality, pornography, witchcraft, etc.—we have to keep our eyes on Jesus and never look back. Sometimes, when things grow weary, people rethink bygone days as if they've somehow sweetened with time. (How many women, after going through a hard break-up, reconsider a former boyfriend?) But when that great day comes, there will be no time for reconsidering bygone days, glancing back at our past sin (none of which has improved with age anyway), or hanging on to our current sins. When Lot left the city of Sodom, fire and brimstone rained from heaven and destroyed all that remained there. So will it be when Jesus returns (see Luke 17:26–30). We must examine the condition of our heart so that we prioritize obedience and resist the allure of our past lifestyles while avoiding spiritual compromise. Both now and in the end days, we must not look back.

End Times Preparation

I'm not suggesting we all build bunkers and stock up on resources, but spiritual preparation is the key. The battle of good versus evil is increasing and will reach an all-time high, perhaps in our lifetime. As the end of the age nears, the opposition will not only increase but also intensify. So, regardless of how close the day, we need to buckle down and prepare. We need to stay alert and let go of any pride. We recognize that God is our strength and He alone will provide our spiritual and emotional fortitude to overcome any obstacles that lie ahead.

Resistance Training

We spend more time standing firm and resisting the enemy on the battlefield than anything else. In the latter days, resisting evil will be an even greater challenge. We have already seen an increase in wickedness, but this is nothing compared to the depravity that is to come. Think of the hardest temptation we could resist, then multiply it by ten thousand forces of darkness. An impossible task? In our own strength, yes, but not so if we're moving in God's power and surrounded by a multitude of angels. Remember where our help comes from. To stand firm and resist the darkness of that day, we'll need to fully submit to God. This requires discipline in obedience to His Word, beginning today and persevering until the end.

Getting Our House in Order

In my prayer time recently, I believe the Lord impressed upon my heart to "get your house in order." He then revealed areas in my life that need attention and correction. To name a few, there was a financial obligation I had forgotten about and needed to address. He also revealed some items that I had hidden away years ago that I needed to burn and dispose of. It's crucial that we immediately confront and repent of each sin as the Spirit brings it to light.

I encourage you to do the same. Ask, "How, Lord?" and trust He'll answer. Just as important is our response by acting upon what He reveals to us. All too often, we get sidetracked and lose sight of what we're supposed to do. We put it off until tomorrow, but then months later, tomorrow still hasn't come. Time is of the essence. Our action is required. Don't delay!

Unity in the Body

Maintaining unity and encouraging one another in the Lord is crucial as we continue toward the end times. Spending time together can lift our spirit, especially during increasingly difficult times, and help us maintain our focus and obedience to God. So long as it's possible, we cannot overlook the importance of gathering to build one another up in faith. As we face spiritual and physical challenges in the days ahead, we find strength in numbers, which enables us to prevail against the forces of this coming darkness. There may come a time when the church will return to its roots as an underground fellowship of believers who connect for prayer, Bible study, and corporate worship.

Communication Training

How wonderful it is to know that when tribulation comes, we have a direct line of communication with God. We serve an interactive God, and prayer is a two-way conversation. We ask and He answers, or He asks and we answer. By conversing with Him on a regular basis, we learn to recognize His voice over any other. We know that communication strengthens a relationship, including our relationship with God.

And how should we pray as time draws nigh? Here are some end times prayers to pray.

- Pray for the day to hasten. Pray for the advancement of the gospel throughout the nations, especially those in remote areas of the world who have not yet heard (see Matthew

24:14). By doing so, we hasten His coming (see 2 Peter 3–12).

- Pray for laborers. Ask the Lord to send laborers out into His harvest to spread the gospel and minister to the people (Matthew 9:38).
- Pray for discernment. Discern the season we are in so that you are ready (Matthew 24:32–35). And discern the spirits that are operating around you (1 John 4:1).
- Pray against being hindered. Pray for your physical condition and that nothing would prevent you from fleeing quickly when Christ returns (Matthew 24:19–20).
- Pray that God will shorten the great tribulation. This way the elite may survive (see Matthew 24:21–22).
- Pray to remain diligent. Keep your lamp full and don't let it run dry (see Matthew 25:13).
- Be serious and watchful in your prayers. Pray that you will love and show hospitality to others, and that God may be glorified through your speaking and ministry (see 1 Peter 4:7–11).
- Pray to be found a faithful servant on that day (see Matthew 24:45–51).

This chapter has highlighted the vital role of preparation in overcoming the growing challenges of the last days, and now the next will look at the need for spiritual discernment as we navigate in a world steeped in wickedness where appearances are deceiving.

CHAPTER 21

War Of The Worlds

An interesting phenomenon occurred while I was writing this book. Nearby in New Jersey, drones began mysteriously appearing in the night sky. They weren't normal recreational drones; these were the size of a compact car and in various shapes. Being exceptionally low-flying crafts, some with flashing red, green, and white lights, they flew right above the treetops. They returned night after night, first surveying North Jersey, then New York and on down the Jersey Shore in the weeks following. Observers spotted some even following a Coast Guard vessel offshore and noted a swarm of them coming inland from over the Atlantic.

They caused quite the stir, starting with regional media and moving to national news. Ironically, it sounded like the sequel of the Orson Welles *War of the Worlds* broadcast, but instead of occurring in the town of Grovers Mill, it had spread throughout the state and beyond. To many, a suspected invasion by aliens seemed a bit more believable considering recent congressional hearings revealed that the US government had recovered non-human "biologics" from UAP (unidentified aerial phenomena)/UFO (unidentified flying object) crash sites. I've always considered UFOs demonic, but why would a fleet of them be hovering over, of all places, New Jersey?

My first thought when the drones appeared in the New Jersey skies was not UFOs but spy balloons, but that seemed unlikely since some video evidence seemed to show rotating wheels enclosed within white circular lights—or could these lit optics actually be eyes? Its movements were quite suspect. Many took notice of their similar appearance to the Ophanim described in Ezekiel's vision (see Ezekiel 1:14–18). The eyed wheels in Ezekiel were beneath the cherubim and carried God's throne, and they also housed the cherubim's spirits. So, what of these unusual wheeled lights rotating in the night sky?

Well, remember, we must be spiritually vigilant and recognize there is a counterfeiter. With that in mind, we have to question the nature of the spirits being housed within these wheels. This is an excellent example of why spiritual discernment is so very important and why I've emphasized its use in this book. Satan is a master imitator, and if we're not careful, we could fall prey to his deception. When faced with determining whether something is of God, the devil, or man, we need to distinguish the truth from the lie.

Lights in the Sky

Years ago, I had what I believe was a close encounter of the first kind while driving home one night with my kids. As we approached the end of my street, I saw what I can only describe as a huge disk-like craft hovering in the clearing just in front of my car. I slowed down, attempting to make sense of what I was seeing. Any chance of diminishing its reality quickly faded with my kids' validation. They asked, "Mom, what's that?" I was speechless. A spotlight came down from its center and began searching around, and I pulled over underneath a tree. It was surreal. The radio stopped working, but stranger still was that I seemed to lose my sense of logic as I just sat there. The craft then moved slowly overhead without a sound, just above the trees, before accelerating and vanishing within seconds.

At the time this occurred, I was a practicing witch. I soon

found out that it was not uncommon to meet other pagans who had UFO encounters. I was told that while UFOs appeared to come from the sky, it was just an illusion to disguise their true habitat—the underworld. Seemingly, that may be a half-truth, because demons have an abode in the earth.

I recently learned that renowned astrophysicist and author of *Lights in the Sky and Little Green Men,* Hugh Ross, who has thoroughly researched the UFO phenomena, has found occult association to be linked with UFO encounters. He suggests that UFOs are not physical craft, but rather interdimensional beings that align with the biblical perspective that God created two species: one that is constrained by the law of physics, such as humans, and one that is not, like the angels. Ross considers these entities demonic, deceptive, and malevolent, and notes that once the doors to the occult have been closed, UFO encounters end.[55] I think my experience substantiates Ross's belief in the connection between the occult and UFO encounters, although I believe the demonic spirits are the manipulators of the craft, not the craft itself. Being bodiless, demons in their limited ability in the physical seek a vehicle to occupy so they can maneuver in the physical world, much in the same way they seek human bodies to fulfill their mission on earth.

The End of Days

Just like in the Orson Welles broadcast, people panic at the thought of the world ending.[56] Whenever something mysterious or unexplainable happens, the thoughts of doomsday arise, but that in itself is nothing new. People have been claiming it's the end of the world all the way back to ancient civilizations. Today is no different. Social media trends surge with current doomsday posts at every new war, every unrest between nations, and every alignment of planets. Social media currently presents terrifying portrayals of the impending apocalypse; it's as if Armageddon's

---

55   Kenneth Samples, Hugh Ross, and Mark Clark, *Lights in the Sky & Little Green Men: A Rational Christian Look at UFOs and Extraterrestrials* (Reasons To Believe, 2012).
56   "The War of the Worlds (1938 radio drama)," Wikipedia, accessed May 5, 2025, https://en.wikipedia.org/wiki/The_War_of_the_Worlds_(1938_radio_drama).

date will begin at midnight, causing an exodus to underground bunkers. This replaces the inspiring novels and movies of the past that once drove sinners to seek repentance. While encouraging a sinner's repentance is good, it's unwise to use the Bible as a scare tactic to bring them into the kingdom. Too many commit to Christ out of fear rather than because of His love for them, so that they can respond and love Him in return (see 1 John 4:19). Then when the Lord tarries, they fall away because "the end" they based their faith on hasn't yet materialized. The book of Revelation shows that this world *will* pass away (see Revelation 21:1). So, the real question in the back of everyone's mind is "When?" We know the answer will come only in real time.

The Book of Revelation

Even a quick read through Revelation amazes us at what is coming to this earth in the last days. If we think we've seen it all, we can think again. When the hidden is unveiled, we will see things in the spiritual realm that our natural eyes have never seen. The book of Revelation depicts a cosmic battle between good and evil, ultimately leading to God's triumph. Opening the scrolls reveals hail and fire raining down upon the earth. The fires in California, Hawaii, and Australia, big as they are, are minuscule compared to the enormity of a fire so severe that a third of the earth is scorched.

Or imagine a burning mountain—perhaps a volcano—that's literally cast into the sea, causing a third of the water to turn to blood, and leading to the death and destruction of a third of the sea creatures and sea vessels. The massive eruption in Yellowstone millions of years ago that left only an enormous crater would pale in comparison.

Or think of stargazing one evening and being stunned by the sight of a giant star falling from heaven and poisoning a third of the rivers and streams. The fallout from such an event would be over three times that of Chernobyl.

As we read further, we discover not only catastrophic natural events, but things our natural minds have a hard time comprehending. One can only imagine an angel opening a bottomless pit and unleashing smoke that obscures the sun, and then monstrous horse-like creatures with human faces and lion-like teeth emerging and swarming like locusts to bring five months of torment and spiritual darkness to the earth. Their leader is Abaddon, the king of the bottomless pit.

We then witness the release of four demonic angels from the Euphrates River, where they have been bound and prepared. Two hundred thousand horsemen, clad in bright and costly armor, follow them. Their horses are fierce like lions and eager to rush into battle, and out of their mouths come fire, smoke, and brimstone that kill a third of mankind.

Those who hold pretribulationist views believe Christians will be raptured well before these events occur. And what a glorious day that would be—but what if their interpretation is wrong?

We need to be ready. In Revelation 3:10, Jesus commends the church of Philadelphia for their perseverance, saying, "Because you have kept My command to persevere, I also will keep you from the hour of trial which shall come upon the whole world, to test those who dwell on the earth." This doesn't say He will remove or rapture us from the earth; rather, He promises to keep or protect us from the coming tribulation, conditional on our faithfulness in keeping His commandments.

If we are here during the tribulation period, how will we know if these unusual events are good or evil? We often assume that if it's formidable, it's unexplainable, and it frightens us, it must be the enemy. But that is not always the case. One of the first things God's angels say to humans who've encountered them is, "Do not be afraid." That's because they're huge and supernatural, and their appearance frightens people. Consider the powerful and majestic quadruple-winged cherubim. These four-faced angelic creatures have the face of a man, a lion, an ox, and an eagle. Or, as we read earlier, the Ophanim, which are celestial beings often depicted as wheels within wheels and covered with eyes. They would bring us pause in the natural, as we wouldn't be able to judge by sight alone, and discernment would quickly become our navigation tool to avoid evil and deception in the last days.

If you haven't received the gift of discernment already, seek the Holy Spirit to bestow it upon you. Begin studying the book of Proverbs, which provides guidance on wisdom and discernment. Familiarize yourself with discerning false teachers, demons, and evil in the world today so that you can make wise decisions that align with God's will when darkness befalls our globe.

End Times Discernment

So, what about the New Jersey drones this chapter opened with? Our government finally released a statement allotting the drones to a Federal Aviation Administration (FAA) project. It's interesting that at first the FAA denied having anything to do with the drones, and went as far as closing down airports amid their sightings, but now they've claimed ownership. It could be their mission was supposed to be secret, though if you were trying to go stealth, why would you expose your craft to millions of people in the evening sky? The explanation provided for its mission was "research and various other reasons," whatever that means. Of course, that's assuming the FAA was transparent and truthful in the intel passed over to our new administration.

During their frequent-flier escapades, I witnessed what I believe was a man-made craft, perhaps a government-classified project, though I'm not totally convinced which government. It was nothing like the otherworldly disk I encountered years ago. I recall the recent reporting of an alarming rise in military-aged men who crossed the then open US–Mexico border. Considering the previous administration's border policy, authorities released them, and they disappeared into the country's interior. For all we know, optimistically speaking, they could be escaping refugees working on a joint mission on a weaponized stealth drone or trading secrets of cyber warfare to defend freedom or worse, and most likely, an opposing country's spies or terrorist group attempting another nefarious operation. Since most of these examples are obviously a physical craft, and some in the technological world of artificial intelligence (AI) cyberspace, then are we safe to say they had nothing to do with demonic entities? I wouldn't be so quick to completely rule out the potential of demonic influence.

Nefarious Forces

Renowned astrophysicist Hugh Ross has described his visit to the Soviet Union during the communist rule. He was there on a speaking engagement to physicists who were heavily involved in the occult and attempting to develop occult weapons to be used against the West. During his first speech, the room erupted in terrifying blood-curdling screams, with some people even curling into a fetal position as they yelled of incredible blasphemous crimes against Jesus. The next day, he returned with a Christian brother who sat in the back and prayed throughout the conference for the demons to be silenced. The room was utterly silent as Ross delivered his speech, and he ended with an invitation to receive and accept Jesus. Ninety percent of those there gave their life to Christ that day.[57]

Back in the 1900s, Nikola Tesla came to the United States from Serbia. Many viewed him as a genius ahead of his time, and his many inventions continue to form the basis of modern technological development. He's responsible for harnessing the power of waterfalls into the first hydroelectric power plant, Niagara Falls, among other things. Tesla aimed to use the earth and its ionosphere as conductors to transmit power and information globally.[58]

Shortly before his death, he claimed to have developed a particle-beam weapon, known as Teleforce, that likely contributed to the disappearance of confidential plans and secret documents from his hotel room along with the conspiracy that the

---

[57] JULIAN DOREY Clips, "Soviet Union's TOP SECRET Occult Studies | Hugh Ross," YouTube, November 14, 2023, https://www.youtube.com/watch?v=9Jh-2QQv2OUo.
[58] "The Miracle Mind of Nikola Tesla from the Tesla Universe Article Collection," Tesla Universe, accessed June 23, 2025, https://teslauniverse.com/nikola-tesla/articles/miracle-mind-nikola-tesla.

US government continued research to develop it.[59] The story of his life warrants further research, but for this book our focus is not on the inventions, but how he received them. Tesla described experiencing intense flashes of light that triggered intense creativity. He claimed his inventions came in holographic detail that he could dismantle piece by piece in his mind, and then he would know how to assemble the invention. He also claimed that otherworldly beings contacted him while he worked on his innovations, and he believed extraterrestrial beings have been controlling mankind since the beginning.[60]

Both the Soviet physicists and Tesla aimed at developing physical weapons and technology by manipulating energies of the earth to advance their agenda. This is called magick. Any physical weaponry obtained by this means would have been influenced by a nefarious source. The Soviets were knowingly using occult practices as the means for their mission, and in so doing, they opened themselves to demonization.

Tesla, on the other hand, may have unknowingly fallen under demonic influence, an interaction he described as receiving a burst of energy into his mind before proceeding to harness the earth's energies to develop his creations. He likely opened the door by his contact with what he thought were otherworldly beings (but were actually demons). This shows that malevolent demonic influence may have caused what we perceive as physical occurrences in our natural environment. It is but another tactic of the enemy deviously enlisting mankind in his army to fight against God in the approaching end times battle.

Heed the Words of Jesus

As darkness increases upon the earth, it will become increasingly harder for us to discern the truth from the lie, and to remain steadfast in the faith. Regardless of when the Lord calls

---

[59] "A machine to end war," Open Tesla Research, accessed June 23, 2025, https://teslaresearch.jimdofree.com/articles-interviews/a-machine-to-end-war-by-nikola-tesla-liberty-february-1937/.
[60] Gheorgita G. I., "Tesla's Secret Time Travel Connection," History, accessed July 16, 2025, https://vocal.media/history/tesla-s-secret-time-travel-connection-xm1fpoi4p.

His church home, the preceding days will be so that even the elite will be led astray (Matthew 24:24). As we prepare for His imminent return, we need to take heed of His promises, instructions, and warnings. Spending time developing a genuine relationship with Jesus will be our best bet to avoid being misled (see Mark 13:5-6). We must be ever mindful not to fall prey to the false prophets or false Christs who claim to be Jesus, despite the display of special powers (see John 14:1-3; Thessalonians 4:13-18). As we know, the true return of Jesus will be a supernatural event, far removed from anything mankind has ever witnessed.

Therefore, we must be on guard as we see things we've never seen before, and experience that which is unfamiliar to us. We must be careful what voice we're listening to so we allow our hearts to align only with biblical teachings. Besides listening, we must be obedient and do exactly as He says including fleeing when He says to flee. If we've prepared for this day, equipping ourselves with the well-oiled, solid-fitting armor of God, and have our feet firmly planted on the Word of God, we will be ready to face the evil of the day. Also, know we must know our Bible. Pray that the Lord will write His words upon your heart so they will be brought to your recollection when they need to be. We can't count on having a physical Bible with us to look up Scriptures when that day comes.

The Last Battle

During hard times, I often encourage myself with the phrase "this too shall pass," meaning nothing, good or bad, lasts forever. It reminds me that no matter how bad it seems at that moment, it's only temporary and the end is in sight. We know that all these things will pass away when the world, as we know it, meets its end. Luke 21:27-28 says, "Then they will see the Son of Man coming in a cloud with power and great glory. Now when these things begin to happen, look up and lift up your heads, because your redemption draws near."

Whether we are upon this earth when the day of the Lord comes, or have already left this earthly plane, one thing we know is we will ride with Him into the last battle. Revelation 19 describes heaven opening to a white horse. Its rider is called Faithful and True. His eyes blaze like fire, and many crowns adorn His head. He wears a robe dipped in blood and His name is the Word of God. Coming out of his mouth is a sharp sword to strike down the nations with.

Here we see Jesus as a powerful Warrior coming to defend His people and destroy the works of darkness forever. "The armies of heaven follow Him, riding on white horses and dressed in fine linen, white and clean" (v. 14). His armies consist of angels and the saints in heaven (including those who have lost their lives during the tribulation) who wear Christ's righteousness, pure and spotless. They have no armor, for they will not wield a sword. Only their King, who wears the bloody garment, will tread the winepress of the fury of God's wrath, and He will destroy the antichrist with the breath of his mouth (see Isaiah 63:3). The inscription KING OF KINGS AND LORD OF LORDS is on his robe and thigh.

Behind the scenes, another army has been gathering. Satan, or the dragon, along with the beast (antichrist) and false prophet, having deceived the nations, rally massive armies of the earth to join demonic forces into one last desperate attempt to war against God. Take note that the Euphrates River is described as having dried up, symbolizing the removal of a barrier, or God lifting His restraint, thus enabling the demonic army invasion of Israel preceding the last battle. In our current day, the average flow of the Euphrates River has decreased to half its original amount and, according to The Iraqi Ministry of Water Resources, is in a crisis of drying up by the year 2040.[61]

The last battle is one that the saints will witness but not fight; rather, we will accompany Jesus (see Revelation 17:14), for He will slay the wicked with the breath of His lips" (Isaiah 11:4). On that day, we have the pleasure of riding into battle alongside Jesus to face the enemy of our souls once and for all. We will stand with

---

[61] A. F. Iyabu, "Tigris and Euphrates Rivers Threatened to Dry by 2040, Iraq Could Experience a Drought," VOI – Waktunya Merevolusi Pemberitaan, accessed June 23, 2025, https://voi.id/en/news/110174.

Him and witness the wrath of God and His power as He avenges the wicked in the greatest battle of all time.

The Church in Philadelphia

One evening about ten years ago, I attended a worship service at an old stone church on a narrow street in Philadelphia. It was the end of a weeklong worship training conference by a well-known worship leader that was open to the public during evening worship. I entered the old building, which opened to a large hall upon entering from street level. The sanctuary was on the second floor and was a typical traditional church set up with wooden pews and the altar at the front of the sanctuary.

I was visiting with a friend, and we looked around wondering if perhaps we were in the wrong place. The crowd was the most diverse I've seen. There were four elderly Black ushers dressed in formal suits and ties, a Ukrainian all-women dance team, and a man with long dreadlocks with a djembe drum. They were a multigenerational, multicultural crowd of believers, all housed in this old, dated church building.

After a collection was taken and a brief introduction was given, the worship leader entered from a door to the side of the altar area. He shared a teaching based on Revelation 4, describing the splendor and awe of the throne room of God in vivid detail. The imagery he provided was phenomenal as he described a colorful rainbow that encircled the throne, its emerald hue intriguing. Constant flashes of lightning illuminated the throne in unison with the powerful and majestic voice of thunder. Before the throne lay a sea of glass, like crystal reflecting all the colors of the rainbow. It was exhilarating. And all in heaven gathered singing, "Holy, Holy is the Lord God Almighty, who was and is and is to come!" Their voices echoed eternally.

After the teaching, he sat behind the keyboard next to a lone drummer. No lights, fog machine, or laser lights, just simplistic worship. The sound of the opening cords of the keyboard rung out and instantaneously transformed the old sanctuary into a sea of exuberant, spontaneous worship. The body of multicultural believers became unified in spirit, leaving behind every ounce of prejudice or division. We were one voice lifted before the Lord God Almighty. His presence fell as the people worshipped. It was as though the heavens were rent and we had transcended beyond this little stone church in Philadelphia.

Then, as quickly as worship began, it ended much too soon. I remember walking out of that small church that night, my spirit still in the clouds, onto the dark streets of Philadelphia that somehow didn't look the same. I imagine this was but a small glimpse of what worshipping our Holy God in heaven will one day be like. Although I've experienced worship to varied levels, nothing has compared to this one night in a place of least expectation—full of Spirit-filled people expecting to be touched by God.

Now, looking back, I see the symbolic footprint of this surreal experience. In the book of Revelation, Jesus spoke so highly of one church that was not large or influential; they were a small, faithful remnant, in which God rewarded them with divine protection during the period of tribulation and granted them salvation and favor, unlocking divine opportunities through the key to the House of David, accessing the kingdom of God. They remained loyal and unshaken in the face of opposition and worldly culture, keeping His Word and never denying His name. Ironically, that church was Philadelphia.

I share this with you as a word of encouragement. While we still live in a world with war, rumors of wars, and famines and earthquakes, and where lawlessness and evil abound, God is with us and inhabits the praises of His people. As our spiritual warfare intensifies, remember to stand firm, remain faithful and look up, for our redemption is near. Nothing we walk through on this earth will be anything like what lies ahead for those who wait upon the Lord.

> Persevere, so that after you have done the will of God,
> you will receive what He has promised.
>
> Hebrews 10:36

APPENDIX

Bondage-Breaking Prayer

The following prayer can be used to break curses brought on by witchcraft and occult involvement. Specifically, this prayer is meant for breaking curses on tools used in initiations that bind you to demonic strongholds. It can also be used to cast out any demonic stronghold connected to an occult item. I recommend using it as a reference guide, ultimately coming before the throne of grace with a repentant heart's cry asking Jesus for forgiveness for any occult involvement and that He would break any curse over you, because of it.

To Break Curses over Yourself

Lord Jesus, I confess all sins I have committed because of my involvement in witchcraft and occult practices, and ask for Your forgiveness and that You would cleanse me of all unrighteous acts that I have done. I ask that you would close any door of access that allowed any foothold or stronghold entrance into my life.

Therefore, by the power and authority of Jesus, I renounce and sever all attachments with the following tools _____ (e.g., book of shadows, cingulum, pentacle, candles, etc.) along with all of their contents and association, in Jesus' name.

I renounce and break any curses spoken over or written upon these tools, in Jesus' name.

In Jesus' name, I renounce and break any cursed symbols carved into or inscribed upon these tools and any personal or bodily items that are attached to them, and I sever all connections and associations with these cursed items, by the authority of Jesus Christ.

I break the power and control of every curse placed upon me through any ritual, dedication, initiation, or elevation, in Jesus' name. Through the blood of Jesus, I break every curse and power transferred to me by any human or demonic being.

In the name of Jesus, I break every legal right, hold, and ground that the enemy had over me, and I break the power over every curse that has come upon me because of any witchcraft involvement.

To Break Curses over Family

I break and remove any curse over my family, my children, and household, and cast out any demonic spirits that have infiltrated my household because of my past occult practice. In Jesus' name and in accordance with Psalm 91, I ask You for the intervention of Your angels to dispel any witchcraft curses that may be affecting my family and me.

Prayer for a High Priest/Priestess or Elder

According to Luke 6:28, which says "bless those who curse you and pray for those who spitefully use you," Lord Jesus, I pray asking for Your blessings and intervention in _____'s life. May their heart be transformed and their eyes be opened to your truth. In Jesus' name, amen.

Also by S. A. Tower

"*A Witch's Encounter with God: Taken from the Night* engages the reader immediately and transports them to the battlefield of the soul. This compelling narrative pulls no punches about church life, family struggles, and the darkness that often parades as light!" ~ **Dr. Ron Phillips**, Senior Pastor of Abba's House and author of over 30 books, including *Our Invisible Allies*

Ms. Tower's first-hand account exposes a thread the enemy uses to entice and ensnare his captive and reveals the unraveling beauty of grace.

Available in paperback and e-book format at your favorite book retailer.

"**From The Craft to Christ** is a powerful demonstration of God's unceasing love to break into the Kingdom of Darkness and liberate those held captive by Satan's power. A must read!" ~ **Robby Dawkins,** International Vineyard Evangelist, Author of *"Do What Jesus Did", Featured in the films "Furious Love" and "Father of Lights"*

From the Craft to Christ" comprises two distinct sections: the first serves as a ministry tool aimed at evangelizing individuals immersed in pagan culture, while the second conveys compelling testimonies from twelve former witches.

Available in paperback and e-book format at your favorite book retailer.

www.ingramcontent.com/pod-product-compliance
Lightning Source LLC
Chambersburg PA
CBHW071858290426
44110CB00013B/1191